UNDERSTANDING ASSET ALLOCATION

In an increasingly competitive world, it is quality
of thinking that gives an edge—an idea that opens new
doors, a technique that solves a problem, or an insight
that simply helps make sense of it all.

We work with leading authors in the various arenas
of business and finance to bring cutting-edge thinking
and best-learning practices to a global market.

It is our goal to create world-class print publications
and electronic products that give readers
knowledge and understanding that can then be
applied, whether studying or at work.

To find out more about our business
products, you can visit us at www.ft-ph.com.

UNDERSTANDING ASSET ALLOCATION

AN INTUITIVE APPROACH TO MAXIMIZING YOUR PORTFOLIO

Victor Canto

Prentice Hall

FINANCIAL TIMES

An Imprint of PEARSON EDUCATION
Upper Saddle River, NJ • New York • London • San Francisco • Toronto • Sydney
Tokyo • Singapore • Hong Kong • Cape Town • Madrid
Paris • Milan • Munich • Amsterdam

www.ft-ph.com

Publisher: Tim Moore
Executive Editor: Jim Boyd
Editorial Assistant: Susie Abraham
Development Editor: Russ Hall
Associate Editor-in-Chief and Director of Marketing: Amy Neidlinger
Cover Designer: Alan Clements
Managing Editor: Gina Kanouse
Project and Copy Editor: Christy Hackerd
Senior Indexer: Cheryl Lenser
Senior Compositor: Gloria Schurick
Manufacturing Buyer: Dan Uhrig

Financial Times Prentice Hall offers excellent discounts on this book when ordered in quantity for bulk purchases or special sales. For more information, please contact U.S. Corporate and Government Sales, 1-800-382-3419, corpsales@pearsontechgroup.com. For sales outside the U.S., please contact International Sales at international@pearsoned.com.

Pearson Education LTD.
Pearson Education Australia PTY, Limited.
Pearson Education Singapore, Pte. Ltd.
Pearson Education North Asia, Ltd.
Pearson Education Canada, Ltd.
Pearson Educatión de Mexico, S.A. de C.V.
Pearson Education—Japan
Pearson Education Malaysia, Pte. Ltd.

Printed in the United States of America

First Printing, March 2006

Library of Congress Cataloging-in-Publication Data

Canto, Victor A.
    Understanding asset allocation : an intuitive approach to maximizing your portfolio / Victor A. Canto.
        p. cm.
    ISBN 0-13-187676-7 (hardback : alk. paper) 1. Asset allocation. 2. Portfolio management. I. Title.
    HG4529.5.C36 2005
    332.6—dc22
                                        2005028621
    ISBN 0-13-187676-7

To Alito, a great mentor, teacher, and economist.
I am proud to be one of his "boys."

CONTENTS

FOREWORD

In November 1996, I wrote, "The single most significant, intergalactic, extra-celestial, interplanetary, and spiritual force behind the global stock market rally is the decline of inflation to rates not seen in over thirty years."[1] I was enthusiastic to say the least, and with good reason. At the time, the U.S. stock market had appreciated 25 percent over the past year and, over a two-year period, stocks had climbed 68 percent. The tax environment was not perfect back then, with Congress having passed what I considered anti-growth and anti-savings tax increases earlier in the decade. Yet, the U.S. economy and stock market were surging at mid-decade, with inflation holding near two percent. My argument, then and now, is that inflation is a tax on savings and investment, and low inflation acts like a tax cut—so much so that it can offset the fiscal drag of the high taxes that might be in place.

I use this example to illustrate top-down thinking, which is not only critical for economists but also for investors of all stripes. In the "macro" top-down world of investing, all the great forces within an economy exert their unique pressures, combining to give an economy its individual stamp—its look, its feel, its function, its promise. Once this stamp is known, one can draw a forecast for the way stocks and bonds will perform, both in the short and long term. Many people make money this way without a good understanding of the way macro forces combine within an economy; however, the same group of indicators can lead investors to underperform. In the same 1996 article, I also wrote, "Growth does not cause inflation; low inflation causes growth." In this statement, you might be able to surmise that not all top-down thinkers think alike. For example, a market bear in 1996 might have written that economic growth and the stock market are inflationary pressures that call for restrictive action from the Federal Reserve. As we know, despite a bump here and there, stocks continued to climb throughout the decade only ending, in my view, when a "low

---

[1] Kudlow, Lawrence A. "'Thankful,' American Abundance: The New Economic and Moral Prosperity." New York: Forbes/AHCP, 1997.

inflation causes growth" Federal Reserve began to act like a growth-causes-inflation central bank.

I'm not one to toss aside bottom-up investment strategies. When looking bottom-up, an investor might say, "Look at this stock: good earnings, good P/E, good management, good product. I need to own it." There is nothing wrong with that at all, and if you select stocks this way you are sure to pick your share of winners. In fact, investors and managers *must* select this way when it gets down to the nitty-gritty of filling a portfolio. However, I caution that anyone who looks too narrowly in their investing life will all too often miss the big picture and the upsides that come with it. Buy low, sell high? Sure. But keep your eyes open, from the top on down.

I have long held that any investor starting out should build an 80/20 portfolio consisting of 80 percent stocks and 20 percent bonds. In the long run, say thirty years, such an investor will almost undoubtedly beat out someone who began with, for example, a 60/40 split. But, a lot can happen along the way. Markets *do* go up and down. Macro environments *do* change. Inflation can trend higher or lower. Tax shifts can come into play, some bullish for stocks, others bearish. Certain investment sectors can rise and fall due to a range of outside factors, as can certain stock sizes and styles. To capture the upside of these shifts, and to avoid the downsides, investors must be willing and able to adjust their allocations based on the top-down macro factors of the day—which brings me to the book at hand.

I go way back with Victor Canto. Around the time I wrote the 1996 inflation article, I had just left California, where I had lived and worked for a very important year in my life. While in California, I got to spend a lot of time with Victor, sometimes talking about life and much of the time doing the things that economists do: reviewing historical data, building forecasting models, and writing papers. Like me, Victor is a top-down guy. He's also an unflinching advocate of low taxation, minimal regulation, and sound money policy, if only because he knows that these macro forces highly favor increased individual freedom and greater prosperity for all. He knows this to be the case because the data prove it time and again. When the tax and regulatory burden is relatively low, the incentive to work, save, and invest proportionately rises.

Everyone prospers in such an environment. But, Victor's also a realist. It's one thing to know what forces can make for an ideal economy, and it's another thing to understand that ideal economies are not always the case. So, the challenges for investors and managers are to adapt their strategies to the economies of the day, understand the way the asset classes in their portfolios can behave from the top on down, and then make adjustments based on that understanding. This is what Victor eloquently maps out in the pages ahead.

The top-down forces within an economy are many. At the very top are those that directly arise from government policy, such as taxes, money supply, and regulations. Moving down a notch, there's the value of the dollar, foreign exchange rates, and trade balances. As noted, there's inflation and the inflation indicators, such as gold prices and Treasury yield curves that speak to the phenomenon of the way money and goods interact. On the corporate level, there's inventory, shipments, and retained earnings. After that, there's employment, productivity, and wage levels. Then there's the abstract, such as supply and demand curves, or the elasticities inherent in different industries and businesses.

The list is long, and highly interrelated, which can be problematic for investors at any level of expertise. If you regularly read the financial papers or watch business television, you already know this because you've seen the same sets of top-down information being interpreted in every way. For instance, if I were to say lower corporate tax rates in the current economic environment can spur greater capital formation, which can in turn elicit business expansion, job growth, and a rising stock market, I would be giving you my very individualized top-down version of the story. And, if another economist were to say that the same lower corporate tax rates can cause an increase in the federal deficit, the impact of which can be higher interest rates, depressed growth, and a falling market, he would be talking top-down as well (although, from where I'd be sitting, he'd very likely be speaking from another planet).

You might detect my particularly macroeconomic bias at this point, and that's fine. I reveal it every night on television. But, it's hard not to be an advocate for what you know works.

Smart investing starts from the top, and Victor Canto reveals both how and why. More, he sets forth just how investors and managers can take advantage of the predictable fluctuations in stocks and bonds that occur in identifiable macroeconomic environments. It all comes down to how well you want to perform. Without question, I know that your investment returns can only improve with Victor leading you along.

Lawrence Kudlow, host, CNBC's *Kudlow & Company*

PREFACE

Thinking about the origins of this book takes me back to my days as a graduate student. I was fortunate to attend the University of Chicago (U of C) during the 1970s, a very special time in the school's history. Back then, there was a future Nobel Prize winner running almost every workshop. Both the teachers and students had an incredible energy level, despite the very high pressure to perform. Graduate students worked hard to be well prepared, and the debates and discussions were phenomenal—regardless of which workshops one attended. The sheer number of high-quality seminars and the luminaries who ran them allowed one to accumulate an incredible breadth of economic knowledge. I was a regular participant in the money and banking, international trade, and public finance workshops run by Milton Friedman, Harry Johnson, and Arnold Harberger, respectively—teachers among the brightest in the economics profession. I also fondly remember Gary Becker's lectures on price theory.

Many faculty members at the U of C, in addition to being outstanding economists, were gifted teachers. But, instruction skills were not restricted to the elder statesmen in the department. There were also some incredible junior faculty members—among them: Robert Barro, Jacob Frenkel, Arthur Laffer, and Jeremy Siegel. In addition to their delivery skills and their content mastery, my professors all shared an interest in policy issues—in particular, the fiscal and regulatory legislation both federal and local elected officials pass. In their lectures, they repeatedly illustrated the way top-down incentives and disincentives affect both economic behavior and the economy's performance. In particular, they taught their students the way to trace government policies' impact through the economy.

I carried much away from my experience at the U of C, but the two sector models' power Harry Johnson drilled into his students highlights my understanding. Gary Becker taught incentives' role in human behavior. It was in Harberger's class, however, I was able to put it all together. He beautifully combined his famous interpretation of the corporate income tax incidence and his general-equilibrium approach's discipline with his analysis of tax rate distortions and waste measurement, applying all to real-world situations. In my opinion, this is where Harberger really excelled. With his incredible depth and range of knowledge, he was able to propose simple and elegant solutions to the problems public policy often relegates to an economy.

I have tried to follow Harberger's example in my professional life. During my years at the University of Southern California (USC), I paid close attention to policy issues and applied many concepts and ideas I learned from "Alito," the name Harberger received from his admiring Latin-American students. In time, my interest in the interconnection of policy and economic behavior evolved. After leaving USC in the mid-1980s, I worked for AB Laffer, VA Canto & Associates, where I focused more and more on government policies' impact and implications. But, it was not until 1997—at which point, I had started my own firm with encouragement from my wife, Ana, and three daughters, Vianca, Victoria, and Veronica—I decided to focus on what I really had become interested in: I had found that seldom does government action analysis apply to the strategies vital to business managers, financial analysts, and investors. With this in mind, I set forth to discover the policy actions' investment implication. My discoveries would certainly be useful to not only investors, portfolio managers, and financial analysts, but also corporate strategists, government officials, and the policymakers themselves. This book represents the sum of this knowledge gained in my professional career. For the reader, I hope it represents a new path for investing—the extra step demanding it be taken.

Along the way, while developing my investing theories, I have met many wonderful people (many of whom have become great friends). Sometimes, during difficult times, people find out who their true friends really are. In 1997, as I began my new firm, Harlan Cadinha, Herb Gullquist, Kevin Melich, Robert Doede, Christian Carrillo, and Danielle Andrews were wonderfully supportive and proved to be exceptional friends. More recently, I have gotten to know David Cleary, Robert Holz, Tom Gangle, Peter Carl, and Peter Mork, and in one way or another,

I have benefited from their friendships. Charlie Parker, Robert Webb, and Larry Kudlow have always been supportive and encouraging.

One person without whom this project would not have become reality is Chris McEvoy. His dedication, initiative, and many editorial suggestions greatly enhanced the manuscript. Andy Wiese and Samir Ghia were outstanding research assistants.

ABOUT THE AUTHOR

Dr. Victor Canto is La Jolla Economic's (LJE) founder and chairman, an economic consulting firm located in La Jolla, California. He has served as A.B. Laffer, V.A. Canto & Associates' president and director of research, a tenured associate professor of finance and business economics at the University of Southern California (1983–1985), an assistant professor of finance and business economics at the University of Southern California (1977–1983), and a visiting professor at the Universidad Central del Este in the Dominican Republic. He was also a visiting professor of economics at the University of California at Los Angeles (1987).

In 1980, Dr. Canto was a consultant to the Financial Council of Puerto Rico. In 1977, he was an advisor to the Economic Studies Division of the Dominican Republic's Central Bank. In 1975, he was technical advisor for Dominican Republic's financial minister.

Dr. Canto has authored, edited, or coedited a number of books. These titles include the landmarks *Foundations of Supply-Side Economics*; *Monetary Policy, Taxation, and International Investment Strategy* (Quorum Books 1990); *Supply-Side Portfolio Strategies* (Quorum Books 1988); and *Currency Substitution: Theory and Evidence from Latin America* (Spring 1987). His articles have appeared in many leading economic journals, including *Economic Inquiry*, *Journal of Macroeconomics*, *The International Trade Journal*, *Journal of Business and Economic Statistics*, *The Southern Economic Journal*, *Applied Economics*, *Weltwirstchaftliches Archiv*, *The CATO Journal*, *Public Finance*, *The Journal of International Money and Finance*, and *The Journal of Wealth Management*. He has also been published in the *Wall Street Journal* and *Investor's Business Daily*.

In addition to writing on his principal fields of interest—international economics, public finance, and macroeconomics—Dr. Canto has authored articles on the energy markets for the *Public Utilities Fortnightly* and the *Oil and Gas Journal*. He has also penned a series of articles on portfolio strategy for the *Financial Analysts Journal*. Dr. Canto contributed the "Exotic Currencies" section for *The New Palgrave Dictionary of Money and Finance* (MacMillan Press Limited 1992). He is currently a contributing financial editor for *National Review Online*.

Dr. Canto is the recipient of the Supremo de Plata, awarded by the Dominican Republic JC to the Outstanding Young Man of 1983, and the University of Southern California University Scholar award. He is a member of Chi Epsilon (the civil engineering honorary society).

Dr. Canto received a B.S. in civil engineering from the Massachusetts Institute of Technology in 1972 and a M.A. and Ph.D. in economics from the University of Chicago (1974 and 1977, respectively).

INTRODUCTION: YOU CAN DO BETTER

The critical variable in meeting an investment goal is asset distribution between classes. This is no secret. But, achieving success in asset allocation is easier said than done. I believe a better asset-allocation framework exists than most investment firms offer today. In short, where most plans tend to be rigid, flexibility is what investors most need. The majority of plans limit choices, but nothing should be taken off the table—although investors should have the best framework in which to make their decisions.

Of course, every investment plan is set up so the investor comes out ahead. But you can do *better* than just come out ahead.

Investments are made to meet the investor's goals and lifestyle needs and not necessarily to beat industry benchmarks. But, making an allocation decision between equities and bonds or large- and small-cap stocks requires not just a return assumption, but also a conviction in the likelihood of success. That's why the asset-allocation process needs to be probability based. First, asset-class return probabilities need to be formulated. Second, those probabilities need to be applied to an investor's long-term goals, producing a recommended asset allocation. Third, this allocation needs to be run through a quantitative framework that overweights the opportunistic sectors and underweights the overvalued ones. All this ensures there are no unintended bets made in a portfolio.

Historical data can be a guide to future returns. But, risks change and valuation and timing matter. How does a shift in real interest rates affect small-cap stocks? If taxes and governmental regulations rise, what does that mean for bonds? A forward-looking view one can tie together such important variables is critical to the asset-allocation process. But, the process needs to differentiate itself in two additional ways: The first way has to do with the versatility of the framework. The second way has to do with actively using passive vehicles (also known as index funds).

When I talk about the framework's versatility, I mean the asset-allocation model can be changed to find opportunity. For example, I do not view the nontraditional sector as the hedge fund's exclusive domain. To me, it is a place for any investment decision that does not correlate with traditional capital-market indices but does have value. This sector can include hedge funds, but it can also include investments in discounted closed-end funds and industry-sector funds, or specific securities representing good long-term value.

Next, there's actively using passive vehicles. You may have noticed the debate over whether to "index" or go "active." This discussion is conducted in the context of strategic asset allocation (SAA), which requires an active manager to consistently outperform the market over the long run. But what if a manager regularly outperforms the market during certain cycles and underperforms the rest of the time? It's quite possible the manager's long-run performance is not much different from the index's performance.

This argument suggests indexing is indeed the superior strategy for SAA. Indexing alone, however, produces inferior results to a strategy that focuses on taking advantage of the different asset classes' relative performances during *cycles*. I'm not talking about a traditional tactical asset allocation (TAA). Rather, I am talking about a somewhat intermediate step between SAA and TAA. Call it cyclical asset allocation (CAA).

Such a strategy emphasizes different asset classes as well as active-versus-passive management, as cycles dictate. When markets do not provide much in terms of selection opportunities for securities, the index fund is a cost-efficient tool with which to access broad market moves. But, market efficiency has cycles, too. Correspondingly, reallocating index funds is another source of value that can be added through the asset-allocation process.

There is a time for everything. There is a time for active management and a time for passive management; a time for value stocks and a time for growth stocks; a time for large-caps and a time for small-caps.

Constructing major stock indices provides an excellent illustration of this. In general, stock indices are capitalization weighted, meaning larger stocks tend to get more weight in an index. For example, at one point during the 1990s' bubble days, the 10 largest S&P 500 holdings accounted for roughly 50 percent of that index's capitalization. Thus, when the top 10 holdings outperformed the index, the 490 stocks accounting for the bottom 50 percent underperformed (on average). Hence, the odds of an active manager outperforming during this period would have been low. The implication is an index strategy during a large-cap cycle is superior.

On the other hand, during a small-cap cycle, the same 490 S&P stocks would have outperformed (on average). In this case, even randomly selecting small cap stocks would have a good chance of beating the market. So, during a small-cap cycle, an active strategy is most likely the desirable approach.

Size and weighting schemes alter the odds an active management strategy can outperform an index. But, when the odds are in your favor to outperform, I believe you should take the chance. This is based on a conviction in the likelihood of your success.

Style differences also count. Take any index, such as the S&P 400, S&P 500, or S&P 600. In each, the number of value stocks is much larger than the number of growth stocks. That said, numerous studies exist showing the way value stocks, on average, tend to beat their respective broad-based indices. Even if this result holds true, however, it may not be advisable to pursue an active value strategy. Here's why: An active management strategy invariably leads to a concentrated portfolio in relation to the value stocks universe. Equally important, by the nature of the value-selection criteria, when misses occur, they can be disastrous to a portfolio.

A simple example illustrates this point: A stock is undervalued at $15 and its price declines to $12. Is it now even more undervalued? Should you increase your exposure to this stock? Not so fast. The value approach can, in some cases, induce you to double-up on a loser. On the other hand, growth investors have a natural way of preserving their gains: when growth slows down, they get out of a stock.

Again, there's a time for everything.

I take the view that, on a risk-adjusted basis over the long-term, no single asset-allocation strategy should dominate another. Sometimes, an active approach works. Other times, passive is the way to go. Sometimes, it's large-caps; other times, it's small. As cycles persist, there are times when each strategy outperforms.

Hence, an investment plan shouldn't behave as if it has one hand tied behind its back. Instead, it should be free and flexible, with all the investment alternatives at its disposal. When this is the case, an asset-allocation consultant who can identify the different strategies' relative attractiveness over time should administer it.

Of course, a broad range of advice can be found in today's investment community. Some of it is good, if limited in scope, and some of it is bad. For instance, an overdependence on historical data and quick-fix universal solutions does not always served investors well.

I believe historical relationships, combined with information contained in the futures markets, can provide the signals necessary to develop a forward-looking world view that, on average, correctly anticipates the turning points in various return cycles. More, a top-down global view focusing on policy changes at the government level and a range of geopolitical events are also useful in identifying and anticipating some of the secular and cyclical changes in relative performance both domestically and across countries.

Armed with such information, decision rules can be developed for determining how and when to choose an investment's style, location, and/or size, and whether to do so in a passive or active mode. You can call this whole process the value-timing approach to asset allocation.

Any investor faces capital-market risk. Managing that risk, evaluating opportunities in the context of your goals, and efficiently accessing specific investments requires broad, objective, close-to-the-capital-markets thinking. Indeed, an asset-allocation framework does not need to be a black box that processes a large number of statistical variables and spits out an investment plan. It should be a logical framework that lays out the investors' choices. Stocks or bonds? Domestic or international? Large or small? Index or active? Traditional or nontraditional?

Committing to a single strategy can only guarantee you mediocrity in the long run. Don't limit your options. You can do better.

1

IN SEARCH OF THE UPSIDE

I t is striking how little most people understood about risk as recently as three decades ago. Risk, of course, is that piece of information all investors need to know—and should desire to keep as low as possible in relation to the returns they expect to see on their investments. Fortunately, developments in modern portfolio theory provide a framework for addressing the ways risk can affect expected returns.[1] The developments have been nothing short of dramatic.

The Measurement of Risk

We now have the Sharpe ratio at our disposal, a well-known formula useful for evaluating alternative investments and determining when to add additional assets to a portfolio.[2]

The *Sharpe ratio* summarizes two measures—mean return and variance—within a single measure. *Mean return* can be considered the average return an investment or investment class is expected to deliver over time, while *variance* can be considered the average range of asset performance around the mean return. To calculate the Sharpe ratio, subtract the *risk-free rate* returns (that is, Treasury bill [T-bill] returns) from the asset returns in question and divide that result by the standard deviation of the return of the asset class in question less that of the risk-free rate. In this manner, risk is pinpointed. One way to think of this is to consider a person who borrows money to invest. After doing so, that person's net gain is the difference between the return of the investment and the funds borrowed; the greater the difference (on the positive side), the greater the reward. Similarly, the higher the Sharpe ratio, the lower the risk in relation to the reward. The Sharpe ratio is calculated using the mean and standard deviation of an excess return. That is the net of the asset class return and the risk free rate (that is, three months' T-bill yields). A related measure is obtained when the ratio is calculated based on the mean and return of a single investment. This ratio is also known as the *information ratio*.

Then, there's the *capital asset pricing model* (CAPM), which similarly looks at the relationship between an investment's risk and its expected market return—or, more specifically, the ways investment risk should affect its expected return.[3]

One major insight of the CAPM is that not all risks should affect asset prices. As would be the case if two assets moved in the same direction, the volatility of the portfolio consisting of the two assets would remain the same as the individual assets. In contrast, if the two assets move in the opposite direction, the volatility of a portfolio consisting of the two assets would be much lower than that of each of the assets by themselves. The latter represents an example of a risk that can be diversified away by combining it with other assets in a portfolio, which should not be considered a risk. Hence, when considering adding asset to a portfolio, one needs to take into account whether the asset moves with the portfolio and whether the addition of the asset will reduce or increase the volatility of the portfolio. If the asset does not add to the volatility of the portfolio, it should not be priced for risk, or more plainly, investors would not demand an additional return or premium over and above the current expected return. The only risk that should be priced is the risk that cannot be diversified away, the *residual risk* or *systematic risk*. The CAPM is firm on this point. What should matter to the investor, therefore, is the incremental impact on the overall portfolio volatility—not the individual investment volatility. With this in mind, an investor can effectively apply the Sharpe ratio: When adding an asset to a portfolio improves the Sharpe ratio, the asset adds to the return of a portfolio over and above the increased volatility of the new overall portfolio.

Investing suddenly seems very simple. Indeed, in the days of the Sharpe ratio and the CAPM, the *market portfolio*—a portfolio that has bought the market (given that the overall market is in equilibrium)—has become the efficient portfolio. An *efficient portfolio* is a portfolio that contains returns that have been maximized in relation to the risk level that individual investors desire. In a market that is in equilibrium, where the number of winners and losers must balance out, adding one additional asset class or stock does not increase the portfolio's risk return ratio. This means the portfolio containing risky assets with the highest Sharpe ratio must be the market portfolio.

Asset Allocation and Retirement

Will efficiency do the trick over the long haul? Do modern advancements in the financial world guarantee that the returns to an investment plan or portfolio are going to be high enough to generate sufficient funds to meet future obligations?

In a word: no. That's why the *asset-allocation consultant* was created.[4] This consultant examines contributions to a plan and expected future outlays and, assuming the past is a good guide to the future, uses historical returns and volatility measures to come up with an optimal investments mix—a mix that most likely satisfies future outlays with a minimal contribution level.

As a person plans for his golden years, he generally has two important things in mind: a picture of the lifestyle he would like to enjoy in retirement and his current net worth. Working backward, the desired lifestyle determines the cash flow required for his golden years. Depending on the expected returns of the various investment classes, one can figure out the target wealth he needs to reach his planned lifestyle. In turn, current wealth level and expected rates of return determine how much an investor must set aside each period so he can meet his long-term objectives.

Conceptually, all this appears fairly simple—but this is the real world. Uncertainty plays a major role in every aspect of life, and investing is no exception. We don't know what the future holds for our income paths, nor do we know what the income purchasing power will be down the road. We also don't know what health or family issues can arise in the years ahead, or what extraneous and unforeseen costs will cut into our plans for a second home or year-long vacation abroad. Similarly, we cannot know the actual future paths of the different asset classes that are available for our portfolios. An investor must, therefore, first find out whether the person managing her portfolio has a realistic plan—even before discussing the desirability of alternative asset mixes for a portfolio. She must ask, "Are the long-term objectives you set out for me feasible?"

Pension Plan consultants hoping to answer this question must make a series of assumptions and they can start by assuming *mean reversion*, or that, ultimately, asset-class returns converge along their long-run historical averages. Consultants know assets tend to return to their means, or averages, after running to their extremes, and with this knowledge, they are able to use the past as a guide to what will likely happen in the future. Advisors can also assume there will be a frequency to the strategy rebalancing of a portfolio and a portfolio will most likely be annually revisited. Armed with these two assumptions, consultants can go back in time, figure out the range of variation in returns for the different asset classes considered for inclusion in a portfolio, and calculate the likely ranges of outcome.

Ranging the Possibilities: Monte Carlo Simulations

With the advent of computers and the decline in the price of computing power, it is now easy for financial advisors to set up simulations that calculate all the possible permutations and combinations of past returns for every available asset class. In the financial world, these simulations often take the form of

Monte Carlo simulations, computer calculations that take into account chance and randomness (hence the casino quality of the name). This can sound very sophisticated—and the computer spreadsheets that such models spit out indeed excite the eye—but these simulated results are nothing more than the possible combinations and permutations of past outcomes.

Although Monte Carlo simulations can be informative, they can also be hazardous. For instance, although asset classes tend to return to their means (or historical averages) over time, they do not necessarily perform in sync with market conditions on all occasions. The following example helps illuminate this discussion: During a period of sustained economic expansion and low inflation, one expects the performance of the various asset classes, as well as the level of returns of those asset classes, to be very different from those observed in a slow-growth, inflationary environment. Historically, gold has been considered a great inflation hedge as well as, for the cautious, a refuge. Thus, during inflationary times, gold and other commodities are expected to outperform not only the market, but also their historical rates of return. Separate industries, in other words, respond differently to changing economic conditions. That's why we have a multitude of classifications for assets, such as *cyclical stocks,* stocks closely tied to the ups and downs of the economy; *value stocks,* stocks that tend to trade at a lower price relative to its fundamentals (that is, dividends, earnings, sales, and so on) and are thus considered undervalued by a value investor; *growth stocks,* stocks that look attractive because of the potential earnings growth of the company; and so on. Each classification is intended to capture some characteristic that relates a group of stocks to the changing economic environment. It follows that because separate economic variables (such as policy changes like tax rate cuts or shocks such as natural disasters) affect stocks differently; one must pay attention to the combination of policy changes or shocks to determine the impact of a changing economic environment on a particular asset class.

Depending on an economic shock's nature, asset classes sometimes move together, although at other times, they travel in different directions. So, the degree of synchronization among asset-class returns depends in great part on the nature of economic policies (or the shocks they produce). This insight is different from the one a Monte Carlo simulation provides. As for the former, the reasoning goes that when times are good, asset classes should perform in an expected manner (with most rising and perhaps those that typically hedge against the bad times underperforming). This is not a bad generalization, but it leaves much to be desired. If this reasoning is actually the case, it means the separate outcomes of the individual asset classes are not truly independent of each other. Taken to the next degree, this would mean the joint occurrences of asset-class returns are not truly independent of each other either. So, if a Monte Carlo simulation can only mimic occurrences where each of the assetclass returns are independent of each other, what good is it other than to illustrate generalized fluctuations? This leaves investors with another question they must ask their financial advisors: "How good is your simulation program and how well do you use it?"

A Poor Man's Monte Carlo Simulation

Thankfully, a simple alternative to the Monte Carlo and other simulations exists. Importantly, the alternative does not require any assumptions in addition to the original two. If one is willing to assume the past is a good guide to the future and portfolios should be annually rebalanced, one has a straightforward way to generate a range of outcomes that takes into account the joint outcomes of the actual returns of the different asset classes. Such a solution is located in the periodic table of asset returns, a feature of most asset-allocation presentations.

My version of the periodic table can be found in Table 1.1. For ease of illustration, I only consider seven asset-class returns that will be defined in later chapters. Each asset class's annual performance is ranked in descending order, with the best performer ranked the highest and the worst the lowest. Because the returns shown on the periodic table are those the market generates at a certain point in time, it follows that the joint occurrence of the outcomes is a feasible combination because it already occurred in the past. Thus, looking at the individual returns jointly, we avoid the potential pitfall of many simulation procedures.

To begin, the periodic table can be used to calculate possible ranges of outcome for all asset classes. As shown in Table 1.2, if you chose the top-performing asset class each year for the past three decades, $1 invested in 1975 would have grown to $2,919.50 today. In contrast, $1 invested in the worst-performing categories since 1975 would have declined to $0.24 at the end of 2004. That is quite a range of possible outcomes. In the context of rates of return, the outcomes range goes from a gain of 30 percent per year during this period to a decline of 4.7 percent per year. Again, that's quite a range. Investors, however, who required a rate of return higher than 30 percent during this period would have been out of luck—to reach their long-term objectives, they would have had to either revise their expectations or their current savings.

Table 1.1

Periodic table of asset returns.*

Rank	1975	1976	1977	1978	1979	1980
1	S 52.8	S 57.4	S 25.4	ROW 27.6	S 43.5	S 39.9
2	V 43.4	V 34.9	ROW 12.6	S 23.5	V 21.2	G 39.4
3	L 37.2	L 23.8	TB 5.1	TB 7.2	L 18.4	L 32.4
4	G 31.7	B 16.8	B -0.7	G 6.8	G 15.7	V 23.6
5	ROW 26.9	G 13.8	V -2.6	L 6.6	TB 10.4	ROW 19.8
6	B 9.2	TB 5.1	L -7.2	V 6.2	ROW 6.3	TB 11.2
7	TB 5.8	ROW -0.6	G -11.8	B -1.2	B -1.2	B -4

Rank	1981	1982	1983	1984	1985	1986	1987	1988	1989
1	TB 14.7	B 40.4	S 39.7	B 15.4	ROW 47.7	ROW 62.7	ROW 22.8	ROW 25.8	G 36.4
2	S 13.9	S 28	V 28.9	V 10.5	G 33.3	B 24.4	G 6.5	S 22.9	L 31.5
3	B 1.9	G 22	L 22.5	TB 9.9	L 32.2	V 21.7	TB 5.5	V 21.7	V 26.1
4	V 0	L 21.4	ROW 21	L 6.3	B 31	L 18.5	L 5.2	L 16.8	B 18.1
5	L -4.9	V 21	G 16.2	G 2.3	V 29.7	G 14.5	V 3.7	G 11.9	S 10.2
6	ROW -6.5	TB 10.5	TB 8.8	ROW 0.6	S 24.7	S 6.9	B -2.7	B 9.7	ROW 9.8
7	G -9.8	ROW -4.2	B 0.7	S -6.7	TB 7.7	TB 6.2	S -9.3	TB 6.4	TB 8.4

Rank	1990	1991	1992	1993	1994	1995	1996	1997	1998
1	TB 7.8	S 44.6	S 23.4	ROW 30.1	ROW 5.8	G 38.1	G 24	G 36.5	G 42.2
2	B 6.2	G 38.4	V 10.5	S 21	TB 3.9	L 37.4	L 23.1	L 33.4	L 28.6
3	G 0.2	L 30.6	B 8.1	V 18.6	G 3.1	V 37	V 22	V 30	ROW 17
4	L -3.2	V 22.6	L 7.7	B 18.2	S 3.1	S 34.5	S 17.6	S 22.8	V 14.7
5	V -6.8	B 19.3	G 5.1	L 10	L 1.3	B 31.7	TB 5.2	B 15.9	B 13.1
6	S -21.6	ROW 10.1	TB 3.5	TB 2.9	V -0.9	ROW 9.6	ROW 5.2	TB 5.3	TB 4.9
7	ROW -24.4	TB 5.6	ROW -14	B 1.7	B -7.8	TB 5.6	B -0.9	ROW 0.7	S -7.3

Rank	1999	2000	2001	2002	2003	2004
1	S 29.8	B 21.3	B 6.9	B 14.1	S 38.8	S 22.5
2	G 28.2	TB 5.9	TB 3.4	TB 1.7	ROW 36.2	ROW 17.8
3	ROW 26.2	S -3.6	S 2.5	S -15.3	V 31.8	V 15.5
4	L 21	V -9.6	V -13	ROW -17.4	L 28.7	L 10.7
5	V 12.6	L -9.9	L -13.1	V -22.5	G 25.7	B 9.3
6	TB 4.7	ROW -14.4	G -13.2	L -23.7	B 1.3	G 6.0
7	B -9	G -17	ROW -22.6	G -24.5	TB 1.2	TB 1.2

Key
S—Small
V—Value
L—Large
G—Growth
R—Rest of the World
B—T-Bonds
TB—T-Bills

* The figures included in this table are percentages.

Table 1.2

Growth of $1 invested in the top-, second-, third-, fourth-, fifth-, sixth-, and seventh-ranked asset classes each year: 1975–2004.

	Value of $1	Return
Top	$2,919.50	30.0%
Second	$365.57	21.7%
Third	$92.48	16.3%
Fourth/Median	$31.89	12.2%
Fifth	$11.43	8.5%
Sixth	$1.75	1.9%
Seventh	$0.24	–4.7%

Source: Research Insight, Morgan Stanley Capital Management and Ibbotson Associates

LIKELIHOOD OF CHOOSING THE TOP-PERFORMING ASSET CLASS

After a range of outcomes is determined, the obvious next step is to figure a likelihood of the various outcomes. Again, using the periodic table (and some high school-level math), one can easily do this. Because we are only considering seven asset classes, the likelihood of randomly choosing the top-performing asset class in any one year is 1 in 7, or 14.29 percent. The chance we choose the top asset class for two years is a little more complicated, as we need to figure out how many possible outcome combinations exist. For the first year, seven possibilities exist: T-bills, Treasury bonds (T-bonds), large-caps, small-caps, value stocks, growth stocks, and international stocks. When you work out all the possibilities for two years, there are 49 feasible outcomes (that is, T-bills and T-bills, T-bills and T-bonds, T-bonds and large-caps, large-caps and international stocks, and so on). Hence, the chance of randomly picking the winner two years in a row is 1 in 49, or 2.04 percent. The chance of picking the winner three years in a row is 1 in 343, or 0.29 percent. So, the odds of choosing the winner declines quickly as the number of years increases.

In Table 1.3, the odds of choosing the top performer are calculated each year for 30 consecutive years (the results are listed using scientific notation). It is safe to assume most people do not achieve the 30 percent annual return that the top asset class of the last 30 years produces because the odds of doing so are small. My best guess is that people should not plan their retirements with the idea that they will hit the top-performing asset class each and every year.

Table 1.3
Likelihood of randomly selected various outcomes.

Top rank every year	4.44E-26
Top and bottom rank every year	2.01E-49
Above median every year	9.13E-12
Above median 29 out of 30 years	3.65E-10
Above median 28 out of 30 years	7.06E-09
Above median 27 out of 30 years	8.79E-08
Above median 26 out of 30 years	7.91E-07
Above median 25 out of 30 years	5.49E-06
Above median 24 out of 30 years	3.05E-05
Above median 23 out of 30 years	1.39E-04
Above median 22 out of 30 years	5.34E-04
Above median 21 out of 30 years	1.74E-03
Above median 20 out of 30 years	4.87E-03
Above median 19 out of 30 years	1.18E-02
Above median 18 out of 30 years	2.49E-02
Above median 17 out of 30 years	4.60E-02
Above median 16 out of 30 years	7.46E-02
Above median 15 out of 30 years	1.06E-01
Above median 14 out of 30 years	1.33E-01
Above median 13 out of 30 years	1.46E-01

continues

Table 1.3 continued

Above median 12 out of 30 years	1.40E-01
Above median 11 out of 30 years	1.18E-01
Above median 10 out of 30 years	8.65E-02
Above median 9 out of 30 years	5.49E-02
Above median 8 out of 30 years	3.00E-02
Above median 7 out of 30 years	1.39 E-02
Above median 6 out of 30 years	5.41 E-03
Above median 5 out of 30 years	1.73 E-03
Above median 4 out of 30 years	4.44 E-04
Above median 3 out of 30 years	8.76 E-05
Above median 2 out of 30 years	1.25 E-05
Above median 1 out of 30 years	1.15 E-06

Still, this cloud—as with every cloud—has a silver lining. It can be difficult to choose the best performer every year, but it is just as difficult to choose the worst performer every time. Indeed, investors should not worry too much about the worst-case scenario presented in Table 1.3 because there is simply little chance of averaging a 4.8 percent annual decline for 30 years.

Let's take this line of thinking a little further. The periodic data also sheds some light on the long–short strategy whereby there is money to be made on both the winners and the losers. If one has perfect foresight, one is able to pick not only the top performer each year, but also the worst performer. Shorting the latter would enhance the return (for our sample period) to 34.7 percent per year, which is a nice increase. As shown in Table 1.3, however, the chance of choosing both the winner and the loser each and every year for 30 years is almost the square of choosing the winner each year, which is an unlikely event.

So, while still using the same logic, let's relax the performance requirements a little bit. Because seven asset classes reside in our universe, it follows that every year there will be three asset classes that come in above the median return. In other words, the chances of selecting an asset class that performs above average are 3 in 7, or 42.86 percent. This clearly is a more likely event than choosing the top- or worst-performing asset class each year. The chances of choosing an asset class that performs above the median for two years in a row are 9 in 49, or 18.36 percent. Table 1.3 shows that the chances of choosing an above-median performer for 30 years in a row are 14 *orders of magnitude* higher than the chances of choosing the top performer each year during this period. (An order of magnitude means that the number is 10 times larger. For example, 20 is an order of magnitude larger than 2 while 200 is two orders of magnitude larger than 2. Note that 14 orders of magnitude round out to about 200 trillion.)

Still, in spite of the huge increase in the likelihood of randomly choosing an above-median performer for 30 years in a row, the odds of doing so are still minuscule. As Table 1.3 shows, they are about 9 in 1 trillion.

Table 1.3 also illustrates the impact of relaxing the conditions on either outcome likelihood. For instance, you are 40 times more likely to choose an above-median performer in 29 out of 30 years than in 30 out of 30 years (see Figure 1.1 for a visual representation). The data show that as one reduces the requirement regarding the number of years an above-median asset has to be selected, the likelihood of choosing an above-median asset improves. For example, although it is difficult to choose the winners, it is just as difficult to choose the losers. Put another way, one can consistently choose the loser just as easily as one can consistently choose the winner. Beyond 13 out of 30 years, however, this likelihood begins to decline. Table 1.3 also shows the most likely outcome is for performance to come in near the average number of years. In fact, the likelihood of being above the median for 15 years out of the 30-year horizon is 10.6 percent. Furthermore, if events are independent, as I assume, we can calculate the intervals of likelihood. For example, the likelihood of being above the median between 11 and 15 years is 64 percent.

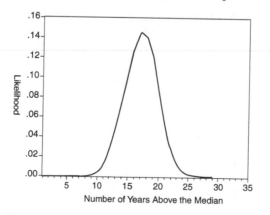

Figure 1.1   Likelihood of randomly choosing an above-median performer.

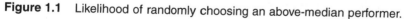

Summary

One can already find a number of morals of the asset-allocation story at this point. One deduction can be that those who rotate among the various asset classes are in for a rough ride. The data show that it is extremely difficult to randomly select the top performers each and every year. Although this can be somewhat discouraging, an upside does exist: It is also extremely difficult to choose the worst-performing asset class every single year. As well, it is fairly easy to randomly be above the median almost half the time, which means one-year buy-and-hold strategies are likely to generate average returns.

One question immediately comes to mind: Why not buy and hold a single asset all the time? The data provides the answer. Table 1.2 reports the average returns realized for each year by selecting the top-ranked asset class, the second-ranked class, and so on, for each year. Holding one asset class for 30 consecutive years (see Table 1.4) contrasts these returns with the returns produced. Looking at the 30-year example, it is apparent that the best-performing asset class—small caps—would only rank in the second or third tier of a strategy that chose the top-performing asset class each year. Large-cap, value, and growth stocks rank in the third (median) tier, while fixed income and international stocks rank in the fourth (median) tier. These results suggest rotating among the asset classes has the potential of expanding the upside, as no single asset held for all 30 years would take one to the top of the heap. On the other hand, one pays a price for increasing the upside: The downside is also increased. Each asset class, if held for the last 30 years, would have produced a performance well above those asset classes in the bottom two tiers, as reported in Table 1.2.

Table 1.4
Growth of $1 invested in each of the seven asset classes: January 1975–December 2004.

	Growth of $1	Returns
Small-Cap	$184.38	18.99%
Value	$61.23	14.70%
Large-Cap	$47.70	13.75%
Growth	$33.39	12.41%
International	$16.96	9.90%
T-Bonds	$15.49	9.61%
T-Bills	$5.98	6.14%

So, what have we discovered? A traditional strategic asset allocation can easily deliver a performance that is about average over a long horizon. A strategic allocation, however, that does not rotate among the various asset classes precludes it from capturing the upside the returns of the asset classes the top tier generates. Hence, if the upside of asset returns is to be realized, an active strategy that enhances strategic asset allocation must be developed.

2

THE CASE FOR CYCLICAL ASSET ALLOCATION

I f you read enough of today's economic literature, you find the financial community has come to agree that, on average, small-cap and value investments outperform their large-cap and growth cousins.[1] Using monthly returns for the various asset classes since 1975, I find some interesting data that can put these rather firm conclusions into question, while also surprising many investors who came of age in the 1990s.[2]

Not that small-cap and value investments haven't performed—they've done extremely well. In the three decades since 1975, small-cap stocks have not only outperformed large-cap stocks, they've beaten *all* other asset classes. Figure 2.1 shows that, on January 1, 1975, $1 invested in small-cap stocks grew to $184.38 by December 31, 2004. In contrast, $1 invested in large-cap stocks grew to only $47.70 during the same time period. The size difference is profound. As for the style difference, $1 invested in value stocks in 1975 grew to $61.43 in 30 years. Meanwhile, $1 invested in growth stocks grew to only $33.39 (see Figure 2.2). As for domestic, the stocks of U.S. companies versus international stocks, the stocks of companies located outside the U.S., $1 invested in domestic stocks garnered $47.70 over 30 years, while $1 invested in international stocks produced only $16.96 (see Figure 2.3). As for fixed income, $1 invested in three months' T-bills matured to $5.98, while $1 invested in 10-year Treasury bonds (T-bonds) produced $15.68 (see Figure 2.4).

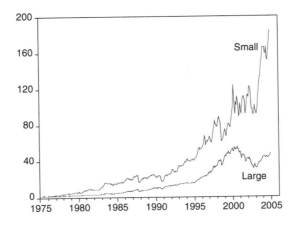

Figure 2.1 Growth of $1 invested in 1975 in small- and large-cap stocks.

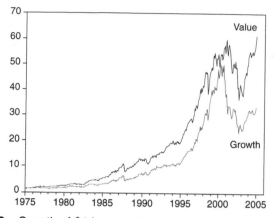

Figure 2.2   Growth of $1 invested in 1975 in growth and value stocks.

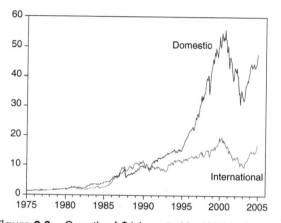

Figure 2.3   Growth of $1 invested in 1975 in domestic and international stocks.

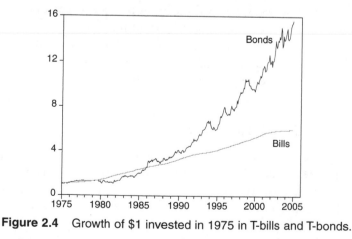

Figure 2.4   Growth of $1 invested in 1975 in T-bills and T-bonds.

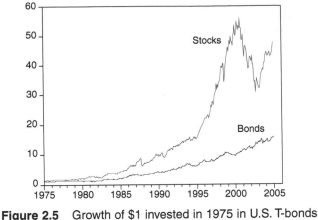

Figure 2.5 Growth of $1 invested in 1975 in U.S. T-bonds and large-cap stocks.

The data raise a number of issues for financial practitioners. One such issue is the question of whether room for growth stocks exists in a style-based asset-allocation strategy. The optimal strategic allocation for the two styles (value and growth) is another issue that immediately comes to mind. A third issue is whether there are any benefits to a cyclical or tactical asset-allocation strategy. By cyclical asset allocation, we mean a strategy allowed to deviate from the long-run allocation to take advantage of predictable fluctuations in the market as opposed to a tactical asset allocation, defined in this discussion as a shifting of capital between asset classes in relationship to a policy benchmark based on perceived valuation discrepancies in a reasonably efficient market. Looking at Figures 2.1 through 2.5, one notices secular upswings, prolonged increases in the series sometimes lasting several years, in each series point to the positive returns the markets have produced over the last three decades. The data also reveal some cyclical fluctuations in the returns, a result consistent with the mean-reversion hypothesis. The *mean-reversion hypothesis* holds that although assets at times perform better or worse than their long-run averages, they tend to revert to their averages. If these fluctuations, however, are predictable, they present an opportunity: A cyclical strategy can add value to an investor's asset-allocation objectives.

Selecting the Different Asset Classes

Using large-cap stocks as the benchmark point of reference, Table 2.1 shows small-cap stocks (with a 17.52 percent average annual return) and value stocks (with a 13.79 percent average annual return) are the only asset classes with returns high enough to beat the 12.95 percent produced by large-cap stocks. Clearly, those lucky enough to put all their eggs in the right baskets during this period realized significant returns. Common sense, however, suggests returns should not be the sole criteria of an investor's allocation decisions. Risk also must be accounted for.

Table 2.1
**Annual rates of return and standard deviations for various asset classes:
1975–2004.**

	Growth of $1 Invested in 1975	Annual Returns	Standard Deviation
T-Bills	$5.98	5.98%	2.00%
T-Bonds	$15.48	9.21%	10.70%
Small-Cap	$184.38	17.52%	21.11%
Large-Cap	$47.70	12.95%	15.23%
Growth	$33.39	11.75%	16.70%
Value	$61.23	13.79%	14.81%
International	$16.96	9.47%	16.92%

Source: Research Insight, Morgan Stanley Capital Management, and Ibbotson Associates

Looking at Table 2.1, it is apparent value stocks would clearly have been the best choice over the last three decades. Value stocks had a higher average annual return during the sample period and showed lower volatility than large-cap stocks. On the other hand, growth stocks had a lower return and showed higher volatility than the benchmark large-cap stocks, a combination that would probably disqualify them. But small-cap stocks offered the most intriguing choice: They delivered a much higher annual rate of return during the sample period—but with greater volatility. So, the question is straightforward: Do higher rates of return compensate an investor for the added risk?

Arguably, systematic risk is the most important risk measure for investors who are considering the addition of an asset class to a diversified portfolio.[3] According to the capital asset pricing model (CAPM), the only risk priced (that is, a risk that requires a higher rate of return) is risk correlated with the market. This is otherwise known as *systematic risk*, or *market risk*. Risk not correlated with the market is not priced because it can be diversified away. The CAPM offers a way to estimate *systematic risk for different asset classes*—what is known as *beta*. It also offers a precise measure of the *additional return* provided by the asset class over that required to compensate for the systematic risk—or what is known as *alpha* (or *Jensen's alpha*).

With this in mind, the statistics reported in Table 2.2 provide some new insights. A somewhat surprising finding is that the beta coefficient for the small-cap index is virtually one—meaning that it is in sync with the market—although the alpha coefficient is positive and significant. This suggests small-cap stocks, although delivering higher returns than large-caps during the sample period, were no more risky than large-caps. At the other end of the spectrum, we find growth stocks have a beta in excess of one while posting a negative alpha. The higher beta here suggests growth stocks had a higher systematic risk than the market. To make matters worse, this higher risk did not lead to superior risk-adjusted returns as measured by Jensen's alpha. In fact, the large-cap growth portfolio for this period had a negative statistically significant coefficient; not only were growth stocks riskier, they also delivered a lower return. Given these 30-year statistics, one would be hard-pressed to make a case for the inclusion of growth stocks in a portfolio.

Table 2.2
Risk measurements: 1975–2004.

	Risk-Adjusted Annual Returns	Beta	Jensen's Alpha	T-Statistics	Sharpe Ratio
Small-Cap	13.79%	1	5.64%	2.07	0.65
Large-Cap	8.13%	1	0.00%		0.53
Growth	7.17%	1.06	−1.46%	1.87	0.43
Value	8.91%	.93	0.81%	1.67	0.60
International	4.91%	.62	−1.27%	0.04	0.29

Source: Research Insight, Morgan Stanley Capital Management, and Ibbotson Associates

As for value stocks, they produced a somewhat lower beta than the market during the sample period, suggesting they have a lower systematic risk than the market. Value stocks also appear to have shown a positive alpha, but only enough to be considered marginally significant at best. Once again, taken at face value, the results suggest value stocks have a lower systematic risk than the market but quite possibly offer higher risk-adjusted returns.

International stocks exhibited what appears to be significantly lower beta and alpha coefficients for the period, with the alpha coming in at just about zero. This means that although international stocks offered a much lower systematic risk for the period, they did not produce additional excess return. One conclusion is this: The only possible contribution international stocks can make to a portfolio is as risk-reducing or diversification mechanisms.

Based on the statistics presented in Table 2.2, the CAPM investment implications are fairly straightforward: Avoid growth stocks in your portfolio, include some international stocks as a risk-reduction measure, take some value stocks also as a risk-reduction measure as well as an excess-return-producing measure, and add in small-cap stocks to generate some risk-adjusted excess returns (alpha).

In the process of developing traditional, and optimal, asset allocations for their clients, investment advisors typically have looked to the long-run historical expected returns for the various asset classes as well as the historical *variance–covariance matrix*, which shows the ways market variables either move away from one another or travel in tandem. In turn, these statistics are used to generate an *efficient frontier*, which is the combination of different asset classes that, given the historical returns of the mix, also produce the lowest standard deviation or volatility from which an optimal portfolio is selected.

Finding the Optimal Combinations

I am taking a more direct approach—some call this approach pedestrian, but it is easier to articulate and is hopefully clearer and more user-friendly. To explore further the style, size, and location choices for a strategic asset allocation (in short, an allocation based on historical, expected returns), I have built a set of 11 portfolios—one for each possible asset choice using the S&P 500/BARRA value and S&P 500/BARRA growth monthly returns from 1975 on. The first portfolio allocates 100 percent of assets to value stocks, and each additional portfolio reduces the value exposure by 10 percentage points. The process continues until 100 percent is allocated to growth stocks. I have also constructed 11 size-related portfolios, 11 location-based portfolios, and 11 balanced portfolios.

First, a word on the S&P/BARRA indices. According to BARRA, they "are constructed by dividing the stocks in an index according to a single attribute: book-to-price ratio. This splits the index into two mutually exclusive groups designed to track two of the predominant investment styles in the U.S. equity market."[4] These styles are value and growth, a distinction William Sharpe found valid.[5]

The Sharpe ratio, named after William Sharpe (the 1990 Nobel Prize in Economics winner), divides a portfolio's excess return (return less riskless T-bill return) by its volatility. In effect, the Sharpe ratio treats each asset class as a separate portfolio, focusing on the standard deviations that measure total risk. If the portfolio in question represents the entire investment of an individual, volatility matters—and the Sharpe ratio is an appropriate comparison tool. As such, the Sharpe ratio provides an apt way to compare and evaluate the size, style, location, and balance of portfolios.

The Optimal Value Stocks/Growth Stocks Mix

The style portfolios I produced are reported in Table 2.3. Please note that *12* different portfolios are reported here. The 11 previously mentioned maintain consistent allocations to growth and/or value stocks for the 1975 through 2004 period. For example, the "20%" portfolio consists of a 20 percent growth allocation and an 80 percent value allocation for the 30-year period. The "100%" portfolio consists of all growth stocks and the "0%" portfolio consists of all value stocks. The 12th, or "Best" portfolio, was constructed a bit differently. For this portfolio, I assume perfect foresight and choose (on an ex-post basis, or after the fact) the best allocation for each calendar year. Hence, the "Best" portfolio consists of a time-changing allocation to value and growth stocks that maximizes the Sharpe ratio for each of the sample years.

Table 2.3

Sample period risk-adjusted average annual returns, standard deviations, and Sharpe ratios for selected style portfolios.

Growth Allocation						
1975–2004	100%	90%	80%	70%	60%	50%
Average Annual Return	7.17%	7.34%	7.52%	7.69%	7.86%	8.04%
Standard Deviation	16.73%	16.34%	15.99%	15.68%	15.41%	15.19%
Sharpe Ratio	0.428	0.449	0.470	0.491	0.510	0.529
1975–2004	40%	30%	20%	10%	0%	Best
Average Annual Return	8.21%	8.39%	8.56%	8.74%	**8.91%**	11.65%
Standard Deviation	15.02%	14.90%	14.83%	14.81%	**14.84%**	15.78%
Sharpe Ratio	0.547	0.563	0.577	0.590	**0.600**	0.738

Source: Research Insight, Morgan Stanley Capital Management, and Ibbotson Associates

The numbers show that the portfolio consisting solely of value stocks returned an 8.91 percent average annual return on a risk-adjusted basis (Table 2.3: 0 percent growth allocation). The growth portfolio in this group returned 7.17 percent per year. Again, common sense suggests returns alone should not be the sole criteria of an investor's allocation decisions, and risk also must be accounted for. In Table 2.3, the second row shows the estimated standard deviation (or volatility) of the returns for each portfolio. At 14.84 percent, the volatility of the all-value style portfolio (or 0 percent growth) is a bit lower than the 16.73 percent standard deviation of the all-growth portfolio. Higher return and lower volatility is a compelling argument in favor of value stocks. In the third row of the same table, I simply calculated the risk-adjusted portfolio returns ratio to their standard deviation (that is, I plugged in the Sharpe ratio). The idea is the portfolio with the highest return-to-standard-deviation ratio offers the highest reward-to-risk ratio. The data show that the portfolio consisting solely of value stocks generated the highest reward-to-risk ratio.

The results presented in Table 2.3 are consistent with the various findings reported in the academic literature indicating that value stocks have outperformed growth stocks over the last 30 years.[6] The results are also consistent with those reported in the previous section when we found —when compared to the market—growth stocks had higher risk and negative value-added, while value stocks had lower risk and positive value-added. The data suggest that a 100 percent allocation to value stocks is the optimal allocation for a long-run or strategic style allocation.

The Optimal Large Stocks/Small Stocks Combination

The size portfolios are reported in Table 2.4. The summary statistics show what we already know: Across the sample, small-cap stocks produced higher returns than large-cap stocks (13.79 percent versus 8.13 percent per year). We also can see small-caps had a higher volatility than their larger counterparts (21.20 percent versus 15.26 percent). Looking at the Sharpe ratios, we get some expected results. Small-cap stocks have a higher Sharpe ratio than large-cap stocks. As such, they would be considered more attractive to a portfolio than large-caps, although the data also show that a portfolio consisting of between 70 and 80 percent small-cap stocks and between 20 and 30 percent large-cap stocks would generate the *highest* Sharpe ratio. The latter is a new result and suggests, as one adds 20 to 30 percent large-cap stocks to a portfolio, the reduced volatility is sufficient to offset the reduced returns generated by the large-cap stocks.

Table 2.4

Sample period risk-adjusted average annual returns, standard deviation, and Sharpe ratio for selected size portfolios.

Small Allocation						
1975–2004	**100%**	**90%**	**80%**	**70%**	**60%**	**50%**
Average Annual Return	13.79%	13.22%	**12.66%**	**12.09%**	11.53%	10.96%
Standard Deviation	21.20%	20.21%	**19.28%**	**18.42%**	17.64%	16.95%
Sharpe Ratio	0.650	0.654	**0.657**	**0.657**	0.654	0.647
1975–2004	**40%**	**30%**	**20%**	**10%**	**0%**	**Best**
Average Annual Return	10.39%	9.83%	9.26%	8.70%	8.13%	16.09%
Standard Deviation	16.36%	15.89%	15.54%	15.33%	15.26%	18.55%
Sharpe Ratio	0.635	0.619	0.596	0.567	0.533	0.867

Source: Research Insight, Morgan Stanley Capital Management, and Ibbotson Associates

The Optimal Domestic Stocks/International Stocks Portfolio

The location portfolios are reported in Table 2.5. The numbers show that the portfolio consisting solely of U.S. stocks, on a risk-adjusted basis, returned an average of 8.13 percent per year (first row, 0 percent international allocation) over the sample period. The portfolio of foreign stocks, at 4.91 percent, under-performed the domestic stocks during the period. The second row in the table shows the estimated standard deviation of the returns for each portfolio. At 16.97 percent, the foreign portfolio volatility is a bit higher than the 15.26 percent standard deviation of the domestic portfolio. Thus, it is clear the domestic-stock portfolio, with higher return and lower volatility, is the superior alternative. The question faced by investors is whether a combination of the two portfolios, when compared to the pure-domestic portfolio, would yield sufficient risk-reduction to compensate for the lower return. The data suggest the answer is a resounding *no*. It thus appears that during the sample period, the optimal strategic location allocation was to go 100 percent with domestic stocks.

Table 2.5
Sample period risk-adjusted average annual returns, standard deviation, and Sharpe ratio for selected location portfolios.

International Allocation						
1975–2004	**100%**	**90%**	**80%**	**70%**	**60%**	**50%**
Average Annual Return	4.91%	5.23%	5.56%	5.88%	6.20%	6.52%
Standard Deviation	16.97%	16.17%	15.48%	14.92%	14.50%	14.22%
Sharpe Ratio	0.290	0.324	0.359	0.394	0.428	0.459
1975–2004	**40%**	**30%**	**20%**	**10%**	**0%**	**Best**
Average Annual Return	6.84%	7.17%	7.49%	7.81%	**8.13%**	12.25%
Standard Deviation	14.11%	14.16%	14.37%	14.74%	**15.26%**	14.94%
Sharpe Ratio	0.485	0.506	0.521	0.530	**0.533**	0.820

The Optimal T-Bond/Equity Combination

The equity/fixed-income choice is explored in Table 2.6. T-bonds delivered 3.75 percent per year with 10.70 percent average volatility. In contrast, stocks (or the 0 percent T-bond portfolio) produced a risk-adjusted 8.13 percent per year over the period with 15.26 percent volatility. The data show the returns and volatility for T-bonds are much lower than those for stocks. More important, the data also suggest the greater risk-reduction in the T-bond portfolio cannot be large enough to offset the portfolio's lower returns. The Sharpe ratio of the T-bond portfolio is 0.35 versus 0.53 for the equity portfolio. This result should not be surprising, given Jeremy Siegel's popular book, *Stocks for the Long Run*, in which he basically confirms that equities far outperform T-bonds over the long haul.[7] Looking, however, at the various stocks and T-bonds combinations, it appears a mixture provides a higher return-to-risk ratio. A portfolio consisting of 60 percent equities and 40 percent T-bonds yields the highest Sharpe ratio.

Table 2.6
Sample period risk-adjusted average annual returns, standard deviation, and Sharpe ratio for selected T-bond/equity portfolios.

Bond Allocation						
1975–2004	**100%**	**90%**	**80%**	**70%**	**60%**	**50%**
Average Annual Return	3.75%	4.19%	4.63%	5.06%	5.50%	5.94%
Standard Deviation	10.70%	10.10%	9.74%	9.65%	9.84%	10.29%
Sharpe Ratio	0.350	0.415	0.475	0.525	0.559	0.577
1975–2004	**40%**	**30%**	**20%**	**10%**	**0%**	**Best**
Average Annual Return	**6.38%**	6.82%	7.26%	7.69%	8.13%	11.44%
Standard Deviation	**10.97%**	11.85%	12.87%	14.02%	15.26%	12.37%
Sharpe Ratio	**0.581**	0.575	0.564	0.549	0.533	0.925

Source: Research Insight, Morgan Stanley Capital Management, and Ibbotson Associates

Putting It All Together

Naïvely reading financial literature of course provides you with some clear-cut ways to allocate to asset classes. The literature suggests value stocks are the way to go and suggests there is no benefit to a strategic asset-allocation strategy (based on historical, expected returns) or tactical strategy (which at times deviates from the long-run plan to take advantage of short-run opportunities). My own data, to this point, suggest just about as much. Based on the 30-year sample period, the optimal style choice for a portfolio is to allocate 100 percent to value stocks. In terms of location, the optimal allocation is to put 100 percent into domestic stocks. The numbers also point to a less than 100 percent allocation for the size and equity/fixed-income choices. In the case of the size choice, the most favorable allocation is 70 to 80 percent small-cap stocks, while the optimal allocation for T-bonds versus stocks is 40 to 50 percent T-bonds. These are somewhat surprising results based on the conventional wisdom—one would expect to find the opposite result, which would be a 60 percent allocation to large-cap stocks in both cases. The question now becomes whether 30 years is a long enough span to generate a long-run result. If the sample period is not long enough to establish long-run returns, the results can suffer from sample-selection bias.

Indeed, there are some reasons to question the impact of the sample period on the results. First, on theoretical grounds, one can argue that if markets are reasonably efficient, the market portfolio that buys the market should be on the efficient frontier—that owning a historically proven asset class mix is the best bet for every investor. Hence, growth stocks, although not the historical high performers value stocks are, should be included in such a portfolio. Second, looking at the data, we know the 1990s were not kind to value stocks. So, the growth stocks' performance during this time forces one to rethink the "absolute" superiority of value stocks.

In the next few paragraphs, I develop an alternative view that, although consistent with the data regarding the historical superiority of value stocks over growth stocks, argues that room exists for growth stocks in a portfolio.

The results in Table 2.3 suggest the case for growth stocks would at best rest on a cyclical (or tactical) style asset-allocation strategy—again, a strategy allowed to deviate from the long-run allocation to take advantage of predictable fluctuations in the market. But, even here, the academic literature is not encouraging. Researchers have looked at the relative performance of the two styles (value and growth) during down and up markets as well as during slow and fast growth periods of real gross domestic product (GDP).[8] The results are universal: The value portfolio outperforms the growth portfolio.

Style Cycles

Borrowing from financial estimation techniques, I decided to calculate the average monthly returns and standard deviations for each calendar year in our sample 30-year period. Table 2.7 reports the average monthly returns ratio to the standard deviation for each of the 11 portfolios' returns during each calendar year for which data were available. The bold-faced numbers in Table 2.7 identify the portfolio combinations chosen using perfect foresight. A visual inspection of the table shows that, during 13 of the years, the optimal style portfolio was one consisting solely of growth stocks, although for 15 other years, the best possible portfolio consisted solely of value stocks. This is eye-opening: The frequency of the 100 percent growth portfolios is only slightly less than that of the value portfolios. More important, the results show that for 28 of the 30 years, the optimal portfolio consisted of a corner solution (which is to say, the choice of all of one and none of the others).

Table 2.7

Sharpe ratio for selected style portfolios, 1975–2004.

	Growth Allocation										
	100%	90%	80%	70%	60%	50%	40%	30%	20%	10%	0%
1975	1.183	1.265	1.347	1.430	1.511	1.590	1.663	1.729	1.788	1.836	**1.874**
1976	0.611	0.740	0.873	1.011	1.152	1.297	1.446	1.598	1.753	1.910	**2.068**
1977	-1.364	-1.360	-1.351	-1.335	-1.309	-1.272	-1.220	-1.153	-1.069	-0.969	-0.856
1978	**0.064**	0.060	0.055	0.051	0.046	0.040	0.035	0.029	0.023	0.016	0.010
1979	0.423	0.459	0.495	0.530	0.565	0.598	0.631	0.662	0.693	0.723	**0.751**
1980	**1.187**	1.159	1.127	1.091	1.050	1.005	0.955	0.900	0.840	0.776	0.707
1981	-1.468	-1.463	-1.455	-1.445	-1.430	-1.411	-1.387	-1.356	-1.319	-1.273	-1.218
1982	**0.590**	**0.589**	**0.588**	0.586	0.583	0.580	0.576	0.572	0.567	0.562	0.556
1983	0.637	0.752	0.872	0.997	1.125	1.253	1.381	1.505	1.623	1.733	**1.833**
1984	-0.438	-0.387	-0.333	-0.279	-0.223	-0.166	-0.110	-0.054	0.001	0.055	**0.107**
1985	1.582	1.611	1.640	1.670	1.700	1.731	1.761	1.791	1.821	1.849	**1.875**
1986	0.491	0.529	0.568	0.607	0.646	0.684	0.721	0.757	0.792	0.825	**0.857**
1987	**0.191**	0.182	0.172	0.162	0.151	0.140	0.129	0.117	0.105	0.093	0.080
1988	0.531	0.619	0.708	0.798	0.888	0.978	1.065	1.151	1.233	1.312	**1.387**
1989	**1.811**	1.781	1.749	1.713	1.674	1.631	1.585	1.536	1.483	1.427	1.367

	Growth Allocation										
	100%	90%	80%	70%	60%	50%	40%	30%	20%	10%	0%
1990	**-0.281**	-0.325	-0.371	-0.418	-0.466	-0.516	-0.566	-0.618	-0.670	-0.723	-0.777
1991	**1.657**	1.619	1.577	1.532	1.482	1.427	1.368	1.305	1.238	1.166	1.090
1992	0.216	0.286	0.360	0.436	0.512	0.587	0.659	0.725	0.784	0.836	**0.879**
1993	-0.093	0.085	0.292	0.532	0.804	1.107	1.428	1.751	2.050	2.302	**2.492**
1994	**-0.027**	-0.062	-0.097	-0.131	-0.165	-0.197	-0.228	-0.257	-0.285	-0.312	-0.337
1995	**5.206**	5.298	5.339	5.323	5.253	5.132	4.971	4.780	4.570	4.352	4.132
1996	1.443	1.459	1.474	1.485	1.494	1.500	1.503	**1.502**	1.497	1.488	1.475
1997	1.561	1.567	1.573	1.577	1.580	1.581	1.580	1.577	1.572	1.563	1.552
1998	**1.558**	1.456	1.352	1.246	**1.580**	1.033	0.926	0.820	0.715	0.611	0.508
1999	**1.418**	1.391	1.353	1.301	1.235	1.155	1.060	0.955	0.841	0.723	0.604
2000	-1.212	-1.163	-1.098	-1.015	-0.910	-0.780	-0.627	-0.453	-0.269	-0.085	**0.089**
2001	**-0.646**	-0.664	-0.683	-0.702	-0.720	-0.739	-0.757	-0.774	-0.790	-0.805	-0.818
2002	-1.323	-1.299	-1.272	-1.243	-1.213	-1.180	-1.147	-1.112	-1.077	-1.041	-1.006
2003	**2.599**	2.510	2.424	2.343	2.266	2.194	2.127	2.064	2.006	1.952	1.902
2004	0.634	0.760	0.891	1.026	1.162	1.298	1.433	1.565	1.691	1.811	**1.923**

Again assuming perfect foresight, I calculated the returns and standard deviations of a strategy that correctly anticipated the best annual portfolios. The results, reported in Table 2.3's last ("Best") column, suggest knowledge of annual cycles would have added 23 basis points per month over the amount allocating 100 percent of assets to value stocks generates. This adds up to approximately 274 basis points per year. A *basis point* is one-hundredth of one percent. More important, during the first 15 years of the sample period, there were nine years in which a 100 percent allocation to value stocks was optimal. But, on the other hand, the last 16 years, were more favorable to growth stocks. In nine of those 16 years the portfolio of 100 percent growth stocks produced the highest Sharpe ratio.

The magnitude of these potential benefits suggests it can be worthwhile to spend some resources on trying to correctly anticipate growth cycles. To be sure, the timing and distribution of the optimal allocations during the various years does not appear to be random. The question is now: What explains the pattern of results?

I believe one style's predominance over another for the past 30 years reflects changes in the economic environment. My analysis suggests that, during the bulk of the 1970s and part of the 1980s, the economic environment favored value stocks over growth stocks. It is, therefore, not surprising to see that most empirical literature has found that value stocks outperform growth stocks. It seems increasingly clear, however, that the results reported in the literature suffer from sample-selection bias. Value stocks did well because of the economic policies adopted over the past three decades. If this is in fact the case—as I believe it is—there is no guarantee the overall economic environment in the future will favor value stocks at all times. My analysis suggests it behooves investors to pay attention to the economic environment and suggests growth stocks—when the environment warrants—can have an important impact on the total return of a style-based asset-allocation strategy.

Size Cycles

Size cycles also matter. Following the methodology outlined in the previous section, I calculated 11 size-related portfolios for each of the 30 years for which data were available. The results are reported in Table 2.8. Again, as in the case of the style choices, the optimal allocation for size portfolios is more often than not a corner solution. For 12 years, the highest Sharpe ratio is produced by allocating 90 to 100 percent of a portfolio's assets to small-cap stocks and for another 12 years, the same applies to large-cap stocks. More notably, if one looks at the timing, one finds the bulk of the allocations to small-cap stocks occur before 1983 or after 1999. Viewed this way, it appears the 1980s and 1990s were—by and large—favorable to large-cap stocks, an apparent anomaly based on the historical experience. Also, assuming perfect foresight, identifying the optimal allocation during each of the years in the sample would have increased the returns produced by the size allocation to 16.09 percent per year from 12.66 percent. Anticipating the correct allocation would have produced a net gain of 343 basis points per year, a figure that should be large enough to capture any investor's attention.

Table 2.8
Sharpe ratio for selected size portfolios: 1975–2004.

| Small Allocation → | 100% | 90% | 80% | 70% | 60% | 50% | 40% | 30% | 20% | 10% | 0% |
Large Allocation →	0%	10%	20%	30%	40%	50%	60%	70%	80%	90%	100%
1975	1.381	1.409	1.438	1.467	1.496	1.523	1.547	1.566	1.577	1.576	1.562
1976	1.433	1.439	1.443	1.447	1.448	1.446	1.438	1.421	1.389	1.335	1.251
1977	1.363	1.202	1.018	0.809	0.575	0.313	0.025	-0.286	-0.613	-0.949	-1.281
1978	0.604	0.580	0.551	0.519	0.480	0.434	0.380	0.315	0.238	0.147	0.042
1979	1.222	1.191	1.157	1.118	1.073	1.021	0.961	0.892	0.810	0.714	0.603
1980	0.953	0.964	0.974	0.985	0.995	1.006	1.015	1.024	1.031	1.036	1.039
1981	0.045	-0.060	-0.176	-0.303	-0.441	-0.591	-0.751	-0.918	-1.088	-1.256	-1.417
1982	0.917	0.887	0.856	0.823	0.790	0.755	0.720	0.684	0.648	0.612	0.577
1983	1.665	1.680	1.691	1.696	1.691	1.672	1.634	1.574	1.486	1.372	1.233
1984	-0.998	-0.926	-0.852	-0.774	-0.695	-0.613	-0.529	-0.443	-0.355	-0.266	-0.175
1985	1.080	1.147	1.215	1.285	1.356	1.427	1.497	1.566	1.634	1.698	1.759
1986	0.112	0.187	0.259	0.327	0.393	0.455	0.513	0.569	0.620	0.669	0.714
1987	-0.248	-0.214	-0.179	-0.142	-0.104	-0.065	-0.025	0.016	0.058	0.101	0.144
1988	1.152	1.170	1.184	1.192	1.194	1.185	1.166	1.133	1.087	1.028	0.959
1989	0.206	0.382	0.558	0.730	0.894	1.050	1.194	1.326	1.445	1.550	1.64

	Small Allocation									Large Allocation	
	100%	90%	80%	70%	60%	50%	40%	30%	20%	10%	0%
1990	-1.446	-1.370	-1.289	-1.203	-1.113	-1.019	-0.921	-0.819	-0.715	-0.607	-0.498
1991	**2.104**	2.070	2.027	1.976	1.917	1.850	1.775	1.695	1.609	1.519	1.427
1992	1.090	1.103	1.114	1.124	**1.130**	1.125	1.101	1.043	0.936	0.769	0.557
1993	1.754	**1.757**	1.754	1.742	1.719	1.681	1.623	1.541	1.433	1.298	1.140
1994	**-0.032**	-0.049	-0.067	-0.085	-0.102	-0.119	-0.135	-0.151	-0.166	-0.179	-0.191
1995	2.598	2.831	3.094	3.388	3.711	4.057	4.408	4.733	4.990	5.136	**5.145**
1996	0.716	0.790	0.873	0.964	1.062	1.164	1.265	1.357	1.431	1.478	**1.495**
1997	0.948	1.051	1.157	1.263	1.362	1.449	1.519	1.567	1.592	**1.596**	1.581
1998	-0.335	-0.220	-0.099	0.027	0.159	0.296	0.439	0.587	0.741	0.899	**1.061**
1999	1.168	1.210	1.252	1.292	1.329	1.356	**1.369**	1.361	1.327	1.267	1.183
2000	**-0.079**	-0.118	-0.166	-0.223	-0.294	-0.379	-0.479	-0.589	-0.694	-0.773	-0.810
2001	**0.746**	0.643	0.530	0.407	0.274	0.129	-0.026	-0.191	-0.365	-0.545	-0.729
2002	**-0.606**	-0.675	-0.745	-0.814	-0.882	-0.946	-1.006	-1.060	-1.107	-1.147	-1.179
2003	**3.035**	3.009	2.975	2.931	2.875	2.806	2.722	2.620	2.499	2.358	2.197
2004	1.073	1.090	1.108	1.128	1.150	1.173	1.199	1.225	1.253	1.279	**1.300**

Location Cycles

Now for location. The performance of the 11 location-based portfolios for the 30 years in question is reported in Table 2.9. In line with previous results, most optimal annual allocations are either pure-corner solutions (all eggs in one basket) or allocations of more than 90 percent to one location (most eggs in one basket). I find this to be the case in 24 of the 30 years. But one new result has to do with the distribution of the corner solutions: Although it is optimal to allocate 100 percent to U.S. stocks most of the time, in only nine years is it desirable to invest 90 percent or better in international stocks. So, the data suggest that, when in doubt, tilt to U.S. stocks. The more interesting result, however, is the allocations to U.S. stocks appear to run in bunches, lending more credibility to the cycle hypothesis.

Table 2.9

Sharpe ratio for selected location portfolios: 1975–2004.

International Allocation										
	100%	90%	80%	70%	60%	50%	40%	30%	20%	10%	0%
1975	1.00	1.06	1.12	1.18	1.24	1.31	1.37	1.43	1.48	1.53	**1.56**
1976	−0.28	−0.14	0.00	0.16	0.33	0.50	0.66	0.83	0.98	1.12	**1.25**
1977	**1.30**	1.08	0.79	0.45	0.09	−0.25	−0.56	−0.81	−1.01	−1.16	−1.28
1978	1.24	**1.25**	1.24	1.19	1.09	0.94	0.74	0.53	0.34	0.18	0.04
1979	−0.68	−0.54	−0.40	−0.26	−0.11	0.02	0.16	0.28	0.40	0.51	**0.60**
1980	0.46	0.54	0.63	0.71	0.79	0.86	0.92	0.96	1.00	1.02	**1.04**
1981	**−0.97**	−1.04	−1.12	−1.19	−1.26	−1.33	−1.39	−1.43	−1.45	−1.44	−1.42
1982	−0.74	−0.63	−0.51	−0.37	−0.22	−0.07	0.09	0.23	0.36	0.48	**0.58**
1983	1.34	1.40	1.45	1.48	**1.49**	1.47	1.44	1.40	1.35	1.29	1.23
1984	**−0.15**	−0.15	−0.16	−0.17	−0.17	−0.17	−0.18	−0.18	−0.18	−0.18	−0.18
1985	4.06	4.29	**4.45**	4.45	4.25	3.88	3.42	2.93	2.48	2.09	1.76
1986	2.28	**2.29**	**2.29**	2.26	2.17	2.03	1.82	1.56	1.27	0.98	0.71
1987	**0.76**	0.71	0.65	0.58	0.52	0.45	0.38	0.32	0.26	0.20	0.14
1988	1.19	1.24	1.29	1.34	**1.38**	1.41	1.40	1.35	1.25	1.11	0.96
1989	0.12	0.24	0.38	0.53	0.69	0.87	1.05	1.23	1.39	1.53	**1.64**

continues

Table 2.9 continued

	International Allocation										
	0%	10%	20%	30%	40%	50%	60%	70%	80%	90%	100%
1990	**-0.50**	-0.63	-0.75	-0.86	-0.93	-0.99	-1.02	-1.04	-1.05	-1.05	-1.05
1991	**1.43**	1.35	1.26	1.15	1.04	0.91	0.79	0.66	0.54	0.43	0.32
1992	**0.56**	0.29	-0.02	-0.32	-0.58	-0.78	-0.92	-1.02	-1.10	-1.15	-1.19
1993	1.14	1.43	1.59	1.64	**1.64**	1.60	1.57	1.53	1.49	1.46	1.43
1994	-0.19	-0.14	-0.10	-0.05	0.00	0.04	0.09	0.13	0.16	0.20	**0.23**
1995	**5.14**	4.56	3.86	3.15	2.52	1.97	1.52	1.14	0.82	0.56	0.34
1996	**1.49**	1.41	1.32	1.21	1.08	0.94	0.77	0.58	0.38	0.16	-0.07
1997	**1.58**	1.45	1.30	1.13	0.94	0.75	0.54	0.34	0.14	-0.05	-0.23
1998	**1.06**	1.04	1.02	1.00	0.97	0.93	0.89	0.85	0.81	0.76	0.71
1999	1.18	1.25	1.31	1.37	1.42	1.47	1.50	1.51	**1.52**	1.52	1.50
2000	**-0.81**	-0.89	-0.97	-1.06	-1.14	-1.23	-1.31	-1.39	-1.46	-1.52	-1.56
2001	**-0.73**	-0.81	-0.90	-0.98	-1.07	-1.16	-1.25	-1.34	-1.43	-1.52	-1.61
2002	-1.18	-1.18	-1.17	-1.16	-1.15	-1.14	-1.12	-1.10	-1.07	-1.04	**-1.01**
2003	2.20	2.21	2.21	2.21	2.21	2.20	2.18	2.17	2.15	2.13	2.10
2004	1.30	1.36	1.40	1.45	1.49	1.52	1.55	1.57	1.59	1.61	**1.63**

Again, the issue is whether we can anticipate these cycles, a topic addressed in the next chapter. For now, it suffices to show the potential benefits of anticipating these cycles. The correct annual location-based allocation increases from 8.13 percent per year (generated by investing solely in domestic stocks) to 12.25 percent per year when international stocks are strategically included. Once again, a potential gain of 412 basis points per year is enough to tempt most people to find a way to anticipate these cycles. Even if one does not capture a full cycle, the gains can be large enough to make it worth pursuing such a strategy.

Equity/T-Bond Cycles

Finally, let's look for evidence of equity/T-bond cycles. The equity/T-bond choice turns out to be the one with the least amount of corner solutions. As shown in Table 2.10, only during 11 of the 30 sample years is a 100 percent equity allocation the optimal choice. The same number of years holds for an optimal T-bond allocation of 90 percent or higher. For six out of eight years, 100 percent T-bond-allocation is optimal. Importantly, these years (1981–1982, 1990–1991, and 2000–2001) are associated with U.S. recessions. The data clearly suggest knowledge of a coming recession would have been quite useful to an investor interested in a balanced allocation over the sample period. Assuming perfect foresight once more, correctly anticipating these cycles would have increased returns from 6.38 percent per year (40/60 equity/T-bonds) to 11.44 percent per year. The potential gains of such a strategy average are a whopping 506 basis points per year. If that does not support the cyclical allocation strategy, nothing does. All one needs to do is anticipate the economic slowdowns.

Table 2.10

Sharpe ratio for selected T-bond/equity portfolios location portfolios: 1975–2004.

	T-Bonds										
	100%	90%	80%	70%	60%	50%	40%	30%	20%	10%	0%
1975	0.420	0.711	0.963	1.160	1.301	1.398	1.462	1.505	1.532	1.550	**1.562**
1976	2.287	**2.393**	2.320	2.149	1.958	1.784	1.635	1.511	1.409	1.323	1.251
1977	**-0.974**	-1.090	-1.183	-1.251	-1.295	-1.318	-1.326	-1.322	-1.312	-1.297	-1.281
1978	-1.764	-1.372	-1.021	-0.745	-0.535	-0.376	-0.252	-0.155	-0.076	-0.012	**0.042**
1979	-0.981	-0.815	-0.641	-0.463	-0.285	-0.112	0.053	0.208	0.352	0.483	**0.603**
1980	-0.610	-0.499	-0.361	-0.193	0.004	0.221	0.440	0.641	0.810	0.942	**1.039**
1981	**-0.443**	-0.511	-0.587	-0.672	-0.765	-0.867	-0.977	-1.092	-1.208	-1.318	-1.417
1982	**2.309**	2.122	1.914	1.701	1.493	1.299	1.121	0.960	0.817	0.690	0.577
1983	-0.640	-0.490	-0.321	-0.133	0.070	0.282	0.497	0.706	0.902	1.079	**1.233**
1984	**0.497**	0.450	0.391	0.320	0.240	0.156	0.075	-0.001	-0.068	-0.126	-0.175
1985	1.688	1.763	1.830	1.885	1.924	**1.943**	1.941	1.919	1.879	1.824	1.759
1986	1.013	**1.015**	1.011	0.998	0.977	0.948	0.911	0.867	0.819	0.767	0.714
1987	-0.746	-0.741	-0.619	-0.417	-0.238	-0.110	-0.022	0.039	0.084	0.118	**0.144**
1988	0.349	0.421	0.493	0.565	0.636	0.703	0.766	0.824	0.876	0.921	**0.959**

| T-Bonds | | | | | | | | | | | |
	100%	90%	80%	70%	60%	50%	40%	30%	20%	10%	0%
1989	1.110	1.344	1.562	1.734	1.840	**1.878**	1.866	1.823	1.766	1.704	1.644
1990	**-0.126**	-0.198	-0.259	-0.311	-0.354	-0.389	-0.419	-0.444	-0.465	-0.483	-0.498
1991	1.991	**2.056**	2.037	1.967	1.877	1.783	1.694	1.615	1.544	1.482	1.427
1992	0.642	0.668	0.689	0.703	**0.707**	0.701	0.685	0.660	0.629	0.594	0.557
1993	1.985	2.014	**2.030**	2.026	1.993	1.925	1.819	1.677	1.509	1.326	1.140
1994	-1.337	-1.248	-1.145	-1.031	-0.908	-0.780	-0.652	-0.527	-0.408	-0.296	**-0.191**
1995	3.036	3.413	3.845	4.326	4.830	5.303	5.663	**5.826**	5.760	5.506	5.145
1996	-0.598	-0.378	-0.139	0.112	0.365	0.610	0.837	1.040	1.218	1.368	**1.495**
1997	1.110	1.256	1.374	1.461	1.521	1.560	1.581	1.591	**1.592**	1.588	1.581
1998	1.154	1.817	**2.396**	2.322	1.964	1.667	1.459	1.312	1.205	1.124	1.061
1999	-2.431	-1.898	-1.320	-0.769	-0.292	0.101	0.418	0.672	0.878	1.045	**1.183**
2000	**2.415**	1.828	1.236	0.727	0.322	0.007	-0.238	-0.430	-0.583	-0.708	-0.810
2001	**0.030**	-0.159	-0.418	-0.670	-0.803	-0.829	-0.815	-0.791	-0.767	-0.746	-0.729
2002	**1.460**	1.429	1.275	0.745	-0.095	-0.633	-0.890	-1.022	-1.098	-1.146	-1.179
2003	0.096	0.288	0.520	0.796	1.108	1.436	1.739	1.975	2.122	2.189	**2.197**
2004	0.899	1.006	1.125	1.252	1.376	1.478	**1.536**	1.538	1.488	1.402	1.300

The Optimal Long-Run Allocation

The *efficient market theory* tells us the market portfolio, in an idealized situation, is on the efficient frontier—or the point where the expected return is maximized for the level of projected risk. But if this were truly the case, we would have found that after applying the tools of modern finance—such as the CAPM and Sharpe ratio measures—*all* asset classes would be included on the efficient frontier. Table 2.11 reports the results of the optimal mix for each of the two asset classes combinations reported in the previous paragraphs. The pair-wise allocation are based on the Sharpe ratio produced by the data during the 1975 through 2004 period. Yet the summary statistics produced by the full 30-year sample show that as one separates assets by style, size, location, and equity/T-bond choice, value stocks are superior to growth stocks and domestic stocks are superior to international stocks. Taken at face value, these statistics suggest there is no room for growth stocks and international stocks in a well-diversified portfolio. These results produce two competing alternatives: One is the market portfolio is not on the efficient frontier and the other is the sample period is not long enough to estimate long-run mean returns and standard deviations. If the sample period is too short, it could include some temporary deviations from the long-run trends. This could be dangerous, as the sample-selection bias could result in a strategic asset allocation mistakenly overweighing or underweighing some asset classes. Because the mean-reversion hypothesis—as most people articulate it—assumes random disturbances around the mean (assuming no fundamental change in the process generating the returns), the solution to the sample-selection bias is to use the longest time period possible.[9]

Table 2.11

Optimal allocation based on the Sharpe ratio produced by the historical returns: 1975–2004.

Size	Small	Large
	80.0%	20.0%
Style	Value	Growth
	100.0%	0.0%
Location	USA	Rest of the World
	100.0%	0.0%
Equity/Fixed	Equity	Fixed Income
	60.0%	40.0%

Figures 2.6 through 2.10 show that, when one looks at the relative perform-ance of the various asset classes, distinct patterns emerge. (Small-caps versus large-caps is shown in Figure 2.6, value versus growth in Figure 2.7, domestic versus international in Figure 2.8, T-bonds versus T-bills in Figure 2.9, and stocks versus T-bonds in Figure 2.10.) This patterning raises the possibility of nonrandom cyclical behavior, in which case an asset-allocation strategy that alters allocations over cycles produces results superior to a strategic asset allocation that ignores cyclical fluctuations and focuses only on the long run. Thus, the data presented in Figures 2.6 through 2.10 and Tables 2.7 through 2.10 suggest a strategic allocation produced by looking at the long-run sample is not stable. Simply put, a great deal of variation in the year-to-year allocation in the three-decade sample exists. In fact, looking at the data, in the best cases (that is, the best location and style choices), *the long-run allocation is correct only 50 percent of the time.* In all other cases, it is correct far less than that. Looking at the yearly choices, the results reported in Tables 2.7 through 2.10 suggest the pattern and preponderance of corner solutions for the optimal yearly allocation are unlikely to be random. Uncovering the causes of the pat-terns presents us with an opportunity to develop a cyclical asset-allocation strategy that would take advantage of the patterns identified in the data.

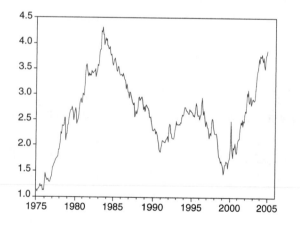

Figure 2.6 Ratio of small-caps to large-caps: cumulative total-return index.

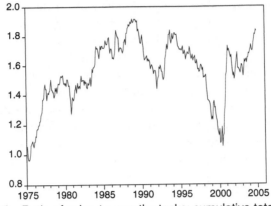

Figure 2.7   Ratio of value to growth stocks: cumulative total-return index.

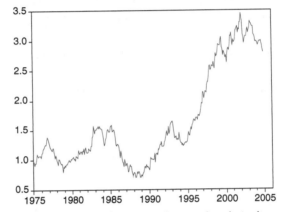

Figure 2.8   Ratio of domestic to international stocks: cumulative
total-return index.

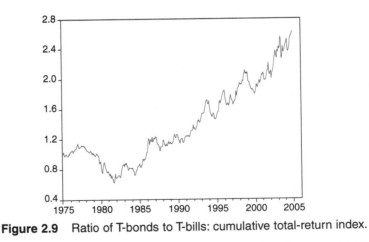

Figure 2.9   Ratio of T-bonds to T-bills: cumulative total-return index.

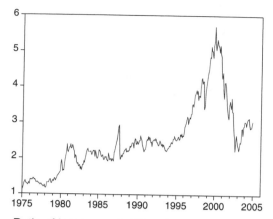

Figure 2.10   Ratio of large-caps to T-bonds: cumulative total-return index.

Summary

So far, I have argued that many asset-allocation recommendations today are sample-driven by the way the data are analyzed, and in a later chapter, I argue that the relative performance of asset classes is due to the macroeconomic environment. For instance, the value stocks just reviewed did well for a 30-year period because of economic policies adopted during different time periods. With this in mind, there is simply no guarantee the overall economic environment favors value stocks at all times in the future. In fact, the data suggest it behooves investors to pay attention to the economic environment and suggest growth stocks, when the situation warrants, can have an important impact on the total return of a style-based asset-allocation strategy. It all comes down to knowing ways to spot cycles. In later chapters, I show ways a top-down approach can help do this and ways style cycles, once identified, can be used to implement a successful tactical asset-allocation strategy. In the process, I also develop and illustrate a theory as to why the traditional finance approach has failed to identify the different asset-class cycles—a circumstance that has left many an investor short.

Now, let's give cycles a closer look.

3

THINKING IN CYCLES

s mentioned, the periodic table (see Table 3.1) of asset returns is a very effective tool commonly used for marketing asset-allocation services. By way of Table 3.1, potential investors are shown that the top and bottom asset-class performers vary from year to year. It is then commonly asserted that because the temporary deviations from historical patterns are random and unpredictable and because the whole process is mean-reverting—that is, ultimately, asset-class returns converge along their long-run historical averages—investors are better off using historical returns as well as the historical relationships among the variables as a guide to the future. The logical implication of this is that historical relationships, such as market returns and the variance–covariance matrix, constitute the relevant data for strategic asset allocation. Under these conditions, identifying the historical mix that best suits an investor's needs, in theory, best serves that investor over the long run. In a way, the mean-reversion hypothesis is the indexing version of the asset-allocation strategy, the idea being there is a *single* asset allocation that optimizes an investor's long-run returns.

This logic is understandable, but I question a couple of the assumptions. We don't know the length of sample one needs to obtain the long-run estimates of the variance–covariance matrix that describes the interrelationships of the different variables.[1] To be sure, one can have good reasons to question estimates obtained from the last 30 years of data. For the sample portfolios in the previous chapter, I used the 1975–2004 period because (as explained in Endnote 2 in Chapter 2, "The Case for Cyclical Asset Allocation") I desired the mutually exclusive definitions of the size, style, and location classifications the S&P/BARRA as well as the Morgan Stanley Capital MSCI indices offer. Unfortunately, this data set is not available for a long period of time, so I was locked into this 30-year period. Equally important, and noted in the previous chapter as well: What if mean-reversion is not random, but predictable? What if the deviations of asset classes from their long-run historical paths do not occur in a haphazard way? What if we can forecast just when a class of stocks or bonds will shift up or down? If this scenario is the case, an active allocation policy that deviates from the long-run strategic allocation can produce superior results. The search for predictable patterns is the subject of this chapter.

Table 3.1
Periodic table of asset returns.*

Rank	1975	1976	1977	1978	1979	1980
1	S 52.8	S 57.4	S 25.4	ROW 27.6	S 43.5	S 39.9
2	V 43.4	V 34.9	ROW 12.6	S 23.5	V 21.2	G 39.4
3	L 37.2	L 23.8	TB 5.1	TB 7.2	L 18.4	L 32.4
4	G 31.7	B 16.8	B -0.7	G 6.8	G 15.7	V 23.6
5	ROW 26.9	G 13.8	V -2.6	L 6.6	TB 10.4	ROW 19.8
6	B 9.2	TB 5.1	L -7.2	V 6.2	ROW 6.3	TB 11.2
7	TB 5.8	ROW -0.6	G -11.8	B -1.2	B -1.2	B -4

Rank	1981	1982	1983	1984	1985	1986	1987	1988	1989
1	TB 14.7	B 40.4	S 39.7	B 15.4	ROW 47.7	ROW 62.7	ROW 22.8	ROW 25.8	G 36.4
2	S 13.9	S 28	V 28.9	V 10.5	G 33.3	B 24.4	G 6.5	S 22.9	L 31.5
3	B 1.9	G 22	L 22.5	TB 9.9	L 32.2	V 21.7	TB 5.6	V 21.7	V 26.1
4	V 0	L 21.4	ROW 21	L 6.3	B 31	L 18.5	L 5.2	L 16.8	B 18.1
5	L -4.9	V 21	G 16.2	G 2.3	V 29.7	G 14.5	V 3.7	G 11.9	S 10.2
6	ROW -6.5	TB 10.5	TB 8.8	ROW 0.6	S 24.7	S 6.9	B -2.7	B 9.7	ROW 9.8
7	G -9.8	ROW -4.2	B 0.7	S -6.7	TB 7.7	TB 6.2	S -9.3	TB 6.4	TB 8.4

Rank	1990	1991	1992	1993	1994	1995	1996	1997	1998
1	TB 7.8	S 44.6	S 23.4	ROW 30.1	ROW 5.8	G 38.1	G 24	G 36.5	G 42.2
2	B 6.2	G 38.4	V 10.5	S 21	TB 3.9	L 37.4	L 23.1	L 33.4	L 28.6
3	G 0.2	L 30.6	B 8.1	V 18.6	G 3.1	V 37	V 22	V 30	ROW 17
4	L -3.2	V 22.6	L 7.7	B 18.2	S 3.1	S 34.5	S 17.6	S 22.8	V 14.7
5	V -6.8	B 19.3	G 5.1	L 10	L 1.3	B 31.7	TB 5.2	B 15.9	B 13.1
6	S -21.6	ROW 10.1	TB 3.5	TB 2.9	V -0.9	ROW 9.6	ROW 5.2	TB 5.3	TB 4.9
7	ROW -24.4	TB 5.6	ROW -14	G 1.7	B -7.8	TB 5.6	B -0.9	ROW 0.7	S -7.3

Rank	1999	2000	2001	2002	2003	2004
1	S 29.8	B 21.3	B 6.9	B 14.1	S 38.8	S 22.5
2	G 28.2	TB 5.9	TB 3.4	TB 1.7	ROW 36.2	ROW 17.8
3	ROW 26.2	S -3.6	S 2.5	S -15.3	V 31.8	V 15.5
4	L 21	V -9.6	V -13	ROW -17.4	L 28.7	L 10.7
5	V 12.6	L -9.9	L -13.1	V -22.5	G 25.7	B 9.3
6	TB 4.7	ROW -14.4	G -13.2	L -23.7	B 1.3	G 6.0
7	B -9	G -17	ROW -22.6	G -24.5	TB 1.2	TB 1.2

Key
S–Small
V–Value
L–Large
G–Growth
R–Rest of the World
B–T-Bonds
TB–T-Bills

* The figures included in this table are percentages.

The Fixed-Income Cycles

Although it is true a casual look at the periodic table seems to support the randomness of the mean-reverting patterns (it may just be the lack of synchronization giving the table this random appearance), a closer look at the asset classes' performance by size, style, and location suggests otherwise. The data presented in Figure 3.1 show an apparent persistence in differential performances. More important, these cycles of persistent performance are not synchronized across size, style, and location. This is promising, but it is only a first step. To take advantage of all the possible asset-class cycles, one must first document their existence and find a way to either identify or anticipate them early on—a tall order. The potential payoff, however, of uncovering and anticipating cycles merits a good effort.

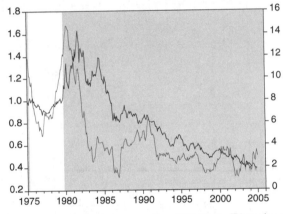

Figure 3.1   Cumulative returns ratio of T-bills to T-bonds versus the trailing 12-month U.S. inflation rate.

Let's start out by sharpening our eyes. If you closely inspect the relative-performance tables in Table 3.2, you can see a fairly interesting pattern between T-bill and T-bond returns. Note: Bills outperformed bonds for a string of years prior to 1981. Since 1981, however, bills have not been able to put together a two-year string. I have a very simple explanation for this relative performance. It has to do with the change in operating procedures at the Federal Reserve—commonly referred to as the Fed—started by Paul Volcker in the 1980s and continued by his successor, Alan Greenspan. Looking at the inflation rate's performance during the 1970s, it is apparent the existing Fed policies were not working. After taking the chair at the Fed under President Carter, Volcker initially tried to control the quantity of the money supply, thereby controlling the underlying inflation rate. Perhaps as a response to the failure of this quantity approach, Volcker changed the Fed operating procedures and began focusing on the inflation rate. This new procedure became known as *price-rule targeting*. Whenever inflation rose above an unspecified target level, the Fed understood this to be *prima facie* evidence that there was too much money in the system and the excess liquidity was causing inflation. The policy response was to lower the quantity of money through open-market operations, meaning the central bank sold bonds in the open market and received cash in exchange, thereby draining the excess cash from the pipeline. Conversely, when the inflation rate fell below the target inflation rate, the Fed added liquidity to the system. This price-rule targeting worked, and the U.S. inflation rate began a secular decline toward the long-run Fed target rate, which I surmise to be around 2 percent. Although it is true the decline in the inflation rate has not been smooth, the secular trend is apparent.

In the early 1980s, those who understood the impact of the Fed policy changes were able to anticipate the secular decline in the underlying inflation rate about to come. As T-bonds have a longer duration than T-bills, the price of T-bonds presumably adjusts to bring yields in line with the market's underlying inflation rate. Shorter-duration instruments, such as T-bills, are less sensitive to changes in underlying inflation because they mature in a shorter period of time and new instruments are issued at the prevailing market rate. In the extreme, the shortest-duration instruments suffer little price appreciation or depreciation. The strategy is then clear: A secularly declining inflation rate benefits the longer-maturity instrument over the shorter-maturity one (that is, T-bonds over T-bills). Figure 3.1 reports the cumulative returns of the ratio of T-bills to T-bonds versus the U.S. inflation rate. The relationship is evident: The decline in the inflation rate favored T-bonds.

The data in Figure 3.1 show that although changes in operating procedures at the Fed can help direct the secular allocation between the two assets in question, cyclical deviations remain. If you refer to the relative performance in Table 3.2, you can see T-bills outperformed T-bonds during time periods when the economy was experiencing a slowdown, either because we were entering a recession or were phasing in a tax-rate cut. It seems, during these times, the Fed deviated from its price-rule operating procedures in an attempt to ameliorate the slowdowns. Thus, the data suggest a simple strategy for fixed-income allocation: As long as the Fed remains on a price rule, bonds should be favored. One needs to be alert, however, to the Fed's temporary departures from the price rule; during these periods, an increased exposure to T-bills may be warranted.

Table 3.2
Relative performance of various asset classes.*

Equity versus Bonds

Rank	1975	1976	1977	1978	1979	1980	1981	1982	1983	1984	1985	1986	1987	1988	1989
1	L 37.2	L 23.8	B -0.7	L 6.6	L 18.4	L 32.4	B 1.9	B 40.4	L 22.5	B 15.4	L 32.2	B 24.4	L 5.2	L 16.8	L 31.5
2	B 9.2	B 16.8	L -7.2	B -1.2	B -1.2	B 4	L -4.9	L 21.4	B 0.7	L 6.3	B 31	L 18.5	B -2.7	B 9.7	B 18.1

Rank	1990	1991	1992	1993	1994	1995	1996	1997	1998	1999	2000	2001	2002	2003	2004
1	B 6.2	L 30.6	B 8.1	B 18.2	L 1.3	L 37.4	L 23.1	L 33.4	L 28.6	L 21	B 21.3	B 6.9	B 14.1	L 28.7	L 10.7
2	L -3.2	B 19.3	L 7.7	L 10	B -7.8	B 31.7	B -0.9	B 15.9	B 13.1	B -9	L -9.9	L -13.1	L -23.7	B 1.3	B 9.3

Domestic versus International

Rank	1975	1976	1977	1978	1979	1980	1981	1982	1983	1984	1985	1986	1987	1988
1	L 37.2	L 23.8	ROW 12.6	ROW 27.6	L 18.4	L 32.4	L -4.9	L 21.4	L 22.5	L 6.3	ROW 47.7	ROW 62.7	ROW 22.8	ROW 25.8
2	ROW 26.9	ROW -0.6	L -7.2	L 6.6	ROW 6.3	ROW 19.8	ROW -6.5	ROW -4.2	ROW 21	ROW 0.6	L 32.2	L 18.5	L 5.2	L 16.8

Rank	1989	1990	1991	1992	1993	1994	1995	1996	1997	1998	1999	2000	2001	2002	2003	2004
1	L 31.5	L -3.2	L 30.6	L 7.7	ROW 30.1	ROW 5.8	L 37.4	L 23.1	L 33.4	L 28.6	ROW 26.2	L -9.9	L -13.1	ROW -17.4	ROW 36.2	ROW 17.8
2	ROW 9.8	ROW -24.4	ROW 10.1	ROW -14	L 10	L 1.3	ROW 6.3	ROW 5.2	ROW 1.8	ROW 20.3	L 21	ROW -14.4	ROW -22.6	L -23.7	L 28.7	L 10.7

Large versus Small

Rank	1975	1976	1977	1978	1979	1980	1981	1982	1983	1984	1985	1986	1987	1988	1989
1	S 52.8	S 57.4	S 25.4	S 23.5	S 43.5	S 39.9	S 13.9	S 28	S 39.7	L 6.3	L 32.2	L 18.5	L 5.2	S 22.9	L 31.5
2	L 37.2	L 23.8	L -7.2	L 6.6	L 18.4	L 32.4	L -4.9	L 21.4	L 22.5	S -6.7	S 24.7	S 6.9	S -9.3	L 16.8	S 10.2

Rank	1990	1991	1992	1993	1994	1995	1996	1997	1998	1999	2000	2001	2002	2003	2004
1	L -3.2	S 44.6	S 23.4	S 21	S 3.1	L 37.4	L 23.1	L 33.4	L 28.6	S 29.8	S -3.6	S 2.5	S -15.3	S 38.8	S 22.5
2	S -21.6	L 30.6	L 7.7	L 10	L 1.3	S 34.5	S 17.6	S 22.8	S -7.3	L 21	L -9.9	L -13.1	L -23.7	L 28.7	L 10.7

Value versus Growth

	1975	1976	1977	1978	1979	1980	1981	1982	1983	1984	1985	1986	1987	1988
1	V 43.4	V 34.9	V -2.6	G 6.8	V 21.2	G 39.4	V 0	G 22	V 28.9	V 10.5	G 33.3	V 21.7	G 6.5	V 21.7
2	G 31.7	G 13.8	G -11.8	G 6.2	G 15.7	V 23.6	V -9.8	V 21	G 16.2	G 2.3	V 29.7	G 14.5	V 3.7	G 11.9

	1989	1990	1991	1992	1993	1994	1995	1996	1997	1998	1999	2000	2001	2002	2003	2004
1	G 36.4	G 0.2	G 38.4	V 10.5	V 18.6	G 3.1	G 38.1	G 24	G 36.5	G 42.2	G 28.2	V -9.6	V -13	V -22.5	V 31.8	V 15.5
2	V 26.1	V -6.8	V 22.6	G 5.1	G 1.7	V -0.9	V 37	V 22	V 30	V 14.7	V 12.6	G -17	G -13.2	G -24.5	G 25.7	G 5.978

Bills versus Bonds

	1975	1976	1977	1978	1979	1980	1981	1982	1983	1984	1985	1986	1987	1988	1989
1	G 9.2	B 16.8	TB 5.1	TB 7.2	TB 10.4	TB 11.2	TB 14.7	B 40.4	TB 8.8	B 15.4	B 31	B 24.4	TB 5.5	B 9.7	B 18.1
2	TB 5.8	TB 5.1	B -0.7	B -1.2	B -1.2	B -4	B 1.9	TB 10.5	B 0.7	TB 9.9	TB 7.7	TB 6.2	V -2.7	TB 6.4	TB 8.4

	1990	1991	1992	1993	1994	1995	1996	1997	1998	1999	2000	2001	2002	2003	2004
1	TB 7.8	B 19.3	B 8.1	B 18.2	TB 3.9	B 31.7	TB 5.2	B 15.9	B 13.1	TB 4.7	B 21.3	B 6.9	B 14.1	B 1.3	B 9.3
2	B 6.2	TB 5.6	TB 3.5	TB 2.9	B -7.8	TB 5.6	B -0.9	TB 5.3	TB 4.9	B -9	TB 5.9	TB 3.4	TB 1.7	TB 1.2	TB 1.2

Key

S–Small
V–Value
L–Large
G–Growth
R–Rest of the world
B–T-Bonds
TB–T-Bills

* The figures included in this table are percentages.

Table 3.3 shows $1 invested in T-bills in 1975 grew to $5.98 by the end of 2004, while $1 invested in T-bonds fetched $15.48. In turn, $1 invested in the best performer (T-bonds or T-bills) each year grew to $42.25. In contrast, that $1 grew to only $2.19 if it were annually invested in the worst of the two. Put another way, choosing the better of these two assets would have produced a 13.3 percent average annual return—409 basis points better than the best-performing asset (T-bonds). The upside, however, is not without risk. Choosing the worst performing of the two assets would have delivered a 2.6 percent average annual return, or 338 basis points less than the T-bill returns.

Table 3.3
Annual rates of return for the combination of various asset classes: 1975–2004.

	Growth of $1 Invested in 1975	Annual Return
T-Bills	$5.98	5.98%
T-Bonds	$15.48	9.21%
Best	**$42.25**	**13.3%**
Worst	**$2.19**	**2.6%**
T-Bonds	$15.48	9.21%
Large-Caps	$47.70	12.95%
Best	**$201.27**	**19.3%**
Worst	**$3.77**	**4.5%**
Small-Caps	$184.38	17.52%
Large-Caps	$47.70	12.95%
Best	**$498.11**	**23.0%**
Worst	**$12.33**	**8.7%**

	Growth of $1 Invested in 1975	Annual Return
Growth	$33.39	11.75%
Value	$61.23	13.79%
Best	**$125.54**	**17.5%**
Worst	**$13.93**	**9.2%**
Large-Caps	$47.70	12.95%
International	$16.96	9.47%
Best	**$199.94**	**19.3%**
Worst	**$3.46**	**4.2%**

The Equity/Fixed-Income Cycles

To be sure, the equity/fixed-income choice is the most important portfolio allocation decision an investor can make.[2] So, it makes sense to focus the search for persistent patterns in relative performance. The one common element among the periods of equity underperformance reported in the relative-performance (see Table 3.2) is they all coincide with economic slowdowns. In some cases, the slowdowns were bona fide recessions (1981, 1982, 1990, and 2001). In other cases, nonrecessionary slowdowns were produced by the phase-in of tax-rate cuts (the second round of the Reagan tax cuts hit in 1986) or tax increases (such as those in 1992 and 1993). The data suggest recessions and tax-rate changes are major indicators of turning points in stock/bond relative performance. A declining growth rate for real gross domestic product (GDP) is a pretty good indicator of a fixed-income cycle—irrespective of the monetary system organization, the pre-announcement and implementation of tax-rate changes, or any other macroeconomic shock. In GDP, we've found a core indicator of cycles.

Now, observe a corollary between GDP and real interest rates. A rising real interest rate is in general a harbinger of future stock appreciation and bond depreciation and is thus bullish for equities and bearish for fixed-income instruments such as bonds and bills. My explanation for this result is straightforward: Fixed-income instruments are like stocks with fixed earnings. An increase in the real interest rate leads to a higher discount rate and thus produces a lower value for the discounted coupon payments on fixed-income instruments. So, an increase in the real rate causes a decline in the value of fixed-income instruments. On the other hand, an upward change in the real rate, although eliciting an increase in the discount rate, also elicits changes in the real economy. It is fairly easy to show shifts in aggregate demand over aggregate supply lead to a higher real interest rate as well as higher output and higher overall profit-levels in the economy. Under these fairly general conditions, one can show the value of equities must also increase. But what we know for sure is the value of fixed-income instruments declines more than equities. Thus, a rising real interest rate is an indicator of an equity cycle, while a declining real rate is an indicator of a fixed-income cycle. To anticipate such a cycle, all one needs to do is correctly forecast the path of the real interest rate in the economy.

Again, as shown in Table 3.3, the potential benefits of a strategy that correctly anticipates relative performances are significant. Selecting the best-performing asset produces a 19.3 percent average annual return, or 635 basis points better than the large-cap equity returns. The potential price for choosing the worst-performing asset class each year is high. Being wrong each year returns 4.5 percent per year, or 470 basis points less than the returns delivered by bonds.

The Size Cycles

Let's give equity classes a closer inspection.[3] I believe the small-cap effect is the result of attempts to protect against unwanted inflation (inflation hedging), tax avoidance (tax sheltering), and minimizing the impact of regulations (regulatory skirting). My rationale is again straightforward: Congress and tax collectors like to go after big game. As a consequence, our tax code and regulations are primarily aimed at large corporations. In fact, many laws are written in such a way as to exempt smaller companies from compliance. This means smaller companies are able to morph themselves to take advantage of changes in the tax code and government regulations. Changes in tax rates, regulations, and the inflation rate affect the performance of small-capitalization companies to a greater degree relative to large-cap companies.

On the other hand, our larger firms benefit from increased certainty, which makes corporate planning easier. If events are fully anticipated, corporations are able to plan ahead to minimize their long-run expenses while maximizing their long-run profits. In this way, I argue the reduction of uncertainty has a distinct "size" effect: It favors larger-capitalization stocks. An article a few years back in *Barron's* illustrates this point.[4] The argument of the piece was that a large component of General Electric's (GE) profits was being generated by the company's investments, making GE a hedge fund in drag. The article suggested then-CEO

Jack Welch was timing the realization of investment profits to keep GE's profits above analyst expectations. Thus, in support of my point, GE was doing what every well-run firm should do: It was taking advantage of a reduction of uncertainty to maximize profits and thus shareholder value. (This article also illustrates how much the world has changed in a short period of time. Only a few years ago, it was okay to say GE was managing its earnings. Saying so now could get a company in trouble.)

There's a simple explanation for the relative performance of small- and large-cap stocks over the last 30 years. The 1970s were characterized by high and climbing inflation, rising tax rates, and ever-mounting regulations. Small-caps outperformed in this environment (see Table 3.2). The economic cycle came to an end with the presidential election of Ronald Reagan. After his economic program—lower taxes and regulations—became fully effective in 1984, large-cap stocks began a cycle of outperformance, which was only briefly interrupted by the phase-in of the second Reagan tax-rate cuts. The regulatory and tax-rate increases of Reagan's successors, George H.W. Bush and William J. Clinton, put an end to the large-cap cycle. It was not until the Republican Congressional takeover in 1995, and the divided government that ensued, that large-caps once again began to outperform. "Gridlock" slowed regulation and tax-hiking to a halt, so gridlock was good for large-cap stocks. Then came 1999, the year in which Fed Chairman Greenspan began to worry about "irrational exuberance" in the economy. He tightened the credit markets, the regulatory burden increased, and the market rotated to small-cap stocks. The election of George W. Bush and the temporary tax-rate cuts that followed in 2001 did nothing to arrest the burden on large-cap corporations.

Correctly anticipating the size cycles would have generated a 23 percent average annual return, or 548 basis points in excess of the small-cap returns. Selecting the wrong size would have lowered the annual returns to 8.7 percent, or 425 basis points below the returns of the large-cap stocks.

The Style Cycles

We can use a similar basket of indicators to determine style cycles.[5] Low interest rates—which are the product of sound monetary policy, in my view—have resulted in a lengthening of investor horizons. This, in turn, has had a powerful effect on market valuation. When investors have longer horizons, rather obviously, they can incorporate events into their valuation schemes that are further in the future. The result in this circumstance is investors become more patient. Because future profits carry higher relative weight than current profits, the lengthening of market events affecting only the current economy has a smaller impact on the financial markets than on the real economy. Thus, longer horizons favor growth stocks over value stocks.

To illustrate the powerful effects of monetary policy on investor horizons, consider the effect of changes in interest rates on a stream of yearly payments of $1 in perpetuity. At an interest rate of 10 percent, the discounted net-present value of the income stream is $10; in other words, at a 10 percent rate, an investor is willing to pay $10 for an income stream that produces $1 in perpetuity, or the equivalent of 10 years of income at a 0 interest rate. At an interest rate of 5 percent, the net-present value of the stream raises to $20—the equivalent of 20 years of income when the rate is 0 (see Figure 3.2).

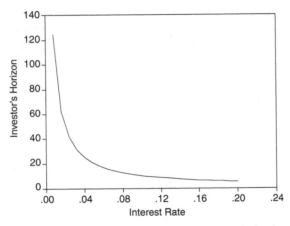

Figure 3.2 Interest rates versus the investor's horizon.

As we saw in the size effect, uncertainty—be it economic, political, or financial—is a very important variable that significantly affects market valuation. Increased uncertainty unambiguously reduces investor horizons, meaning short-term profits get an increased weighting in the valuation of different assets. In uncertain environments, value stocks are the choice over growth stocks.

Taxation is another variable in the relative performance of value and growth stocks. Corporate income taxes affect the amount of cash firms have to reinvest. As a result, an increased effective corporate tax rate takes a bigger bite out of growth stocks. Hence, I argue that a rising marginal tax rate favors value stocks over growth stocks. Putting it all together, I believe the value/growth relative performance is influenced by interactions between the tax code, the government regulations, and the inflation rate.

Parenthetically, despite the relative performance of value and growth stocks for the last 30 years, William Sharpe's seminal article on style investment was not published until 1992.[6] It is probable that Sharpe's paper circulated a couple of years prior to its publication, but for all practical purposes, the style performance of equities up to that point (as reported in the historical series) is nothing more than calculations after the fact. In other words, before 1992, most financial managers or consultants would not have made an explicit portfolio style decision. That said, looking at data since the late 1980s, it follows that value stocks outperformed as the economy went into a recession and there was uncertainty regarding the tax code. Growth stocks next outperformed during the gridlock period, when moves to higher taxes and regulation were arrested by a divided government. Add to that low and steady inflation and there was little uncertainty during the mid- and late 1990s. When the corporate scandals broke, and the stock market bubble popped, uncertainty crept back in and value stocks reigned once again.

The Location Cycles

Before I get into location cycles, I need to make some assumptions about exchange rates. In the long run (by this, I mean the economy will approach its equilibrium in the long run), *purchasing power parity* (PPP) will be restored. PPP is the point at which exchange rates have adjusted based on the purchasing power of currencies.[7] If the world we live in were frictionless, all adjustments would be instantaneous. This is, unfortunately, not the case. Shocks give rise to temporary disturbances that push economies away from old equilibriums and into new ones. There are adjustment costs to this process, meaning it can take some time for the economy to reach its new equilibrium. More, the path the economy takes to reach its new equilibrium depends on numerous factors. Nevertheless, at any point in time, the value of the exchange rate can reflect adjustments to previous and current market conditions.

So, if one agrees with this interpretation of major inflection points, it is easy to see two location-based appreciation cycles. One begins around 1983–1984 when the Reagan tax rates were being implemented, and the other begins around 1995 when the Republicans took over Congress (see Table 3.2). The stories are similar: Early on, in each case, the U.S. economy behaved like a growth stock. Investors—both domestic and international—flocked to the U.S., and the capital inflows produced a higher stock market. In the early hours, as net worth increased relative to disposable income, the U.S. trade balance worsened. Still, the U.S. outperformed the rest of the world. As investors tried to acquire dollars to invest in the U.S., the dollar appreciated above its

PPP value. Over time, as investment continued, the rate of return in new investments declined and, eventually, rates of return went back to their long-run equilibriums. PPP was once again restored.

Because the price rule essentially eliminates monetary disturbances as the source of exchange-rate fluctuations, it follows that the bulk of dollar fluctuations reflects U.S. terms of trade or relative rates of return. Thus, early on, as the rate of return increases, the dollar appreciates. If PPP is to be restored, however, the dollar has to experience a round trip. More important, the price rule also ensures fluctuations in the dollar do not alter the underlying inflation rate in any significant way.

In both cases—1983–1984 and 1995—the exchange rate behaved like an inverted *V*. Thus, the location rule is as follows: When the U.S. dollar is in its rising phase, you can expect the U.S. market to outperform the rest of the world; during the declining phase of the dollar, you can expect the U.S. stock market to underperform. The idea is that a positive relationship exists between the relative performance of the U.S. equity markets and the foreign exchange value of the dollar. The data reported in Figure 3.3 document this point.

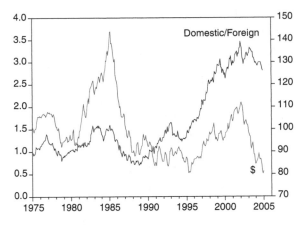

Figure 3.3   Ratio of domestic to foreign stock indices versus the foreign exchange value of the dollar.

To my surprise, correctly identifying the location (domestic versus international) during the 30-year period would have added 635 basis points over the performance of the large-cap stocks. This result surprises given that international stocks exhibit lower average returns and higher volatilities than large-cap stocks, as well as lower Sharpe ratios within the equity asset classes. The numbers illustrate the power of diversification. A lack of synchronization between the domestic and foreign markets offers a potential upside to an active global strategy.

The Case for a Cyclical Asset-Allocation Strategy

In brief, those are your cycles. Now, let's draw a few early conclusions. From 1995 to 1999, large-cap stocks outperformed small-caps while the growth stocks' dominance over value stocks began a year earlier and ended a year later. The fact that large-cap growth companies ruled during the 1995–1999 time period represents a dramatic shift in performance; for the 30-year period ending in 2004, small-cap value stocks ruled the investment world.

As the 1995–1999 experience unfolded, there was a major debate in the investment community, with some suggesting a long-lasting shift in relative equity valuations was occurring while others pointed to a string of unexpected temporary shocks. The issue had important implications for portfolio allocation decisions. Some managers espoused a mean-reversion hypothesis while others voiced a new-economy view. The investment implications of the two are quite different. Under the mean-reversion hypothesis, the 1995–1999 years (large-cap growth) were an aberration and the economy would eventually revert to historical patterns (small-cap value). An implication of this assumption was that even though temporary deviations from historical patterns can be observed, historical variances and covariances of returns would be stable over the long run. This suggests historical relationships—such as market returns and the variance–covariance matrix—constitute the relevant data for strategic asset allocation; identifying the optimal historical mix serves the investor best over the long run. Once again, mean-reversion becomes the asset-allocation version of indexing. Meanwhile, the *new-economy view* argued that the shifts in relative performance during the 1995–1999 period represented permanent change that would require new long-run allocating.

Proponents of mean-reversion point to the last five years as evidence in support of their view: In the most recent period, we have in fact reverted to a small-cap value environment. This shift damages the new-economy view, but it does not in any way harm the hypothesis *deviations from the long-run mean are not random*. More, if this is the case (as I believe it is), a third alternative emerges neither group considered: *These shifts are cyclical*. So, to the extent these cycles can be identified, a strategy that cyclically alters an investor's asset-allocation mix can produce results superior to a traditional long-run strategic allocation.

The data presented in the relative-performance tables (see Table 3.2) clearly identify some persistent cycles for the various asset-class choices. The cycles are visible to the naked eye and suggest a strategy anticipating these cycles would have been able to increase the returns of a domestic investment portfolio. Such a strategy could have been solely based on a well-diversified domestic portfolio or an optimal long-run portfolio generated by the variance–covariance matrix of the historical returns. But the strategy would have adjusted with the cycles. In other words, I believe an active allocation strategy is capable of producing returns that are superior to those of a passive, mean-reversion–generated strategy.

It is important to note the strategy being presented here is different than a *tactical asset-allocation* (TAA) formula. A TAA is defined in this discussion as a shifting of capital between asset classes in relation to a policy benchmark based on perceived valuation discrepancies in a reasonably efficient market. As I interpret TAA, it is a strategy focusing on high-frequency events. Yet what I have in mind is a cyclical strategy focusing on the impact of policy changes and other economic shocks. I hold that adjustment costs in the economy result in persistent cycles. In addition, to the extent the economy responds differently to different cycles, the sector/industry reaction relative to the overall economy (that is, the beta parameters, which I discuss in depth in later chapters) changes. It is the latter my strategy aims to capture.

A few more observations: Looking at the last 30 years as a whole, I have come to the conclusion that although a strategic asset allocation based on the long run would have done an adequate job, an ideal asset-allocation strategy would have tilted around the long-run allocation. (Table 3.2 makes this very clear.) Such a strategy would have taken advantage of the cyclical fluctuations in relative returns and produced an even better performance. The results reported in Tables 2.7 through 2.10 in Chapter 2 show that the optimal size, style, location, and/or equity/fixed-income allocation was a corner solution approximately 80 percent of the time. Using location as an example, either the U.S. or the rest of the world would have made up 90 percent or more of the overall portfolio 24 times during the sample period. This means, on average and for all practical purposes, only in six of those years did a combination of the two markets generate the optimal mix. The actual numbers suggest more often than not that an *all-or-nothing strategy*—a strategy choosing solely one of two possible asset-class choices—maximizes returns. The problem with all-or-nothing, however, is when you miss, you miss big on a relative basis. (Table 3.3 shows the potential upside and downside of an all-or-nothing strategy.) A risk-adverse investor may not be able to live with such a bipolar strategy; it can simply be too volatile to stomach. Again, for such a risk-averse investor, it may be desirable to minimize the long-run volatility relative to the long-run average return. One way to investigate this is to look at the portion of time funds would have been allocated to either asset-class choice if an investor had perfect foresight.

Table 3.4

Sharpe ratio for selected location portfolios: 1975–2004.

| | International Allocation | | | | | | | | | | |
	100%	90%	80%	70%	60%	50%	40%	30%	20%	10%	0%
1975	1.00	1.06	1.12	1.18	1.24	1.31	1.37	1.43	1.48	1.53	1.56
1976	-0.28	-0.14	0.00	0.16	0.33	0.50	0.66	0.83	0.98	1.12	1.25
1977	1.30	1.08	0.79	0.45	0.09	-0.25	-0.56	-0.81	-1.01	-1.16	-1.28
1978	1.24	1.25	1.24	1.19	1.09	0.94	0.74	0.53	0.34	0.18	0.04
1979	-0.68	-0.54	-0.40	-0.26	-0.11	0.02	0.16	0.28	0.40	0.51	0.60
1980	0.46	0.54	0.63	0.71	0.79	0.86	0.92	0.96	1.00	1.02	1.04
1981	-0.97	-1.04	-1.12	-1.19	-1.26	-1.33	-1.39	-1.43	-1.45	-1.44	-1.42
1982	-0.74	-0.63	-0.51	-0.37	-0.22	-0.07	0.09	0.23	0.36	0.48	0.58
1983	1.34	1.40	1.45	1.48	1.49	1.47	1.44	1.40	1.35	1.29	1.23
1984	-0.15	-0.15	-0.16	-0.17	-0.17	-0.17	-0.18	-0.18	-0.18	-0.18	-0.18
1985	4.06	4.29	4.45	4.45	4.25	3.88	3.42	2.93	2.48	2.09	1.76
1986	2.28	2.29	2.29	2.26	2.17	2.03	1.82	1.56	1.27	0.98	0.71
1987	0.76	0.71	0.65	0.58	0.52	0.45	0.38	0.32	0.26	0.20	0.14
1988	1.19	1.24	1.29	1.34	1.38	1.41	1.40	1.35	1.25	1.11	0.96

continues

Table 3.4   continued

| | International Allocation | | | | | | | | | | |
	100%	90%	80%	70%	60%	50%	40%	30%	20%	10%	0%
1989	0.12	0.24	0.38	0.53	0.69	0.87	1.05	1.23	1.39	1.53	1.64
1990	−1.05	−1.05	−1.05	−1.04	−1.02	−0.99	−0.93	−0.86	−0.75	−0.63	−0.50
1991	0.32	0.43	0.54	0.66	0.79	0.91	1.04	1.15	1.26	1.35	1.43
1992	−1.19	−1.15	−1.10	−1.02	−0.92	−0.78	−0.58	−0.32	−0.02	0.29	0.56
1993	1.43	1.46	1.49	1.53	1.57	1.60	**1.64**	1.64	1.59	1.43	1.14
1994	**0.23**	0.20	0.16	0.13	0.09	0.04	0.00	−0.05	−0.10	−0.14	−0.19
1995	0.34	0.56	0.82	1.14	1.52	1.97	2.52	3.15	3.86	4.56	5.14
1996	−0.07	0.16	0.38	0.58	0.77	0.94	1.08	1.21	1.32	1.41	1.49
1997	−0.23	−0.05	0.14	0.34	0.54	0.75	0.94	1.13	1.30	1.45	1.58
1998	0.71	0.76	0.81	0.85	0.89	0.93	0.97	1.00	1.02	1.04	1.06
1999	1.50	**1.52**	1.52	1.51	1.50	1.47	1.42	1.37	1.31	1.25	1.18
2000	−1.56	−1.52	−1.46	−1.39	−1.31	−1.23	−1.14	−1.06	−0.97	−0.89	−0.81
2001	−1.61	−1.52	−1.43	−1.34	−1.25	−1.16	−1.07	−0.98	−0.90	−0.81	−0.73
2002	**−1.01**	−1.04	−1.07	−1.10	−1.12	−1.14	−1.15	−1.16	−1.17	−1.18	−1.18
2003	2.10	2.13	2.15	2.17	2.18	2.20	2.21	2.21	2.21	2.21	2.20
2004	**1.63**	1.61	1.59	1.57	1.55	1.52	1.49	1.45	1.40	1.36	1.30

Table 3.4 shows that in 15 of the sample years, all funds should have been allo-cated to the U.S. stock market exclusively. In the remaining eight years, funds would have been allocated to the two markets. Using a pro-rated allocation, I estimated funds were allocated to the U.S. market in four of those eight years. My calculation suggests U.S. investing should have accounted for 19 of the 30 years, which is about 63 percent of the time. This approach suggests a 63 percent allocation to the U.S. would be desirable for a long-run purpose. In Chapter 2, using the Sharpe ratio for the sample average reported in Table 2.5 (shown here in Table 3.5), I concluded a 100 percent U.S. allocation would be optimal in the long run. Looking at the reward-to-risk ratio of the returns to the standard devi-ations reported in Table 3.5, we can see a less-than 10 percent difference in the Sharpe ratios of the two allocations. Performing a similar calculation for the other asset classes leads us to a historical allocation closer to the market weights of the different asset classes. Equally important is the result that the Sharpe ratios for these allocations are within 10 percent of the highest Sharpe ratio portfolios. Table 3.6 reports the allocations produced by the pro-rata allocation. If we take the long-run result seriously, an all-or-nothing strategy should generate an aver-age holding closer to the market weights of the different asset classes.

Table 3.5
Sample period risk-adjusted average annual returns, standard deviation, and Sharpe ratio for selected location portfolios.

International Allocation						
1975–2004	100%	90%	80%	70%	60%	50%
Average Annual Return	4.91%	5.23%	5.56%	5.88%	6.20%	6.52%
Standard Deviation	16.97%	16.17%	15.48%	14.92%	14.50%	14.22%
Sharpe Ratio	0.290	0.324	0.359	0.394	0.428	0.459

1975–2004	40%	30%	20%	10%	0%
Average Annual Return	6.84%	7.17%	7.49%	7.81%	**8.13%**
Standard Deviation	14.11%	14.16%	14.37%	14.74%	**15.26%**
Sharpe Ratio	0.485	0.506	0.521	0.530	**0.533**

Source: Research Insight, Morgan Stanley Capital Management, and Ibbotson Associates

Table 3.6
**Percent of the time allocated by size, style,
location, and fixed income versus equity.**

Size	Small	Large
	51.6%	48.4%
Style	**Value**	**Growth**
	48.4%	51.6%
Location	**U.S.**	**Rest of the World**
	63.3%	36.7%
Fixed Income/Equity	**Fixed Income**	**Equity**
	47.1%	52.9%

The simplest way to ensure an active strategy always returns to the long-run allocation is to think of the active strategy as tilting around the long-run values. Only then do you get a time-consistent active strategy. Holding the world weights is consistent with a long-run, mean-reverting, and sensible outcome. We also know more often than not the *ex post* optimal result is a corner solution, where only one style, size, or location is chosen. (The analogy, again, is of putting all eggs in one basket.) But deviating from the long-run solution entails some risk in pursuit of the potential reward. So, we need a signal that tilts us in the proper direction.

Changes to the economic environment (whether caused by taxes, regulation, or fiscal and monetary policy) impact the market and asset prices. The market's reassessment of asset prices generates distinct patterns, and the linkages between the economic environment and the relative performance of the various asset classes can be identified (see Figure 3.4). This outline, combined with the forecast of the economic indicators, suggests the portfolio tilts needed to take advantage of the foreseen economic environment.

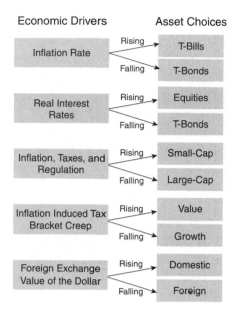

Economic Drivers		Asset Choices
Inflation Rate	Rising	T-Bills
	Falling	T-Bonds
Real Interest Rates	Rising	Equities
	Falling	T-Bonds
Inflation, Taxes, and Regulation	Rising	Small-Cap
	Falling	Large-Cap
Inflation Induced Tax Bracket Creep	Rising	Value
	Falling	Growth
Foreign Exchange Value of the Dollar	Rising	Domestic
	Falling	Foreign

Figure 3.4 Economic drivers and asset choices.

The final element of the cyclical strategy is to forecast the foreign-exchange market. The conviction of this forecast can then be used to tilt a portfolio in favor of the asset class favored by the exchange-rate forecast. How much of the potential gain is captured by this strategy depends on the quality of the forecast and the risk tolerance of the investor. The greater the risk aversion, the less sensitive the tilt around the long-run allocation. This approach suggests a simple way for investors to take advantage of changing conditions over business and economic cycles.

4

TAX TIPS

The corporate story in recent years has been an ugly one. But most black ink dedicated to corporate accounting scandals, questionable capital structures, distorted executive-compensation packages, and rising equity risk premiums has failed to pinpoint an important source of the ugliness: Each undesirable episode was in part influenced by the tax changes that took place over the last two decades. Although the distorting economic effects of the ever-changing tax code impact the way investors, financial managers, and nearly all members of the labor force behave, tax-rate adjustments also help explain shifts in corporate behavior and structure. Identifying and understanding these shifts at the source is critical to developing a cycle-based asset-allocation strategy, which is an asset-allocation strategy that is allowed to deviate from the long-run allocation to take advantage of predictable fluctuations in the market.

Are Enron, WorldCom, Adelphia, and Global Crossing all tax stories? Your first reaction might be to say no; most would say these are stories of greed, human weakness, shifty accounting, and getting caught. You aren't wrong in taking this position, but you aren't 100 percent correct either. There was a certain set of rules by which each company had to play—tax rules, that is. Whether these rules were broken or pushed to their limits, it remains that the tax structure helped determine the corporate actions these firms would take. For each firm, the tax structure favored a push for profits that would raise company stock prices. There's nothing wrong with this, except that each company in its own way "manufactured" profits. When push came to shove, they had little incentive *not* to break the law.

Policy changes in Washington do, in fact, affect corporate behavior, which in turn generates valuation cycles. Tax-rate changes, in particular, are discussed in Congress over long time periods, and anyone following the legislative process can estimate the likelihood proposals on the table will come up for votes and stand a chance of becoming law. Therefore, by tracking the legislative process, one can first identify the potential turning points in tax policy and then focus on the potential impact the legislative changes can have on the returns constellation in the economy. In turn, changes in after-tax income can help investors and financial planners identify the way the behavior of return-maximizing economic agents will also shift.

Although it is easy at first pass to figure out who will be directly affected by a tax change, the elasticities of economic supply and demand are what determine whether an increase or decrease in a tax will be passed on to consumers or to suppliers. If a tax adjustment is costly, it is safe to assume long-run elasticities will be different from short-run elasticities. In this way, a tax-change cycle's length and duration depends on the disturbance's magnitude (that is, the size of a tax-rate change) as well as the supply-and-demand elasticities associated with the disturbance. After all this is settled on, the last step of a strategy identifying tax-change cycles is to anticipate shifts in behavior (across the entire economic spectrum, from the individual laborer to the corporate CEO) caused by proposed legislative changes. The way to anticipate these behavioral shifts is rather simple: Just follow the money.

Government regulation and tax policy, along with corporate governance, affect the marginal cost of various investment *return-delivery vehicles*, which are the ways corporations deliver returns to investors. These vehicles include dividends, capital gains, and corporate debt. Historically, each return-delivery vehicle has been taxed at a different rate, so a change in the tax code alters the after-tax return delivered by each of the three different mechanisms. Some people dismiss the taxes' impact on investments by arguing that these days, the bulk of investments are made by tax-exempt institutions. There are a couple of counterarguments to this view. First, unquestionably, changes in tax rates do affect the way corporate managers and workers behave. Second, "taxable" investors are today's marginal investors—and prices are determined at the margin. Corporate managers, of course, try to use the cheapest return-delivery instrument, rather than a "preferred" instrument. In doing so, they can change a firm's capital structure as well the marginal cost of the instrument used. It follows that changes in the corporate capital structure can trigger regulatory and institutional constraints can further restrict using the return-delivery mechanisms. Equilibrium in this case is only reached when, at the margin, the costs of delivering returns are equated across instruments.

Let's flash back to Enron and other companies: Had each return-delivery mechanism been equalized—that is to say, had the tax structure equally favored dividends, capital gains, and corporate debt—would a handful of companies have worked so feverishly (and corruptly) to increase the returns of but one of those vehicles (namely capital gains)? There's a common thread running through the charges against most companies involved in the corporate scandals that manifested in the early twenty-first century: as digested by *Forbes*, Adelphia "[Overstated results] by inflating capital expenses and hiding debt;" Enron "[Boosted profits] and hid debts totaling over $1 billion by improperly using off-the-books partnerships;" Global Crossing "Engaged in network capacity 'swaps' with other carriers to [inflate revenue];" and WorldCom "[overstated cash flow] by booking $3.8 billion in operating expenses as capital expenses."[1] One can rightly argue the shareholders wouldn't have allowed these digressions to take place if accounting was more transparent, if there was but one set of books shown to both investors and the Internal Revenue Service (IRS). But one can also rightly argue the incentive for these companies to overstate results would have been much less if the return-delivery mechanisms had been equalized.

The potential distorting economic effects of tax changes and their impact on the way investors, managers, and employees behave are numerous:

- If changes in the tax structure produce an after-tax return ranking different from the before-tax ranking, the economy's resources are allocated in a suboptimal way.
- Tax changes alter the way returns are delivered to investors. For example, a financial manager would have an incentive to convert dividend returns into capital-gain returns if the tax on capital gains were reduced in a significant way. The incentive to do so would also generate some creative accounting behavior at the corporate level as well as an increase in resources devoted to the financial engineering of after-tax returns.
- Altering the relative attractiveness of the way returns are delivered to investors also alters the investment composition of individual corporations.

Changes in corporate and investor behavior are most likely noticeable during inflection points in the tax code. If tax-rate changes have the incentive effects I believe they do, the impact of the changes—in the form of behavioral shifts—should be visible to the naked eye. Again, to see these shifts, all one needs to do is follow the money.

Follow the Money

Table 4.1 reports the top income-tax rates since 1979 as well as the retention rate or keep rate after corporate and personal income taxes are netted out for a hypothetical $100 of corporate income delivered to investors as interest income (corporate debt), capital gains, and dividends. In what follows, I ignore the effects of the state and local taxes and the alternative minimum tax.

Table 4.1

Impact of the constellation of tax rates on the incentive structure.

	Top Tax Rate			Retention Rate per $100			Advantage per $100		
	Corporate	Personal	Capital Gain	Debt	Gains	Dividends	Debt/ Gains	Debt/ Dividends	Gains/ Dividends
1979	46.0%	70.0%	28.0%	30.0	38.9	16.2	-8.9	13.8	22.7
1981	46.0%	69.1%	27.7%	30.9	39.0	16.7	-8.1	14.2	22.4
1982	46.0%	50.0%	20.0%	50.0	43.2	27.0	6.8	23.0	16.2
1987	40.0%	38.5%	28.0%	61.5	43.2	36.9	18.3	24.6	6.3
1988	34.0%	28.0%	28.0%	72.0	47.5	47.5	24.5	24.5	0.0
1990	34.0%	31.0%	28.0%	69.0	47.5	45.5	21.5	23.5	2.0
1993	36.0%	39.6%	28.0%	60.4	46.1	38.7	14.3	21.7	7.4
1998	36.0%	39.6%	20.0%	60.4	51.2	38.7	9.2	21.7	12.5
2000	36.0%	39.1%	20.0%	60.9	51.2	39.0	9.7	21.9	12.2
2001	36.0%	38.6%	20.0%	61.4	51.2	39.3	10.2	22.1	11.9
2004	36.0%	35.0%	15.0%	65.0	54.4	54.4	10.6	10.6	0.0

Source: Internal Revenue Service

Corporate Debt

In 1979, the top marginal income-tax rate was 70 percent (see Table 4.1: second column, first row). Because debt is deductible for corporations, $100 of interest income would have delivered the grand amount of $30 after-tax for a T-bondholder (fourth column, second row).

Dividends

The math does not get any better for this delivery vehicle. A corporation earning $100 and choosing to pay all out in dividends would have been subject to a 46 percent corporate tax rate in this example (first column, second row), leaving only $54 for shareholders. In turn, shareholder dividend income, subject to a 70 percent tax rate, would have provided shareholders a lackluster $16.20 after taxes (sixth column, first row).

Capital Gains

This story is a bit more complicated. A firm earning $100 choosing to retain the earnings would have kept $54 in the corporate coffers. In an efficient market, the company's stock price would be expected to rise by $54, thus shareholders would realize a $54 gain. Because capital gains were subject to a 28 percent tax rate in 1979, investors in this case would have been left with $38.90 after all taxes were deducted (fifth column, first row).

Tracking the historical changes in the tax-rate code enables us to make inferences about changes in after-tax cash flows generated by corporate debt, capital gains, and dividends. In turn, these results help explain the changes in market valuations, and indeed in the incentive structure, that have taken place over the last 25 years. Table 4.1 shows an almost secular rise in the after-tax return generated by debt, dividends, and capital gains. But the figures distort the true change on incentives during this period as they do not take into consideration the impact of inflation on bracket creep. For example, during the 1970s—the double-digit inflation years—effective marginal tax rates were much higher than implied by the legislated rates shown in Table 4.1. The opposite was true in the 1990s. During this latter period, the Federal Reserve chairman Alan Greenspan substantially lowered the U.S. inflation rate, which produced a reduction in effective tax rates. Since the 1960s, the effective tax rates on capital gains and dividends have steadily declined, thus increasing the after-tax keep-rate for investors. Since the 1980s, lower tax rates go a long way toward explaining the surge in equity values.

The 1980s Tax-Related Surge in Debt Financing

A piece of information more germane to the current discussion is evident in Table 4.1. As the table's far-right column illustrates, the second round of Reagan tax-rate cuts (the 1986 Tax Reform Act) equalized the tax treatment of capital gains and dividends. After that, the tax policies of Presidents Bush and Clinton brought about a cycle in which capital gains' advantage over dividends steadily increased. Not surprisingly, returns in the 1990s were generated mostly in the form of capital gains as the corporate structure changed to take advantage of the tax laws. Ultimately, corporate behavior also adjusted, with some companies going over the line. All this of course changed when the stock market bubble burst in the late 1990s, subsequently reducing the dividend tax rate. At the present moment, the advantage of capital gains over dividends has been completely eliminated.

Now let's focus again on cycles, beginning with high-yield Treasury bonds (T-bonds). The first round of Reagan tax-rate cuts (The Economic Recovery Tax Act of 1981) represented a major inflection point in the relative rankings of the costs of the return-delivery vehicles. For the first time in the post-war period, corporate debt became the most attractive return-delivering mechanism. (This is clearly visible in Table 4.1, seventh and eighth columns.) Corporate debt significantly increased its advantage over both dividends and capital gains with the Reagan tax-rate cuts of the 1980s. Again, as long as there is differential tax treatment, there will be incentives to use the cheapest vehicles to deliver returns to investors. So, the question is whether the gains from using the cheaper vehicle compensate for the increased regulatory/governance costs. The data provide us with an answer: Debt financing exploded following the first Reagan tax cuts and, for the first time in the post-war period, net equity flows became negative (see Figure 4.1).

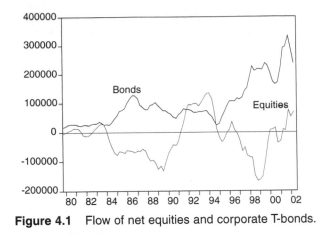

Figure 4.1 Flow of net equities and corporate T-bonds.

Using the relative costs of delivering returns to investors, we can now look back at the 1980s and put a few things in perspective. By 1982, debt had a $23 dollar advantage over dividends per $100 of precorporate-tax income (see Table 4.1: eighth column, third row). This meant corporate financing could deliver a much higher after-tax return than equity financing. A corporate manager, absent any restraint and with shareholder concerns in mind, would have maximized the after-tax return delivered to shareholders by using only corporate debt. But I argue corporate governance would not enable managers to do this. The numbers show the tax structure provided an incentive for corporations to deliver their returns in the form of debt *and* capital gains, which came at the expense of dividends.

Table 4.1 shows the historical advantage of corporate debt over dividends and capital gains, respectively. In the 1980s, the perfect structures for taking advantage of the Reagan tax changes were *leveraged buyouts* (LBOs) and *employee stock-ownership plans* (ESOPs). The beauty of the LBOs, from the perspective of tax-advantage, was that they generated interest payments and little or no dividends. If things worked out, LBOs generated huge capital gains for investors. In effect, LBOs converted dividend income into interest payments and capital gains, the two least-taxed return-delivery mechanisms. Companies or projects with predictable cash flows and/or undervalued assets carried at historical costs were prime candidates for LBOs and ESOPs. These transactions would in effect convert cash flows to interest payments, thereby reducing taxes. Similarly, by taking over companies with assets carried at historical costs, new owners would mark-to-market (that is, value at current market prices instead of carrying them in the books at historical prices) the assets as they sold them, thereby converting to capital gains and thus lowering the effective tax rate on that income.

Value stocks, with their predictable cash flows, were the ideal vehicles for the LBO debt cycle. That is not to say, however, growth stocks didn't also benefit in this period. By computing the tax advantages of debt over dividends, and of capital gains over dividends, we can address a criticism often levied against many "growth" companies. Suppose a growth company repurchased shares and reinvested profits, both of which are ways to create capital gains, during the 1980s. By retaining earnings and paying cap-gains, the corporation would have been able to invest a higher amount, which would then have been taxed at a lower rate than dividend payments. Thus, even if the corporate action produced a lower before-tax rate-of-return, it is possible it would have yielded a higher after-tax return to investors.

This point gets lost on too many financial analysts. Not because of the analysts' arrogance, who (it has been said) often think their tenth best idea is better than the shareholder's best idea, but because too many analysts can't fathom the idea taxes distort the choices people can make and, as a consequence, alter their behavior. A corporate action may not make sense from society's general viewpoint, but it may make perfect sense from the taxation viewpoint. In an extreme way, the same logic applies to tax shelters. Differential tax rates can potentially produce a before-tax return ranking that is much more attractive than the after-tax ranking. Ultimately, when this occurs, tax-sheltering and other frowned-upon things happen within an economy.

But back to the Big 1980s. To make LBOs viable, the market needed a financing instrument. A clever MBA, Michael Milkin, popularized one: the *junk bond*, which is a high-yield bond with a high default risk. Hence, the government created the preconditions for the emergence of Milken, also known as the junk-bond king, and his fellow-travelers. Milken recognized the economic and tax situation and took advantage of it. Those old enough to remember the Milken episode might also recall a lot of the corporate high-yield literature in the 1980s was geared to show the way junk bonds not only paid higher returns, but also had default rates that were historically not much greater than higher-rated obligations. The reason these claims could be made was, early on, LBO operations merely converted existing cash flows to interest payments and capital gains, instead of dividend payments. For a time, the high-yield market prospered and expanded. Unfortunately, as this market became increasingly popular, investment behavior altered in a significant way. The financing mechanism—and not the project's true merit—soon became the determinant as to whether an investment was made, and the investments were made in record proportions. As debt increased, the marginal cost of using the debt rose, leading to a new capital structure. The junk-bond crash was only a matter of time.

In theory, the adjustment mechanism should have been self-correcting. But, alas, in the process of reaching a new equilibrium, excesses were committed. We all know what followed. Milken went to jail, and his firm (Drexel Burnham Lambert) went under. Yet, the tax code in the scandal's wake left the debt-advantage unchanged. So, the debt slowdown during this period was not because the demand subsided. Rather, it was because the financing dried out with the advent of the Savings and Loan (S&L) crisis and Congress's creation of the Resolution Trust Corporation, which was charged with cleaning up the S&L mess. During the Resolution Trust years, the net debt flow became negative. In stylized fashion, the S&L insurance and regulations created a one-sided bet that was a recipe for disaster. The depositors did not worry too much as long as their deposits were insured. Borrowers were willing to invest in ever-riskier projects; if the project worked out, they would keep the gains. If the projects did not work out, the S&L would take over the project. In turn, the S&L, as it expanded its portfolio into ever-riskier loans, was able to charge higher interest rate. The greater its loan portfolio, the greater the leverage on the initial invested capital. Everyone had an incentive to take more risk. They were playing Russian roulette, and we know how that game ends. It was not a question of how, but when.

The Quest for Capital Gains

The tax rate changes enacted during the Reagan administration also steadily erased the capital gains advantage over dividends, and by 1988, any advantage capital gains had over dividends completely disappeared (see Table 4.1: ninth column, fifth row). The tax-rate changes enacted since 1990 have restored and steadily widened the capital gains advantage over dividends. Not surprisingly, we saw a steep decline in the importance of dividends relative to capital gains as a return-delivery mechanism.

Changes in tax rates during the George H. W. Bush/William J. Clinton years, by altering the relative attractiveness of the way returns were delivered to investors (that is, capital gains versus dividends, and so on), altered the investment composition of individual firms. The continued investment shifts away from dividends and toward capital gains during the 1990s, as well as the surge in corporate debt, are well documented today. But unlike most, I happen to think these shifts were in large part tax-induced—and this has far reaching implications. During the previous decade, corporate managers, as noted, had an incentive to convert dividends into capital gains. The incentive to do so generated some creative accounting behavior as well as an increase in resources devoted to engineering after-tax returns rather than generating before-tax returns. In this environment, employers and employees at times found it worthwhile to develop "creative" compensation schemes. Not only were many contracts written in a way that generated capital gains, the contracts also rewarded managers for generating capital gains. So, tax changes affected corporation compensation schemes as well as the way corporate managers behaved. In addition to the legal management of earnings, some corporate managers ventured further into illegal maneuverings.

After the second round of Reagan tax-rate cuts, the top personal income-tax rate and the capital gains tax rate were both 28 percent. In the following years, the capital gain tax rate declined while the personal income-tax rate increased. Although it is true debt during the 1990s remained the most desirable return-delivery instrument, followed by capital gains, Table 4.1 shows capital gains improved in relative standing. Why did this happen? After the economy got back on a growth track in the 1990s, following the brief 1990–91 recession, changes in the capital structure began taking place. Debt surged and equity flows declined (see Table 4.1). But, there's an important difference between the way business was done in the 1980s and 1990s. Instead of the LBOs of the 1980s, equity buybacks through *mergers and acquisitions* (M&As) were the way of the corporate world in the 1990s. The mechanism was different but the effect was the same. Meanwhile, there was a new development with the return-delivery mechanisms—for a brief time period, dividends did in fact close the gap relative to capital gains, yet for the first time in the post-war period, after-tax dividend yields began declining. I attribute this to the increased capital gains tax advantage over dividends. Companies recognized the tax differential and shifted their capital structures in a way that took advantage of it; they became increasingly focused on managing earnings growth to deliver the capital gains the market required.

Earnings are the centerpiece of stock market valuation models, so it is incumbent on investors and portfolio managers to obtain reasonable estimates of the earnings potential of individual company stocks and the overall economy. The two most common aggregate earning sources are the Standards and Poor (S&P) and the National Income and Product Accounts (NIPA). The S&P reports earnings per share for the stocks in its indices. Differences between the two S&P series are readily noticed: The "operating" earnings are much smoother than the "as reported" earnings, while a persistent divergence beginning around 1997 is clearly noticeable (see Figure 4.2). NIPA, however, uses a completely different methodology to estimate and calculate the economy's earnings. Unlike earnings numbers in the S&P 500, an index consisting of 500 stocks with the largest market capitalization, NIPA estimates the combined profits of all the companies in the U.S. economy. The NIPA profits suggest a flat-to-downward trend during the 1997–2000 period (see Figure 4.3). If, as most economists believe, NIPA is less susceptible to manipulations at the corporate level, the fact that its profit trend-line is downward-sloping during the time when the S&P 500 is trending upward hints at the possibility of creative earnings management.

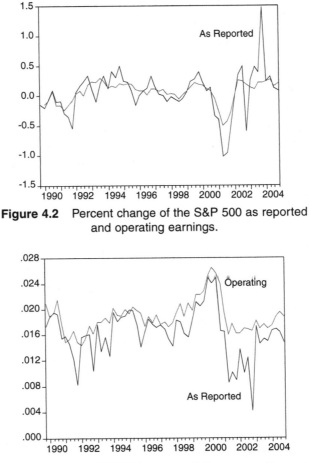

Figure 4.2 Percent change of the S&P 500 as reported and operating earnings.

Figure 4.3 Ratio of S&P 500 as reported and operating earnings to NIPA corporate profits.

To be sure, the data point to a noticeable increase in earnings management during the latter half of the 1990s. Here's another good way to detect this: In the past, I have used the inverse of 10-year T-bond yields (see Figure 4.4) as a proxy for investor horizons, as declining discount rates have had a larger impact on the value of companies with faster earnings growth. With this in mind, a simple way for a company to maximize its price earnings ratio (P/E) is to maximize its predictable earnings growth well into the future, which would also project surprises well into the future. Earnings surprises always have a large impact on stock prices. Thus, in the specific corporate and fiscal environment of the 1990s, it was in the best interest of companies to ensure against negative surprises through earnings management. One way to calculate the P/E for a company is to divide the current stock price by the trailing 12 months' earnings per share.

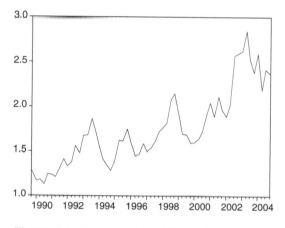

Figure 4.4   Inverse of the 10-year T-bond yield.

The reduction in the capital gains income tax in 1998 added to the corporate incentive to generate capital gains. The advantage of corporate debt over capital gains declined to $9.20 in 1998 from $21.50 in 1990 per $100 of pre-tax income (refer to Table 4.1). In turn, the capital gains advantage over dividends increased to $12.50 in 2000 from $2.00 in 1998. Earnings management and financial engineering became the biggest game in town. Just as in the junk-bond 1980s, the changes at the beginning of this cycle were legitimate. But, as the easy pickings got arbitraged away, the game became a bit more complicated and the temptations for illegal behavior increased. The alternative to illegal behavior was often to suffer the investor's wrath, so the incentive for creative bookkeeping was strong. Just as the market had a spectacular ride in the junk-bond heyday, it soared as excesses were committed by some accountants and CEOs in the 1990s. Both parties, however, came to similar abrupt ends.

Did the Taxes Make Them Do It?

The *1980s* was the greed decade? How wrong we were. It seems during the 1990s, greedy corporate officers paired themselves with unscrupulous accountants to simultaneously mislead shareholders and the IRS. That was quite a feat. Regardless, the problem can be traced directly from tax incentives to many corporate management changes enacted during the last decade. These changes supposedly included the creation of incentives for management to behave like owners and maximize shareholder value.

The motivation for financial engineering generated by compensation plans is fairly straightforward: With the same corporate revenue amount, economies of scale and the tax treatment of different transactions can generate higher after-tax cash flows to investors. So far so good. But add in the accounting treatment of unusual transactions and you have the makings of a very complicated system. Somewhere along the line, managers in the 1990s twisted interpretations. Paper profits, whether real or not, became the name of the game for some managers. The pursuit of these paper profits was all that mattered, with some managers using all legal means to chase them while others used more than legal means.

Looking at selected companies' recent experiences, the profit picnic of the 1990s proved a miserable failure. But, the law of unintended consequences goes a long way toward explaining why the episode was inevitable. The private sector built a structure that did not distinguish between real long-term profits and short-term financially engineered profits. So, corporate managers traveled the path of least resistance. Moralists argue the managers, in general, knew the intent of the incentive structure, and if they were honest, they would have honored its intent. But, this assumption places too heavy a burden on human behavior. The bottom line is, by poorly defining the incentive structure, the relative price of honesty and morality was raised. Not surprisingly, corporate managers, on average, consumed less of it.

That the system was gamed is clearly evident as many corporations reported two sets of books. They used one to show the IRS and another to show shareholders. In recent years, the gap between these two measures substantially widened. Initially, not too many people complained. Everyone hoped for the best, suggesting what the corporations were doing was minimizing their tax liabilities. But, looking back, there may have been another reason for the divergence. Corporate managers were indifferent to whether they reduced a dollar of tax liability or increased a dollar of pro-forma profit. Either way, their compensation increased. Not surprisingly, as managers pushed the envelope on the tax and pro-forma fronts, the gap between the two increased. Looking back, the many who reasoned corporations were only maximizing shareholder wealth were grasping onto a naïve interpretation of events. Once a cheater always a cheater, as the saying goes. If someone you know is cheating someone else, isn't it logical to think, given the chance, they will also cheat you? Our own life experiences clearly suggest this is the case.

Just as incentives made them do it, incentives can stop them from doing it— although it's important to point out not all incentives are created equal. The requirement executives now certify their financial statements' correctness under the threat of being prosecuted criminally if their statements are misleading falls under the rubric of the negative incentive. Negative incentives can reduce fraud and the occurrence of misleading information while punishing illegal behavior. In this regard, the steps being taken to clean up the corporate mess are in the right direction. But negative incentives *do not* encourage good behavior—they merely discourage bad behavior. So, what we need to do now is enact a series of positive incentives that can eliminate the corporate manager's desire to produce financially engineered results and replace it with the desire to pursue true economic profits.

One simple way to move corporate officers and accountants in this direction is to require them to use only one set of accounting reports. I don't care whether the reports are pro-forma or generally accepted accounting principles (GAAP). My view is whatever the investor is shown also should be shown to the IRS, with the appropriate taxes being paid thereafter. If CEOs cook the books to overstate their financially engineered profits, they pay higher taxes, making shareholders unhappy. On the other hand, if CEOs understate profits, the IRS is unhappy. Using a single set of books would force shareholders and the IRS to perform checks and balances on corporate statements. In turn, this would make the accounting process more transparent, while along the way installing a positive incentive for companies to achieve higher real profits.

Regulations and penalties are negative incentives discouraging people from pursuing illegal and/or undesirable activities, and thus, by the elimination process, we get to a "desired" economic behavior. But negative incentives do not stop legal financial engineering, nor do they encourage socially desirable behavior such as maximizing before-tax returns. The only way to move society in this direction is by way of positive incentives, such as a reduction of the distortions the tax code generates. In this case, the benefits to the economy are obvious: As lower tax rates enable investors and shareholders to retain higher after-tax incomes, investors and shareholders have a greater incentive to work, save, invest, and produce. Simply, they put in more when they can keep more of what they earn. Along the way, asset values also rise.

Personal income tax cuts also generate some unintended consequences. As long as a corporate tax exists, a reduction in the personal income tax rate confers an advantage to debt over equity financing. If history is any guide, the market response is to increase the exposure to corporate debt and quite likely the financial system's fragility. One simple way to eliminate these undesirable and unintended consequences is to eliminate the double taxation of income. To date, political realities have not enabled this to be the case. But a second-best option, on the way to an optimal policy, is to make each return-delivery mechanism equally attractive to corporate managers and investors.

The Solution: Realigning Incentives

Equalizing the return-delivery mechanisms' before- and after-tax rankings would send the proper signal for resource allocation. If these were equalized, both productivity and output would rise, which would undoubtedly cause a positive reaction from the markets. Once accomplished, the last step would be to simplify the tax code by moving directly to what it would have already become: a single-rate tax code.

Eliminating the double taxation of dividends would reduce the attractiveness of corporate debt and increase that of dividends. In due course, we would see corporate-debt issuance fall and the net issuance of equity increase. It is important to note, however, eliminating the double taxation of dividends does not punish corporate debt; it only makes equity more attractive.

During the 1990s, generating true economic profits and/or tax saving to produce returns became equally attractive. As profit opportunities were exhausted, creative ways to generate tax savings and capital gains became the order of the day. As we saw, the tax-saving/capital-gain-generating schemes ultimately led to both illegal and ethically questionable behavior. But, fast-forward to the tax-rate changes of 2003 that equalized the attractiveness of delivering returns to investors through capital gains and dividends. This alone removed much of the incentive for the type of behavior that brought on many of the excesses of the last bull market. Lower tax rates in 2003 increased the after-tax income for all forms of return-delivery vehicles. Returning to the example of total taxes paid when $100 of corporate income was delivered, after-tax cash flows for both corporate debt and capital gains increased $4 per $100 of pre-tax corporate income following the 2003 tax cuts. In contrast, the after-tax income for dividend payments increased four times as much, or $16 per $100 of pre-tax income. Given the increase in after-tax income, one should not be surprised both the number of firms paying dividends and the size of dividend payouts increased in the aftermath of the 2003 tax-rate changes. In 2004, U.S. companies paid out a record $113.6 billion in dividends. In addition, 24 more S&P companies are now paying dividends while 421 S&P companies have announced dividend increases. The numbers clearly indicate people respond to incentives.

The impact of the dividend tax cut is even broader than described so far. Many people are fond of pointing out the current dividend yield of approximately 1.8 percent is much lower than the prevailing levels of the 1950s, when yields ranged from 3 percent to 6 percent. But this analysis fails to take into account the impact of taxes on the net dividend received by shareholders. Let's take the high end and compare it to current levels. At a 15 percent dividend tax rate, a 1.8 percent yield produces a 1.53 percent net-of-tax yield. During the 1950s, the top personal income tax rate was 91 percent. Thus, a 6 percent dividend yield before taxes produced only a 0.54 percent after-tax yield a half century ago. Viewed this way, the current after-tax yield is much higher than that of the 1950s. This is one clear case where before-tax yields produce a different result than after-tax yields. Compared with the current situation, the 1950s were not better on an after-tax basis.

Capital gains' tax advantage over dividends, shown in Table 4.1, also explains why the number of companies in the S&P 500 paying dividends declined from 469 to 351 during a 25-year span. With the exception of the period between the second round of Reagan tax-rate cuts and the first Bush administration, capital gains enjoyed a better-than $16 advantage over dividends per $100 of pre-tax corporate income. The second round of Reagan tax-rate cuts eliminated the capital gain advantage temporarily, but tax actions during the Bush–Clinton period that followed restored some of those advantages. It was not until the George W. Bush administration lowered the dividend tax rate and eliminated the capital gains tax advantage that the surge in dividends began.

The 2003 tax-rate changes have also induced, and will still induce, some changes in corporate behavior. As dividends become more popular, we should observe an increase in corporate stocks' dividend yield. One immediate thought is dividend-intensive stocks will greatly benefit from the 2003 tax-rate cuts. This analysis has already proven correct; it is, however, only a first step.

The dividend tax-rate cuts will also make the capital markets more efficient. The simplest way to explain this is to ask and answer the following question: If a corporation can earn a higher rate-of-return than the investor, what would the investor like to see the corporation do? Obviously, the investor would want corporate profits to stay in the form of retained earnings, which would then be invested to earn a higher rate-of-return. Doing so would increase shareholder value. On the other hand, if a corporation could not earn a higher rate of return than the shareholder, the shareholder would demand the corporation return funds to investors in the least costly way. Because dividends and capital gains are now taxed at the same rate, today's investor is presumably indifferent as to the way returns are delivered—capital gains or dividends. Hence, the businesses with fewer opportunities will return funds to investors as dividends, while investors will have the opportunity to deploy their funds in enterprises that project higher rates of return. In this way, the lower dividend tax rate makes the capital markets more efficient as the benefit is not only to the dividend-intensive companies, but also to the fastest-growing companies needing capital.

Prior to the 2003 reduction in the dividend tax rate, corporations had a different incentive. The lower tax on capital gains offered them a tax advantage and sometimes, even if their portfolio investments produced lower returns, they could deliver higher after-tax income to investors as their portfolio investments generated capital gains. Companies could reward investors even when they made less efficient use of capital. Microsoft was the poster child of this behavior—recall the numerous portfolio investments made by the firm during the 1990s. Soon after the tax law changed in 2003, however, Microsoft instituted a dividend policy. As evidence of the way such a well-run company responds to incentives, one need only point out the one-time $3 dividend announced in 2004 was paid out in December 2004. One important reason for this was the pledge by Senator John Kerry, then-Democratic candidate for president, to reverse the Bush 2003 tax-rate cuts. Perhaps hedging its bets, just as a well-managed company should, Microsoft did not risk the possibility of a rollback of the law and an increased tax on the one-time dividend.

According to this interpretation of events, not only can increased dividends be explained by tax-rate changes, so can a decline in corporate malfeasance. A clear side benefit of the 2003 dividend tax-rate cuts is improved corporate governance.

Summary

The different case studies in this chapter illustrate some major points in the cyclical asset-allocation story. As I mentioned earlier, the legislative process does provide advance notice of coming policy changes. This, in turn, enables analysts and investors plenty of time to identify the investment implications and behavioral changes the new legislation will generate. The data also show adjustments are costly and behavioral changes continue long after tax-rate changes are put in place. It is this last point creating the necessary precondition for the cyclical asset-allocation strategy.

By focusing on behavioral changes, one can also understand the type of legislative changes *that need to be enacted* in the future to cure aberrant and undesirable behavior in the corporate sector. This insight is very useful to investors and proponents of the cyclical asset-allocation strategy, as the strategy identifies the type of legislation likely to be proposed in the future. Investors who correctly anticipate such future policy changes can benefit greatly by adjusting their portfolios to the markets those policy changes will produce.

5

LINKING UP

Monetary policy, as wielded by the Federal Reserve (the Fed), affects the economy and stock market in distinct ways. It certainly impacts investor horizons and, once a monetary move is made, it can also reduce uncertainty. But another effect has to do with the interaction between inflation and the tax code. Numerous channels exist through which this interaction occurs. Inflation pushes people into higher tax brackets, creates illusory capital gains, and (given historical depreciation) generates false profits at the corporate level. All these effects suggest inflation alters the economy's marginal tax rate, even if legislated tax rates remain unchanged.

Interaction Between Inflation and the Tax Code

In what follows, I focus only on the interaction between the tax treatment of interest income and inflation. In an unindexed system taxing interest income at ordinary rates, inflation results in an effective tax rate on real interest earned that could be well over the maximum legislated rate. A simple example helps illustrate this point: Assume a 2 percent inflation rate and a nominal (not-inflation-adjusted) 6 percent return on an investment. Doing the simple math, such an investment yields a 4 percent real (inflation-adjusted) rate of return. Under a system taxing nominal returns at 50 percent, the nominal after-tax return is 3 percent, as the inflation rate is 2 percent and the investor nets a 1 percent real return after taxes. Now, compare this to a system indexed for inflation. In this case, the investor is only taxed on his real returns; thus, the tax liability is only 2 percent—leaving the investor a nominal 4 percent return. Comparing indexed and unindexed after-tax nominal returns, it's clear the unindexed system produces a higher tax liability. From this, we can generalize the nature of excess taxation depends on the degree of indexing, the inflation rate, and the tax rate.

To best illustrate this, I calculated the effective tax rate on interest income yielded by U.S. Treasury bills (T-bills) and applied to this the highest personal income-tax rates for each post-war year. The results are shown in Figure 5.1. Clearly, as long as the inflation rate was positive, effective tax rates exceeded legislated tax rates. Notice also, during the Dwight D. Eisenhower years (1953–1961), the effective tax rate declined even though the legislated tax rate remained unchanged. The reason for this was the adoption of the international price rule during the period resulted in a decline in nominal interest rates as well as the measured decline of the inflation component of nominal rates. Therefore, even though the nominal tax rate remained unchanged throughout the Eisenhower years, the effective tax rate lowered. In turn, the reduced effective tax rates produced a rising stock market.

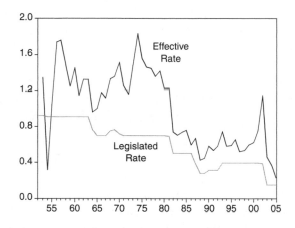

Figure 5.1   Legislated personal income tax rate versus effective personal income tax rate.

The evidence supports the view that marginal tax rates matter. I've expanded this idea, however, to account for policy changes—including monetary policy. Data across Ike's years illustrate monetary policy's power to reduce effective marginal tax rates, lower investor uncertainty, and lengthen investor horizons to produce a strong and vibrant stock market.

Eisenhower's successor, John F. Kennedy, is credited with lowering tax rates, although the rate reduction was posthumously enacted. During the late 1960s, Kennedy tax cut's effect was evident. Unfortunately, during that time, the *Bretton Woods standard* (the dollar–gold currency-exchange standard established in 1944, which in effect made for an international price rule) was falling apart. Meanwhile, the inflation rate began creeping up, as did effective marginal tax rates. Richard Nixon's administration subsequently took the U.S. off the gold standard and the U.S. inflation rate continued to increase. Again, effective tax rates also climbed, with a huge spike taking place in the mid-1970s. During the 1971–1979 period, the inflation rate (as measured by the GDP price deflator) averaged 6.6 percent, ranging from a 4 percent low to a 9 percent high. The real S&P stock index declined at a 4.23 percent annual rate during the period. In short, the economy and the stock market suffered dearly as the disincentives of increased effective tax rates mounted.

During the Ronald Reagan years, the commitment to a *price rule*—the adjustment mechanism whereby shifts in money demand are automatically accommodated by the central bank—was reestablished. Unfortunately, the rule was never (and still has not been) formally announced, and the markets have had to learn its working through experience. Nevertheless, price rule brought inflation down and led to a reduction in the gap between nominal and effective tax rates. The monetary policies put in place during the Reagan years continue to this day. Monetary policy, by the way, minimized the negative impact of the tax-rate increases enacted by President Clinton during his first term. In fact, since 1992, the reduction in the U.S. inflation rate has produced a reduction in effective tax rates. Viewed this way, with the exception of the late 1980s, the U.S. continues to enjoy the lowest tax rates in half a century. Not surprisingly, the stock market has also exhibited its best performance in half a century.

Declining effective tax rates are clearly associated with a rising stock market. This isn't a surprising statement; the surprise is the bulk of the reduction in effective tax rates comes from good monetary policy. When comparing periods with similar inflation rates, my research shows the level of tax rates matter. Thus, I have concluded a policy containing both low tax rates and low inflation (through a price rule) is good policy. It would clearly behoove any investor to put his money in countries following these prescriptions and avoid those countries raising taxes and abandoning the price rule.

The tax story goes a long way toward explaining the 1970s' bear market and the 1980s' and 1990s' extraordinary bull market, and explaining why the so-called equity risk premium increased steadily during the 1980s and 1990s. To best understand the relationship between taxation and the market, we need to modify existing formulas used in both government and financial forecasting.

Market Valuation: The Capitalized Earnings Model

Let's borrow a page from the Fed and use the inverse of the 10-year government Treasury bond (T-bond) yield to value $1 in profits in perpetuity as a proxy for the fair-market-value price-to-earnings ratio (P/E ratio) (see Figure 5.2). The *P/E ratio* is the standard measure for stock valuation whereby stock prices are divided by corporate earnings per share. The essence of the Fed's valuation model is easily derived using a simple high-school algebra formula for the sum of an infinite geometric series. The formula for this follows (B denotes the T-bond's price, c the coupon, and i the T-bond yield):

Equation 1: (1) $B = c/i$

The formula can be used to show the net present value or $1's value in perpetuity, discounted at a 5 percent rate, is $20. The precise formula is nothing more than the coupon rate of the income stream multiplied by the inverse of the discount rate. This formula provides an exact answer for a consol, a T-bond paying a constant coupon in perpetuity. If one is willing to approximate an infinite horizon using the government T-bond, the inverse of the T-bond yield represents the value of $1 in perpetuity discounted at the T-bond yield.

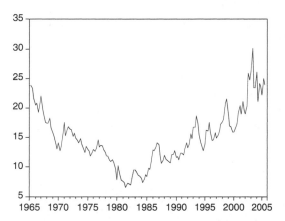

Figure 5.2   The Fed's fair market value measure: the inverse of the 10-year T-bond yield.

Some economists have further extended this model by applying it to equity valuations, the logic being any profitable ongoing concern should have a P/E ratio equal to at least the inverse of T-bond yields. Multiplying the economy's earnings by the inverse of T-bond yields gives us a *fair market value* estimate or the capitalized earnings model valuation; it reflects the price a ready buyer would pay a ready seller when all variables are transparent and known (see Figure 5.3). This interpretation of the capitalized earnings model (CEM) has been attributed to the Fed.

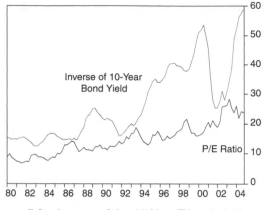

Figure 5.3   Inverse of the 10-Year T-bond yield versus the S&P 500 P/E ratio.

Let's apply some of this math. In 1982, the 10-year T-bond yield was 10.54 percent, producing an implied 9.48 market-wide P/E ratio. By 1988, the yield had declined to 4.65, implying a 21.5 P/E ratio. The T-bond yields alone suggest an expansion of 126 percent for the P/E ratio, well short of the 193 percent realized expansion. In other words, the Fed model suggests a 67 percent P/E overvaluation. Such a calculation, however, ignores lower tax rates' effect on the after-tax yield. The secular decline in tax rates that has taken place during the last few decades has increased the after-tax take of $1 of corporate profit delivered to investors in the form of dividends and/or capital gains.

As shown in Table 5.1, the top corporate income-tax rate between 1980 and 1988 declined from 46 percent to 34 percent while the marginal tax rate on dividend income declined from 70 percent to 28 percent. Following the taxes' impact on $100 of pre-tax income, we can determine the tax-rate changes' affect on equity valuations. Applying 1980's 46 percent corporate tax rate to $100 in pre-tax income would have left a firm with $54. If this amount were doled out as dividend income, the recipient would have been subject to a personal income tax, and at the 1980 rate (70 percent), that person would net only $16. This calculation shows the combined corporate and personal income-tax rate amounted to 84 percent, the effective rate. In contrast, the reduction in tax rates during the Reagan years would have increased the take-home amount to $48 by 1988.

Table 5.1

**Impact of the constellation of tax rates
on the incentive structure.**

	1980	1988	
Personal Income	70%	28%	
Corporate Income	46%	34%	
Dividend	70%	28%	
Capital Gains	28%	28%	
After-Tax Income (Keep Rate)			
	1980	**1988**	**Increase**
Dividends	16%	48%	193%
Capital Gains	39%	48%	22%

Source: Internal Revenue Service

Similar calculations show the keep-rate for retained earnings converted into capital gains also increased during this period, from $39 in 1980 to $48 in 1988. The numbers show the after-tax cash flow increased by 22 percent for capital gains and 193 percent for dividends. Because equity returns are a weighted average of capital gains and dividends, one can safely argue the pre-tax profits' value increased between 22 percent and 193 percent. If one were to assume all the returns during this period were delivered in the form of capital gains (which they were not), one could explain about half the actual P/E ratio expansion not explained in the Fed's model. My calculations would predict at most only a 45 percent overvaluation.

Between the end of 1998 and 2000, the P/E ratio fell from 32.58 to 26.4, a 19 percent decline. The actual decline is much closer to my calculation than the 67 percent decline the Fed's model implies. The math shows secular increases in P/E ratios are much better explained by changes in tax rates than by changes in 10-year T-bond yields. Furthermore, the Fed's math requires more than the interest-rate calculation—it also needs to figure in the tax rate. In short, the Fed analysis is incomplete.

The Fed's CEM remains simple and elegant, but perhaps too simple and elegant for an investor's own good. The CEM's investment implications are fairly straightforward. During overvaluation periods, the market is expected to correct, meaning investors should be out of the market. Similarly, during undervaluation periods, investors should be in the market. But anyone who followed the CEM decision rule over the last three decades would have been quite unhappy. The CEM would have had an investor fully invested during one of the greatest bear markets of the post-war period, and entirely out of the greatest bull market of all time (see Figure 5.3). Elegant or not, the CEM gives lousy investment advice.

Improving the CEM: Accounting for Growth

The CEM's failure is easy to understand. The model assumes current conditions will be repeated in future quarters. To the extent growth takes place, the CEM underestimates the future; conversely, it overestimates the future to the extent that declines take place. Consequently, the model is overly pessimistic during high and/or rising growth periods, and overly optimistic during low and/or declining growth periods. An investor can do better than the CEM, but that doesn't mean the model should be thrown out entirely. Rather, let's build upon the CEM.

For the CEM to be a useful investment tool, we need to correct for the systematic bias produced by its failure to account for earnings growth. Modifying the valuation formula to account for sustainable growth is a trivial adjustment in the formulation. It turns out earnings growth acts to reduce the discount rate on a one-for-one basis. In other words, a $1 income stream in perpetuity discounted at a 5 percent rate has the same value as $1 that grows at 1 percent per year and is discounted at a 6 percent rate. This gives us a generalized formula that takes into account earnings growth.

But, for this operational formula, we need to address some practical issues. First, we must assume T-bond yields provide a first-order approximation of the discount rate. Second, we need to come up with a measure of what constitutes sustainable growth. We know earnings growth, in the long run, is bound by GDP growth, so if earnings grow faster than GDP, they eventually become GDP. Third, we must consider taxation. We know corporate profits in the U.S. are subject to corporate tax rates before they are paid out as dividends or retained as earnings. Hence, it is after-tax profits that are subject to the reinvestment rate.[1] Applying these real-world practicalities to the formula, the growth-modified CEM becomes the following (P denotes the price of equities, E current earnings, i T-bond yields, gdp the GDP growth rate, and t the corporate tax rate):

Equation 2: (2) $P = E/(i-gdp \times (1-t))$

For any formulation to truly act as a guide to the asset-allocation process, it must take into account real-world variables, variables offering a view of the future and not only a reflection of current conditions. Inflation and tax rates are two such variables, and (as the following example shows) all real-world variables must be considered in a sound forecast's construction.

Does the Modified CEM Theory Hold Water?

The stock market's performance during the Clinton administration presented a puzzle for supply-siders at the time. Some argued the Clinton tax-rate increases would be bad for both the economy and the financial markets. But the data show despite Clinton's top personal income-tax rate hike to 39.6 percent from 31 percent (see Figure 5.1), the S&P 500 increased at a 13.76 percent annual rate during his two terms in office. Supply-siders find refuge in the fact that the bulk of those gains occurred after the Republicans took control of Congress in 1995 and moved to keep the nation's fiscal house in order. But the experience of the 1980s weakens this supply-side position. Reagan lowered the top marginal tax rate from 70 percent to 28 percent. During part of the time those rate cuts were in action, the Republicans controlled the Senate; yet from 1984 to 1989, the real S&P 500 index increased at an 8.26 percent annual rate. That's 550 basis points lower than the index's performance during the Clinton years.

Adding insult to injury, the Reagan years came in only 6 basis points better than the Eisenhower years, when the S&P 500 rose at an 8.2 percent annual rate. Remember: The top personal income-tax rate stood at 91 percent for most of the Eisenhower period (see Figure 5.1). Intuitively, the supply-side argument makes sense: Tax rates matter. The stock market's performance, however, during the Eisenhower, Reagan, and Clinton years suggests other variables exist at work. By reviewing these three presidential periods a little more closely, we can find the key to the performance differential.

Let's first look to the inflation rate. The Eisenhower years had the lowest annual inflation rate of the three presidential periods under review. From 1952 to 1960, inflation (as measured by the implicit GDP price deflator) averaged an annual 1.98 percent rate. Inflation during the Reagan years averaged a 3.39 percent annual rate, and the rate during the Clinton years averaged a 2.27 percent annual rate. Next is the real GDP growth rate. The Reagan years produced a 3.77 percent per annum growth rate, followed by the Clinton years at 2.92 percent, and the Eisenhower years at 2.77 percent. From these numbers, we can conclude the higher the tax rate, the lower the real GDP's growth rate, while the lower the inflation rate, the higher the real S&P's performance.

In both the Clinton and Eisenhower years, the U.S. adhered to a price-rule monetary system. During the 1950s, the U.S. was the centerpiece of the Bretton Woods global price rule, while in the Clinton years, U.S. monetary policy had been guided by the Greenspan domestic price rule (which started during the Reagan years). Remember: These two periods exhibited slower economic growth than the Reagan years, from which we can conclude low real GDP growth is not necessarily bad for the market and low inflation is good for the market.

Low tax rates and low inflation produce the best of all possible worlds. If, however, I had to choose one over the other, I would prefer to live in a world of high taxes and low inflation. The Eisenhower years, and to some extent the Clinton years, bear this out.

Policy Changes, Economic Performance, and Market Valuation

Let's link economic policy and economic performance to our valuation models. To complete our theoretical formulations, we need to use a couple of relationships. The first is well-established in the economic literature: It's the well-known *Fisher equation*, or *Fisher effect*, which relates the interest rate levels to the economy's expected real returns and expected inflation rates. Here's the formula (r denotes the expected real rate of return):

$$\text{Equation 3: } I = r + \text{inflation}$$

A second equation does not denote a formal relationship, but it is nevertheless a sensible assumption. Most economic models hold the economy's real rate of return is related to real GDP growth. If aggregate demand shocks dominate the overall equilibrium process, one can easily show increases in real GDP are positively correlated to the real interest rate. Hence, the following equation (a and b denote constant parameters that describe a linear relationship between GDP growth [gdp] and the real rate of return [r]):

$$\text{Equation 4: } r = a + b \times gdp$$

By now, we have accumulated enough relationships to make some inferences regarding equity and fixed-income valuations and determine their relative performance using some simple economic variables, such as the inflation rate, the real GDP growth rate, and tax rates—all commonly used to describe the economic environment. A rising inflation rate, for example, results in higher nominal yields (see Equation 3); for all else, higher nominal yields reduce the discounted value of future nominal income streams (see Equations 1 and/or 2). So, fixed-income streams, such as constant coupon payments, unambiguously decline in value in a higher-inflation environment. To the extent corporate earnings rise with inflation, however, the net effect on equities' valuation is zero. On the other hand, to the extent the tax system is not fully indexed, there is an illusory profits tax, so equities rise by less than the inflation rate. If the effective tax rate is less than 100 percent, one can show equities outperform T-bonds during rising inflation periods. In contrast to a higher inflation rate, an increase in the real rate of return due to higher GDP growth and a higher discount rate lower the fixed-coupon instruments value. On the other hand, higher real rates—under most general conditions—lead to higher equity growth. It is relatively simple to extend this model to account for the valuation of both short-term fixed-income instruments and international equities.

The valuation of the short-term fixed-income instrument is captured in the following equation (*TB* denotes the short-term fixed-income instrument— that is, three-month T-bills—and *s* the short-term yields):

Equation 5: $TB = 1/(1 + s)$

As before, the short-term yields conform to the Fisher equation.

The modified CEM's equity-valuation formula (see Equation 2) also applies to foreign equities—with one caveat: If one uses foreign interest rates and inflation rates, the model's results are denominated in foreign currencies. Hence, to translate these returns to domestic returns, one needs to know whether purchasing power parity (PPP)—the point at which exchange rates have adjusted based on the currencies' purchasing power—holds or not. If PPP holds, the differential inflation rate between two countries matches exchange-rate fluctuations. If (on the other hand) PPP does not hold, real rates of return for the two countries match the exchange-rate fluctuations.[2]

We previously established a link between inflation and real GDP growth rates and the relative valuation of equities and fixed-income instruments. Because most economists (and their economic models) forecast inflation and real GDP growth rates, in Equations 1 through 5, I have developed a way to link these economic forecasts to the relative and absolute valuations of fixed-income instruments and equities. Can these relationships actually be made? The results reported in Table 5.2, based on monthly data going back to 1948, show they can. I used a simple three-month moving average to identify rising and falling interest-rate cycles and a four-quarter moving average for real GDP to determine rising and falling economic growth periods. The data show, as expected, rising inflation and rising economic growth periods are the worst for T-bond returns. In the sample, T-bond returns declined an average 44 basis points per month during such periods. Again, as expected, declining inflation and declining growth periods were the most favorable for fixed-income instruments. During these periods, the T-bond index gained an average 51 basis points per month. The results reported in Table 5.2 also support the assessment regarding equity performance. As expected, declining inflation and rising economic growth periods were the most favorable for equities. During these times, stocks gained an average 117 basis points per month. The worst time periods for equities came when inflation was rising and growth was declining. At these points, equities gained only an average 22 basis points per month.

Table 5.2

Average monthly equity and fixed-income returns during different combinations of rising and falling inflation and rising and falling real GDP growth sample: 1948–2004.

Equity Returns		
	GDP Growth	
	Increasing	Decreasing
Increasing Inflation	0.33%	0.22%
Decreasing Inflation	1.17%	0.87%
T-Bond Returns		
	GDP Growth	
	Increasing	Decreasing
Increasing Inflation	−0.44%	0.17%
Decreasing Inflation	0.30%	0.51%

Source: National Bureau of Economic Research and Ibbotson Associates

So far, the data presented link the two asset classes' (equities and fixed income) relative and absolute returns to the economic environment as described by inflation and GDP growth. Thus, the different inflation and GDP growth combinations can be used to characterize some textbook representations of the world. In the simpler textbooks, the interaction of rising inflation and GDP growth is commonly associated with the *Phillips curve*, where increases in spending—generated by aggregate demand shifts—lead to higher output and higher prices. Declining inflation and real GDP growth periods represent the mirror image, which is described in the simpler textbooks as the result of a decline in aggregate demand.

The negative association between inflation and GDP growth is consistent with a classical model where inflation is too much money chasing too few goods, a relationship often explained in terms of aggregate supply shocks. A bumper crop, for instance, leads to more output and lower prices. On the other hand, a crop failure leads to lower output and higher prices. Viewed this way, the 1970s' *stagflation* (stagnant growth, higher inflation), was just a crop (output) failure caused by supply shocks and/or bad economic policy.

The results reported in Table 5.2, and the implications derived from my valuation models, reveal a classical economic environment in which the highest positive impact on equity returns comes when inflation and growth move in the same direction. In contrast, the *Keynesian Phillips curve* advocates would say such an environment produces the highest range of returns for fixed-income instruments.

The point is knowing the economic-policy package being implemented helps one identify the nature of the shocks that will be imposed on the economy. This knowledge in turn helps one forecast the economy's adjustment, in particular the inflation/GDP-growth combination. After this is known, finding the optimal asset mix is relatively easy.

When random temporary deviations from historical returns patterns are observed, the historical returns' variance and covariance appear stable over the long run. As mentioned earlier, historical returns and the variance–covariance matrix constitute the relevant data for asset allocation. If deviations from trend-lines are random and unpredictable, no benefits can be gained by straying from a long-run strategic asset-allocation strategy. If deviation patterns are not random, however, there are significant potential benefits to cyclical asset allocation (CAA) strategies (defined in Chapter 2, "The Case for Cyclical Asset Allocation") and/or tactical asset allocation (TAA) strategies (defined in Chapter 3, "Thinking in Cycles").

I have argued fiscal and monetary policy produce shifts in the economy's aggregate demand and supply. Depending on the shocks' nature, as the economy returns to a new equilibrium, a new and temporary economic environment is created. To the trained eye, inflation rates and GDP growth rates change in predictable patterns, and (according to the data reported in Table 5.2) so do asset returns. It is the latter giving rise to two different strategies: CAA and TAA.

The CAA strategy is based on the assumption politicians and policymakers have particular world views, and they generally adopt policy measures consistent with these views. This is important because it is the continuity of these responses that can give rise to predictable cycles or deviations from long-term trends. Once these new (and historically true) trends are identified, it is just a matter of tilting portfolios to take advantage of the returns' pattern anticipated by the likely policy responses. Because most economists and investment advisors generate forecasts regarding the inflation rate's and the economy's future path, it follows one can translate these forecasts into forward-looking strategic asset-allocation recommendations.

A Practical Application

How good are such forecasts? Let's make a cursory judgment based on a straightforward illustration. At the beginning of 2004, the *Wall Street Journal*'s consensus economic forecast was for a 2 percent inflation rate and a 4.2 percent real GDP growth rate. A bright forecast, indeed, as low inflation and an expanding economy pointed to a steady improvement in the profit outlook. The economists the *Journal* polled were in fact looking for a 15.9 percent increase in corporate profits, which in this case, I would call a classic supply-side recovery. Historically, a strong growth and low inflation environment (see Table 5.2) has favored stocks. T-bonds, meanwhile, although underperforming, would be expected to post positive returns. Reflecting on 2004's performance, the consensus forecast and the implied tilts for a CAA strategy were right on the money.

The exercise described here illustrates how a basic cyclical investment framework is put into action. By plugging a well-regarded forecast into a practical asset-allocation strategy, an investor can see the clear investment implications for the different asset classes in the period ahead. In this example, I used one of my favorite forecasts—the consensus the *Wall Street Journal*'s panel of economists produced. Investors, over time, may find other forecasts to hang their hats on. That's all well and good. But, the emphasis here is many readily available forecasts exist fitting the various investor world views. Any forecast can easily be modified qualitatively to fit the individual investors' unique preferences and can then be used to generate the asset-allocation tilts that are consistent with the forecast.

The presidential election's outcome was another opportunity to reaffirm a basic CAA strategy's viability. George W. Bush campaigned on a platform of eliminating the income double-taxation. If one took his victory as a signal indicating the likelihood of lower tax rates in the future, the cyclical valuation model would favor stocks over fixed-income instruments. Truth be told, this is exactly what has happened in the aftermath of the 2004 presidential election. This anecdotal example, one of many, again points to an economics-based CAA strategy's benefits—and the potential benefits appear to be quite large.

TAA is a more trade-oriented strategy, but it is based on the same economic approach. The basics of TAA are if we have our economic forecast in hand and have correctly identified existing and forthcoming cycles, we then have a pretty good idea of the relative asset-class returns' likely path. Take once more the case of the *Journal's* consensus forecast for 2004. The weak employment numbers reported at the beginning of the year were at odds with the Wall Street economists' bullish consensus forecast. Thus, either the employment numbers' forward-looking implication or the economists' consensus forecast would be proven incorrect. So, whoever trusted the economists' consensus forecast would have known the market response to the early employment numbers would have to be reversed. This, in turn, presented a trading opportunity.

Mean reversion, the idea asset classes randomly deviate from their long-run averages before returning to those averages, is the asset-allocation version of indexing—a strategy providing good, safe results for an investor, but hardly optimal results. If deviations from trends are totally random, little room exists for a TAA or any other intermediate step in the process. In contrast, if deviations are not totally random, it is worthwhile to spend time forecasting and anticipating the returns patterns. In doing so, investors and financial managers may be able to develop frameworks for making CAA and TAA decisions focused on short-to-intermediate-term horizons.

But, if returns patterns are not random (which I believe to be the case), what causes them? I take the view the returns' deviation from long-run equilibriums reflects the economy's adjustment to various and different shocks and policy changes. Thus, if the cyclical approach is to bear any fruit, we must now develop a simple decision process that incorporates policy's and other economic shocks' effects on the short-, intermediate-, and long-run rates of return in the economy. Only then can we map the path of expected asset returns from which a simple CAA or TAA can be developed. My valuation models do just this.

Summary

In this chapter, we looked at some qualitative arguments as to why policy changes and shifts in the economic environment lead to predictable return cycles. Correctly identifying the economic environment is the first step in deriving economic-based CAA and TAA strategies. Next, through a formal modeling of historical relationships, a more rigorous approach can be developed. From there, we can generate formal decision rules that can guide the CAA/TAA process.

6

TO START, A BENCHMARK

H ere's what we know: Fiscal and monetary policies produce shifts in the economy's aggregate demand and supply. Depending on the nature of the shifts, a new and temporary economic environment is created as the economy returns to a new equilibrium. Along the way, the inflation rate and gross domestic product (GDP) growth rate change in predictable patterns. According to the data reported in the previous chapters, so do the patterns of asset returns (see Table 6.1). The latter is giving rise to cyclical asset allocation (CAA).

But before we can apply a CAA strategy, we need a starting point. In the context of a cyclical strategy, the strategic asset allocation (SAA) constitutes a benchmark from which the CAA temporarily deviates to take advantage of cyclical fluctuations in asset returns caused by policy changes and other economic shocks. Therefore, whether one believes in the mean-reversion hypothesis—that is, whether one does business the way most financial planners do—there is no way to avoid developing an SAA (or, as I prefer to call it, a benchmark portfolio) before applying a cyclical strategy. In short, you need the SAA before you can build the CAA.

Allocations Based on the Last 30 Years

Traditionally, developing an SAA is a two-step process, and a perilous one for the individual investor. The first step uses the asset classes' historical returns and the variance–covariance matrix to build a combination of the various asset classes that leads one to the efficient frontier. This step also leads an investor to the point where maximum expected returns are reached for a determined risk level. The second step determines risk tolerance so an investor can choose the risk/return combination best suiting his or her preferences.

I have two major objections to this process as it is currently practiced. The first objection is simply empirical: How long of a historical sample does one need to determine long-run historical returns and the variance–covariance matrix? In earlier chapters, I used traditional asset-allocation tools to decide whether individual asset classes—Treasury bonds (T-bonds), small-caps, large-caps, value stocks, growth stocks, and domestic/international stocks—would be included on the efficient frontier and thus be potentially included in an investor portfolio. (In Chapter 2, "The Case for Cyclical Asset Allocation," I used the historical Sharpe ratios between asset class pairs to select the optimal mix between the pairs. These results are reported again in Table 6.2.)

Table 6.1
Periodic table of asset returns.*

Rank	1975	1976	1977	1978	1979	1980
1	S 52.8	S 57.4	S 25.4	ROW 27.6	S 43.5	S 39.9
2	V 43.4	V 34.9	ROW 12.6	S 23.5	V 21.2	G 39.4
3	L 37.2	L 23.8	TB 5.1	TB 7.2	L 18.4	L 32.4
4	G 31.7	B 16.8	B -0.7	G 6.8	G 15.7	V 23.6
5	ROW 26.9	G 13.8	V -2.6	L 6.6	TB 10.4	ROW 19.8
6	B 9.2	TB 5.1	L -7.2	V 6.2	ROW 6.3	TB 11.2
7	TB 5.8	ROW -0.6	G -11.8	B -1.2	B -1.2	B -4

Rank	1981	1982	1983	1984	1985	1986	1987	1988	1989
1	TB 14.7	B 40.4	S 39.7	B 15.4	ROW 47.7	ROW 62.7	ROW 22.8	ROW 25.8	G 36.4
2	S 13.9	S 28	V 28.9	V 10.5	G 33.3	B 24.4	G 6.5	S 22.9	L 31.5
3	B 1.9	G 22	L 22.5	TB 9.9	L 32.2	V 21.7	TB 5.5	V 21.7	V 26.1
4	V 0	L 21.4	ROW 21	L 6.3	B 31	L 18.5	L 5.2	L 16.8	B 18.1
5	L -4.9	V 21	G 16.2	G 2.3	V 29.7	G 14.5	V 3.7	G 11.9	S 10.2
6	ROW -6.5	TB 10.5	TB 8.8	ROW 0.6	S 24.7	S 6.9	B -2.7	B 9.7	ROW 9.8
7	G -9.8	ROW -4.2	B 0.7	S -6.7	TB 7.7	TB 6.2	S -9.3	TB 6.4	TB 8.4

Rank	1990	1991	1992	1993	1994	1995	1996	1997	1998
1	TB 7.8	S 44.6	S 23.4	ROW 30.1	ROW 5.8	G 38.1	G 24	G 36.5	G 42.2
2	B 6.2	G 38.4	V 10.5	S 21	TB 3.9	L 37.4	L 23.1	L 33.4	L 28.6
3	G 0.2	L 30.6	B 8.1	V 18.6	G 3.1	V 37	V 22	V 30	ROW 17
4	L -3.2	V 22.6	L 7.7	B 18.2	S 3.1	S 34.5	S 17.6	S 22.8	V 14.7
5	V -6.8	B 19.3	G 5.1	L 10	L 1.3	B 31.7	TB 5.2	B 15.9	B 13.1
6	S -21.6	ROW 10.1	TB 3.5	TB 2.9	V -0.9	ROW 9.6	ROW 5.2	TB 5.3	TB 4.9
7	ROW -24.4	TB 5.6	ROW -14	G 1.7	B -7.8	TB 5.6	B -0.9	ROW 0.7	S -7.3

Rank	1999	2000	2001	2002	2003	2004
1	S 29.8	B 21.3	B 6.9	B 14.1	S 38.8	S 22.5
2	G 28.2	TB 5.9	TB 3.4	TB 1.7	ROW 36.2	ROW 17.8
3	ROW 26.2	S -3.6	S 2.5	S -15.3	V 31.8	V 15.5
4	L 21	V -9.6	V -13	ROW -17.4	L 28.7	L 10.7
5	V 12.6	L -9.9	L -13.1	V -22.5	G 25.7	B 9.3
6	TB 4.7	ROW -14.4	G -13.2	L -23.7	B 1.3	G 6.0
7	B -9	G -17	ROW -22.6	G -24.5	TB 1.2	TB 1.2

Key
S–Small
V–Value
L–Large
G–Growth
R–Rest of the World
B–T-Bonds
TB–T-Bills

* The figures included in this table are percentages.

Table 6.2
Optimal allocation based on the Sharpe ratio produced by historical returns: 1975–2004.

Size	Small	Large
	80.0%	20.0%
Style	**Value**	**Growth**
	100.0%	0.0%
Location	**USA**	**Rest of the World**
	100.0%	0.0%
Equity/Fixed	**Equity**	**Fixed Income**
	60.0%	40.0%

The results were surprising. Based on a 30-year sample period, the optimal style choice was to allocate 100 percent to value stocks and 100 percent to domestic stocks. The numbers also pointed to a less-than 100 percent allocation to the size and equity/fixed-income choices. In the case of the size choice, the optimal allocation was 70 percent to 80 percent small-cap stocks, while the stocks versus T-bonds choice pointed to a 50 percent to 60 percent stock allocation. These two latter results are surprising because, based on the conventional wisdom, one would have expected to find a near-opposite optimal allocation—that is, 60 percent to large-cap stocks in both cases. The asset allocation generated by this approach is reported in Figure 6.1. (In Chapter 3, "Thinking in Cycles," I considered a slightly different variant. I applied the Sharpe ratio to find the optimal allocation for each calendar year and then calculated the average pair-wise allocation for the entire 30-year period. The results are again reported in Table 6.3.)

Table 6.3
Percent of the time allocated by size (large versus small), style (value versus growth), location (domestic versus international), and fixed income versus equity.

Size	Small	Large
	51.6%	48.4%
Style	**Value**	**Growth**
	48.4%	51.6%
Location	**USA**	**Rest of the World**
	63.3%	36.7%
Equity/Fixed	**Equity**	**Fixed Income**
	52.9%	47.1%

(This latter allocation is much closer to the various asset classes' market weights. The asset allocation derived by this process is reported in Figure 6.2.) The question now becomes whether 30 years is long enough to generate a long-run result. If the 30-year sample period is not long enough, the results may suffer from sample-selection bias, which presents a major problem. Even if we were to find the true long-run allocation, fluctuations over the next 30 years may generate a return distribution quite different from those of the long-run returns. In short, the long-run SAA may not be optimal for a finite future time period. This again makes the case for CAA, although we still need the SAA starting point.

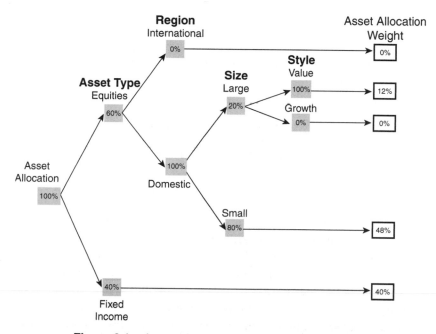

Figure 6.1 Asset allocation produced by the historical returns of asset classes using the Sharpe ratio to select the optimal mix: 1978–2004.

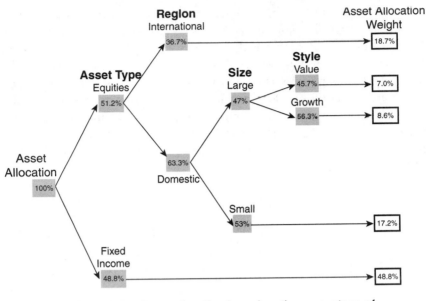

Figure 6.2 Asset allocation based on the percentage of time allocated by the Sharpe ratio to each asset class: 1975–2004.

Market-Based Asset Allocation Weights

Another major objection I have to traditional asset allocation is its partial-equilibrium nature. SAA assumes the individual investor has no market power. In the economic parlance, the individual investor is the quintessential atomistic investor—he is a price-taker and has no influence on prices. Although this can be true at the individual level, what about the possibility that many investors act in a similar manner? If enough investors use the same optimization or asset-allocation process, guess what? They collectively move the market. Although large asset bases can benefit from scale advantages, such as more resources for research and lower expense ratios, they can also erode performance due to the trading costs associated with liquidity. Although a single individual is able to put all his money in his best idea, a large group of like-minded individuals can hit a capacity constraint if an investment is small in relation to the funds the group wants to invest. A large group of small investors can collectively be forced to invest in not-so-good ideas, taking larger-than-optimal positions, thereby eroding market performance.

In some sense, there is an externality to the asset-allocation process and many advisors do not take into account the fact that there can be like-minded investors out there, and that these investors—if numerous enough—have an impact on the market. More important, if capacity differs across investments, the asset-allocation process itself can affect overall returns. One way to solve these problems is to choose incremental investments in such a way that, as more resources are deployed on an asset-allocation strategy, all the components of the strategy reach their capacity at the same time. This is a daunting task for an investor, let alone an individual financial advisor. A simple way, however, exists to approach and solve the problem. The *efficient market theory* tells us that, in an idealized situation, the market portfolio is on the efficient frontier. If this is the case, then all asset classes should be included on the efficient frontier and, therefore, in an economy-wide (or aggregate) SAA portfolio.

As it is true individuals differ regarding their risk-tolerances and investment preferences, it follows their individual asset-allocation plans differ from those of the aggregate economy. Investors, however, cannot collectively avoid economy-wide constraints. Ultimately, a weighted average of individual asset allocations must add up to the market allocation. So, the market allocation is a good place to start building an SAA program.

One can argue the market allocation is the relevant allocation for an infinite number of foundations and trust funds. The allocation also can be optimal for retirement plans (for example, 401[k] plans) that have many participants. But before building a market SAA, one must decide on the equity/fixed-income split—what I consider the most important decision in any asset-allocation process. Conventional wisdom and the market capitalization of these two asset classes suggest a 60/40 split between equities and fixed income. Given the assumption the market is on the efficient frontier, we also take the 60/40 split as an efficient benchmark allocation to equities and fixed income.

In what follows, I use the Morgan Stanley Capital Index (MSCI) as a rough guideline for our global equity allocation. According to the MSCI, the U.S. represents approximately 50 percent of the world's equity markets. Hence, we allocate equities in equal amounts to the U.S. and world markets. With 60 percent of the overall allocation going to equities, 30 percent of the portfolio is allocated to domestic stocks and 30 percent to international stocks.

The U.S. allocation is further subdivided by size and style. The Russell Investment Group tells us large-, mid-, and small-capitalization stocks account for almost 70 percent, 20 percent, and 10 percent of the U.S. equity markets, respectively. Therefore, the 30 percent of the global portfolio allocated to domestic stocks is split as follows: 21 percent large-cap, 6 percent mid-cap, and 3 percent small-cap.

BARRA tells us approximately 50 percent of U.S. stocks are value stocks and 50 percent are growth stocks. Hence, the large-cap allocation is equally split into value and growth stocks, with 10.5 percent of assets going to large-cap value stocks and 10.5 percent to large-cap growth stocks. The allocation to mid-value stocks and mid-growth stocks is 3 percent to each, while the allocation to small-cap value stocks and small-cap growth stocks is only 1.5 percent to each. (In principle, the allocation to international stocks could be further subdivided by country, size, and style, but we ignore this subdivision for the time being.)

Conventional wisdom and approximate market values suggest 10 percent is a good proxy for the short-term fixed-income share of the total fixed-income market value. Given our portfolio's 40 percent allocation to fixed income, it follows we allocate 4 percent to short-term instruments and 36 percent to longer-maturity instruments. (We could further disaggregate the longer-term fixed-income instruments into a global allocation, but for this exercise, we stay domestic.)

Figure 6.3 illustrates the SAA produced by my interpretation of the various asset classes' market weights. Either exchange-traded funds (ETFs), or passively managed low-cost index funds, could fill most buckets in question. ETFs and the low cost-managed index funds are diversified baskets of securities designed to track the performance of well-known indices, proprietary indices or basket of securities. The major differences between the two is that the ETF are traded as individual stocks on major exchanges while the passive funds are subject to the traditional mutual funds-pricing mechanism (that is, at the close of market). They offer diversification or exposure to an entire market index or sector with one security at very low costs (that is, management fees). Each asset class was available at some point over the last three decades. Looking forward, it is readily apparent that—with ETFs' proliferation—investors can now easily expand their choices and further disaggregate the international allocation, the fixed-income allocation, and even the domestic allocation (see Figure 6.4). Indeed, ETFs or low-cost passively managed funds are a must for most investors today. But, to illustrate a market SAA's potential impact, I have restricted our portfolio's allocation to funds that would have been available each year for the past 30 years.

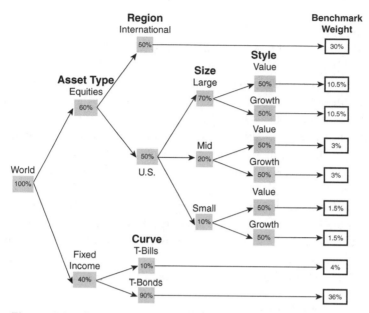

Figure 6.3 Strategic asset allocation—benchmark construction.

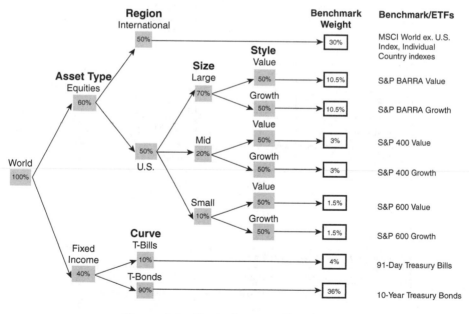

Figure 6.4 Strategic asset allocation.

PERFORMANCE OF THE MARKET-BASED ASSET ALLOCATION WEIGHTS

Let's look at the returns produced by our market SAA, reported in Table 6.4. $1 invested in 1975 using this SAA would have grown to $28.76 by 2004's end, an 11.8 percent annual rate of return. In addition to the SAA returns, Table 6.4 also reports the yearly returns produced by investing in the top-performing asset class, the second-best asset class, and so on. The listing of the returns produced by each asset choice, ranked from the top performer to the bottom performer, is a good approximation of the fancy Monte Carlo simulations financial advisors love to show their clients. Comparatively, the market SAA performed as expected. The portfolio's $28.87 return is near the $31.89 delivered by $1 invested in the median-performing asset class. So, the market portfolio is solidly in line with the Monte Carlo simulations' median performance (the standard computer calculations used by investment advisors taking into account chance and randomness). The first implication of this is that by buying the market portfolio, one can generate median-like returns. The second implication is that to do better, one needs either luck, a better strategy, or the capacity to take more risks.

Table 6.4
Growth of $1 invested in the top-, second-, third-, fourth-, fifth-, sixth-, and seventh-ranked asset class each year versus strategic asset allocation.

	Value of $1	Return
Top	2,919.50	30.5%
Second	365.57	21.7%
Third	92.48	16.3%
Fourth/Median	31.89	12.2%
Fifth	11.44	8.4%
Sixth	1.75	1.9%
Seventh	0.24	−4.7%
Strategic Asset Allocation Based On...		
Period Sharpe Ratio	$72.59	15.35%
Yearly Sharpe Ratio	$34.39	12.5%
Market Weights	$28.76	11.8%

Source: MSCI, Research Insight, and Ibbotson Associates

Table 6.5
Risk measurements: 1975–2004.

	CAPM Beta	Jensen's Alpha	T-Statistics	Sharpe Ratio
Small Cap	1	5.64%	2.07	0.65
Large Cap	1	0.00%		0.53
Growth	1.06	−1.46%	1.87	0.43
Value	0.93	0.81%	1.67	0.60
International	0.62	−1.27%	0.04	0.29
Strategic Asset Allocation Based On...				
Period Sharpe Ratio	0.66	0.03%	24.09	0.72
Yearly Sharpe Ratio	0.52	0.02%	24.58	0.63
Market Weights	0.54	0.1%	27	0.57

Comparing the Historical- and Market-Based Allocations

As I pointed out in Chapter 1, "In Search of the Upside," financial economics developments over the past three decades provide us with the necessary tools to develop risk-adjusted returns in a rigorous and systematic way. Arguably, systematic risk is the more important risk measure for investors who are considering adding an asset class to a diversified portfolio. According to the capital asset pricing model (CAPM), the only sort of risk priced (that is, risk requiring a higher rate-of-return) is systematic risk, which is correlated with the market. The CAPM offers a way to estimate systematic risk for different asset classes (that is, beta) as well as precisely measure the additional return (that is, alpha) provided by an asset class over that required to compensate for the systematic risk. The results reported in Table 6.5 show our market SAA does not produce any additional excess returns (that is, alpha). In fact, the estimated alpha is virtually zero in both magnitude and statistical significance.

But, the results also show the SAA produces a much lower correlation with the market. The diversification in the portfolio seems to produce the highly desirable lower risk outcome without any reduction in returns, something economists call a free lunch.

Ideally, one would then search for those asset classes that would add alpha (that is, excess returns to a portfolio) without increasing beta (that is, the risk of the portfolio in relation to the benchmark).

Now, let's apply the Sharpe ratio. Once more, the Sharpe ratio divides a portfolio's excess returns (returns less risk less Treasury bill returns) by its volatility. In effect, the Sharpe ratio treats each asset class as a separate portfolio, focusing on the standard deviations that measure total risk. If a portfolio in question represents an individual's entire investment, then volatility matters and the Sharpe ratio is a fitting comparison tool. As such, the Sharpe ratio provides an appropriate way to compare and evaluate the size, style, and location choices within our SAA portfolio. For Table 6.5, I applied the Sharpe ratio simply by calculating the ratio of the risk-adjusted portfolio returns to their standard deviation, the idea being that the portfolio with the highest return-to-standard-deviation ratio offers the highest reward-to-risk ratio. Looking at the calculations, our SAA portfolio's performance is comparable to that of large-cap stocks, higher than that of growth and international (that is, location) stocks, and lower than that of small-cap and value stocks.

The tilts produced by the Sharpe ratio, using historical foresight, generate 12.5 percent annual returns and a 15.35 percent period return. The former return is a bit higher than the median asset class, while the latter is approaching the third tier on our performance chart (refer to Table 6.4). By all accounts, the increase in performance is achieved with little or no increase in risk as measured by the CAPM or Sharpe ratio. This exercise illustrates two distinct points. One is that in using actual data to choose the best performing asset mix, sample-selection bias can be shown to truly distort the results. In other words, we should take these results with a grain of salt because this specific allocation cannot produce an optimal long-run mix. In particular, if the near future is different from the near past from which estimates have been calculated, a true long-run estimate is needed. The second point is that the numbers illustrate the potential gains that can be generated by a strategy anticipating relative performance cycles. This is the exciting and promising part of a forward-looking asset-allocation strategy. I argue market-based weights are the appropriate weights, and the CAA strategy should be used to tilt these weights over cycles.

All this turns out to be a strong argument for a market allocation's efficiency. Absent any information about an investor, the market portfolio would be the ideal SAA candidate for most large plans featuring many participants. I did, however, warn such an allocation could lead to capacity issues if too many people adopt it and there is no counterbalance in the economy to offset any deviation from the market allocation. That said, an investor can still choose to pursue an allocation differing from the market allocation. Risk considerations can bring this on. Take the case of workers nearing retirement. They can find it desirable to lower their overall portfolios' Sharpe ratio by reducing their portfolio risk. To do this, they could increase their allocations to fixed-income instruments and decrease their allocations to stocks. For example, rather than a 60/40 equity/fixed-income allocation, near-retirement workers can choose an 80/20 allocation where the 20 percent allocated to equities is invested in safer value stocks. At the other end of the spectrum are young workers with the long horizons. They can find it desirable to allocate a much larger portion of their portfolios to riskier small-cap stocks. If the weighted incomes of the near-retirement workers and the young workers are roughly the same, the two groups' combined allocation equals the market allocation. In this case, there is no market impact (or capacity issues) arising from the combined strategies.

The Lifecycle Allocation

Young investors, of course, still confront the way to make smooth transitions in their asset allocations over time. In some sense, the problem young investors face is relatively simple. We know their beginning portfolios should have an 80/20 allocation of equities to fixed income, and their end portfolios should have a 20/80 allocation of equities to fixed income. Now, if individual workers have expected retirement dates, it would be relatively simple to adjust their portfolio allocations automatically to ensure a smooth transition to the long-run allocations. Let's take the example of workers with 40-year working horizons. In this case, they want to reduce their current 80/20 allocations to 20/80 by their retirement. A simple linear adjustment takes care of this. They need to reduce their equity exposures by 60 percentage points over 40 years, which works out to a 1.5 percent reduction in equity allocations per year. Figure 6.5 illustrates a sample SAA that changes automatically with the worker's lifecycle, hence the name *lifecycle SAA*. The figure's left side describes the asset allocation at the beginning of a working life while the right side illustrates the allocation at the end.

Whether lifecycled or not, in the market SAA, we have our benchmark. Now, we can look to tilt the returns even more in our favor.

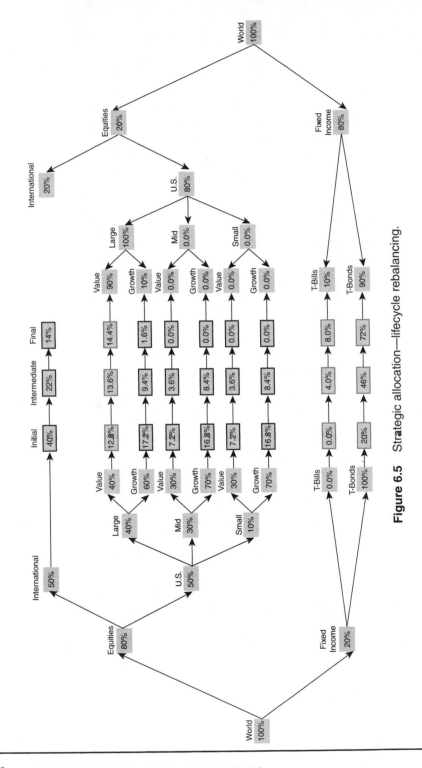

Figure 6.5 Strategic allocation—lifecycle rebalancing.

7

TAKING IT TO THE TILT

Looking at the market data for the last 30 years, I have come to the conclusion that a strategic asset allocation (SAA) based on the long run would have provided more than adequate results for an investor. First, the returns of the SAA would not have been much different from the median returns generated by a Monte Carlo simulation. Second, and equally important, is the SAA would have significantly reduced the portfolio's overall volatility while producing market-like returns. The numbers reported in the previous chapter in fact show the SAA's great benefit, and the diversification produced by the strategy, are best described in risk reduction terms. But, the data nevertheless clearly show the SAA, as promised, delivers a diversified portfolio producing lower risk without sacrificing returns. That's a good deal.

But, if good in this case only means good enough, the good is the enemy of the best. The challenge now is to develop an allocation strategy that delivers even better risk-adjusted returns than the market SAA.

The data reported in Chapter 2, "The Case for Cyclical Asset Allocation," show for approximately 80 percent of the time during our 30-year sample period, the optimal size, style, location, and equity/fixed-income allocation was a corner solution (that is, a 90 percent or greater allocation to one of the choices). The balanced allocation, or equity/fixed-income choice, produced a corner solution in 19 of the 30 sample years (see Table 7.1). During 11 of those years, the optimal allocation was 100 percent stocks, while for another eight years, a 100 percent allocation to Treasury bonds (T-bonds) was best. The style choice produced a corner 28 times (see Table 7.2). During 13 of those years, a 90 percent or better allocation to growth stocks was optimal, while for 15 alternative years, a 90 percent or better allocation to value stocks was best. The size choice produced 24 corner solutions equally split between large- and small-cap allocations (see Table 7.3). During 12 of those years, a 90 percent or better allocation to large-caps was optimal, while for another 12 years, an allocation favoring small-caps was desirable. The domestic/international choice also produced 24 corner solutions (see Table 7.4). During nine of those years, a 90 percent allocation or better to international stocks was the right call, while for another 15 years, a 100 percent allocation to domestic stocks was optimal.

Table 7.1

Sharpe ratio for selected T-bond/equity portfolios: 1975–2004.

	T-Bonds										
	100%	90%	80%	70%	60%	50%	40%	30%	20%	10%	0%
1975	0.420	0.711	0.963	1.160	1.301	1.398	1.462	1.505	1.532	1.550	**1.562**
1976	2.287	**2.393**	2.320	2.149	1.958	1.784	1.635	1.511	1.409	1.323	1.251
1977	**−0.974**	−1.090	−1.183	−1.251	−1.295	−1.318	−1.326	−1.322	−1.312	−1.297	−1.281
1978	−1.764	−1.372	−1.021	−0.745	−0.535	−0.376	−0.252	−0.155	−0.076	−0.012	**0.042**
1979	−0.981	−0.815	−0.641	−0.463	−0.285	−0.112	0.053	0.208	0.352	0.483	**0.603**
1980	−0.610	−0.499	−0.361	−0.193	0.004	0.221	0.440	0.641	0.810	0.942	**1.039**
1981	**−0.443**	−0.511	−0.587	−0.672	−0.765	−0.867	−0.977	−1.092	−1.208	−1.318	−1.417
1982	**2.309**	2.122	1.914	1.701	1.493	1.299	1.121	0.960	0.817	0.690	0.577
1983	−0.640	−0.490	−0.321	−0.133	0.070	0.282	0.497	0.706	0.902	1.079	**1.233**
1984	**0.497**	0.450	0.391	0.320	0.240	0.156	0.075	−0.001	−0.068	−0.126	−0.175
1985	1.688	1.763	1.830	1.885	1.924	**1.943**	1.941	1.919	1.879	1.824	1.759
1986	1.013	**1.015**	1.011	0.998	0.977	0.948	0.911	0.867	0.819	0.767	0.714
1987	−0.746	−0.741	−0.619	−0.417	−0.238	−0.110	−0.022	0.039	0.084	0.118	**0.144**
1988	0.349	0.421	0.493	0.565	0.636	0.703	0.766	0.824	0.876	0.921	**0.959**

continues

Table 7.1   continued

	T-Bonds										
	0%	10%	20%	30%	40%	50%	60%	70%	80%	90%	100%
1989	1.644	1.704	1.766	1.823	1.866	1.878	1.840	1.734	1.562	1.344	1.110
1990	-0.498	-0.483	-0.465	-0.444	-0.419	-0.389	-0.354	-0.311	-0.259	-0.198	-0.126
1991	1.427	1.482	1.544	1.615	1.694	1.783	1.877	1.967	2.037	2.056	1.991
1992	0.557	0.594	0.629	0.660	0.685	0.701	0.707	0.703	0.689	0.668	0.642
1993	1.140	1.326	1.509	1.677	1.819	1.925	1.993	2.026	2.030	2.014	1.985
1994	-0.191	-0.296	-0.408	-0.527	-0.652	-0.780	-0.908	-1.031	-1.145	-1.248	-1.337
1995	5.145	5.506	5.760	5.826	5.663	5.303	4.830	4.326	3.845	3.413	3.036
1996	1.495	1.368	1.218	1.040	0.837	0.610	0.365	0.112	-0.139	-0.378	-0.598
1997	1.581	1.588	1.592	1.591	1.581	1.560	1.521	1.461	1.374	1.256	1.110
1998	1.061	1.124	1.205	1.312	1.459	1.667	1.964	2.322	2.396	1.817	1.154
1999	1.183	1.045	0.878	0.672	0.418	0.101	-0.292	-0.769	-1.320	-1.898	-2.431
2000	-0.810	-0.708	-0.583	-0.430	-0.238	0.007	0.322	0.727	1.236	1.828	2.415
2001	-0.729	-0.746	-0.767	-0.791	-0.815	-0.829	-0.803	-0.670	-0.418	-0.159	0.030
2002	-1.179	-1.146	-1.098	-1.022	-0.890	-0.633	-0.095	0.745	1.275	1.429	1.460
2003	2.197	2.189	2.122	1.975	1.739	1.436	1.108	0.796	0.520	0.288	0.096
2004	1.300	1.402	1.488	1.538	1.536	1.478	1.376	1.252	1.125	1.006	0.899

Table 7.2
Sharpe ratio for selected style portfolios: 1975–2004.

| | Growth Allocation | | | | | | | | | | |
	100%	90%	80%	70%	60%	50%	40%	30%	20%	10%	0%
1975	1.183	1.265	1.347	1.430	1.511	1.590	1.663	1.729	1.788	1.836	**1.874**
1976	0.611	0.740	0.873	1.011	1.152	1.297	1.446	1.598	1.753	1.910	**2.068**
1977	−1.364	−1.360	−1.351	−1.335	−1.309	−1.272	−1.220	−1.153	−1.069	−0.969	**−0.856**
1978	**0.064**	0.060	0.055	0.051	0.046	0.040	0.035	0.029	0.023	0.016	0.010
1979	0.423	0.459	0.495	0.530	0.565	0.598	0.631	0.662	0.693	0.723	**0.751**
1980	**1.187**	1.159	1.127	1.091	1.050	1.005	0.955	0.900	0.840	0.776	0.707
1981	−1.468	−1.463	−1.455	−1.445	−1.430	−1.411	−1.387	−1.356	−1.319	−1.273	**−1.218**
1982	**0.590**	**0.589**	**0.588**	0.586	0.583	0.580	0.576	0.572	0.567	0.562	0.556
1983	0.637	0.752	0.872	0.997	1.125	1.253	1.381	1.505	1.623	1.733	**1.833**
1984	−0.438	−0.387	−0.333	−0.279	−0.223	−0.166	−0.110	−0.054	0.001	0.055	**0.107**
1985	1.582	1.611	1.640	1.670	1.700	1.731	1.761	1.791	1.821	1.849	**1.875**
1986	0.491	0.529	0.568	0.607	0.646	0.684	0.721	0.757	0.792	0.825	**0.857**
1987	**0.191**	0.182	0.172	0.162	0.151	0.140	0.129	0.117	0.105	0.093	0.080
1988	0.531	0.619	0.708	0.798	0.888	0.978	1.065	1.151	1.233	1.312	**1.387**
1989	**1.811**	1.781	1.749	1.713	1.674	1.631	1.585	1.536	1.483	1.427	1.367

continues

Table 7.2   continued

	Growth Allocation										
	100%	90%	80%	70%	60%	50%	40%	30%	20%	10%	0%
1990	**-0.281**	-0.325	-0.371	-0.418	-0.466	-0.516	-0.566	-0.618	-0.670	-0.723	-0.777
1991	**1.657**	1.619	1.577	1.532	1.482	1.427	1.368	1.305	1.238	1.166	1.090
1992	0.216	0.286	0.360	0.436	0.512	0.587	0.659	0.725	0.784	0.836	**0.879**
1993	-0.093	0.085	0.292	0.532	0.804	1.107	1.428	1.751	2.050	2.302	**2.492**
1994	**-0.027**	-0.062	-0.097	-0.131	-0.165	-0.197	-0.228	-0.257	-0.285	-0.312	-0.337
1995	**5.206**	5.298	5.339	5.323	5.253	5.132	4.971	4.780	4.570	4.352	4.132
1996	1.443	1.459	1.474	1.485	1.494	1.500	**1.503**	**1.502**	1.497	1.488	1.475
1997	1.561	1.567	1.573	1.577	**1.580**	**1.581**	**1.580**	1.577	1.572	1.563	1.552
1998	**1.558**	1.456	1.352	1.246	1.140	1.033	0.926	0.820	0.715	0.611	0.508
1999	**1.418**	1.391	1.353	1.301	1.235	1.155	1.060	0.955	0.841	0.723	0.604
2000	-1.212	-1.163	-1.098	-1.015	-0.910	-0.780	-0.627	-0.453	-0.269	-0.085	**0.089**
2001	**-0.646**	-0.664	-0.683	-0.702	-0.720	-0.739	-0.757	-0.774	-0.790	-0.805	-0.818
2002	-1.323	-1.299	-1.272	-1.243	-1.213	-1.180	-1.147	-1.112	-1.077	-1.041	**-1.006**
2003	**2.599**	2.510	2.424	2.343	2.266	2.194	2.127	2.064	2.006	1.952	1.902
2004	0.634	0.760	0.891	1.026	1.162	1.298	1.433	1.565	1.691	1.811	**1.923**

Table 7.3

Sharpe ratio for selected size portfolios: 1975–2004.

	Small Allocation										Large Allocation
	100%	90%	80%	70%	60%	50%	40%	30%	20%	10%	0%
1975	1.381	1.409	1.438	1.467	1.496	1.523	1.547	1.566	1.577	1.576	1.562
1976	1.433	1.439	1.443	1.447	1.448	1.446	1.438	1.421	1.389	1.335	1.251
1977	1.363	1.202	1.018	0.809	0.575	0.313	0.025	-0.286	-0.613	-0.949	-1.281
1978	0.604	0.580	0.551	0.519	0.480	0.434	0.380	0.315	0.238	0.147	0.042
1979	1.222	1.191	1.157	1.118	1.073	1.021	0.961	0.892	0.810	0.714	0.603
1980	0.953	0.964	0.974	0.985	0.995	1.006	1.015	1.024	1.031	1.036	1.039
1981	0.045	-0.060	-0.176	-0.303	-0.441	-0.591	-0.751	-0.918	-1.088	-1.256	-1.417
1982	0.917	0.887	0.856	0.823	0.790	0.755	0.720	0.684	0.648	0.612	0.577
1983	1.665	1.680	1.691	1.696	1.691	1.672	1.634	1.574	1.486	1.372	1.233
1984	-0.998	-0.926	-0.852	-0.774	-0.695	-0.613	-0.529	-0.443	-0.355	-0.266	-0.175
1985	1.080	1.147	1.215	1.285	1.356	1.427	1.497	1.566	1.634	1.698	1.759
1986	0.112	0.187	0.259	0.327	0.393	0.455	0.513	0.569	0.620	0.669	0.714
1987	-0.248	-0.214	-0.179	-0.142	-0.104	-0.065	-0.025	0.016	0.058	0.101	0.144
1988	1.152	1.170	1.184	1.192	1.194	1.185	1.166	1.133	1.087	1.028	0.959
1989	0.206	0.382	0.558	0.730	0.894	1.050	1.194	1.326	1.445	1.550	1.644

continues

Table 7.3   continued

| | Small Allocation | | | | | | | | | | Large Allocation |
	100%	90%	80%	70%	60%	50%	40%	30%	20%	10%	0%
1990	−1.446	−1.370	−1.289	−1.203	−1.113	−1.019	−0.921	−0.819	−0.715	−0.607	**−0.498**
1991	**2.104**	2.070	2.027	1.976	1.917	1.850	1.775	1.695	1.609	1.519	1.427
1992	1.090	1.103	1.114	1.124	**1.130**	1.125	1.101	1.043	0.936	0.769	0.557
1993	1.754	**1.757**	1.754	1.742	**1.719**	1.681	1.623	1.541	1.433	1.298	1.140
1994	**−0.032**	−0.049	−0.067	−0.085	−0.102	−0.119	−0.135	−0.151	−0.166	−0.179	−0.191
1995	2.598	2.831	3.094	3.388	3.711	4.057	4.408	4.733	4.990	5.136	**5.145**
1996	0.716	0.790	0.873	0.964	**1.062**	1.164	1.265	1.357	1.431	1.478	**1.495**
1997	0.948	1.051	1.157	1.263	**1.362**	1.449	1.519	1.567	1.592	**1.596**	1.581
1998	−0.335	−0.220	−0.099	0.027	0.159	0.296	0.439	0.587	0.741	0.899	**1.061**
1999	1.168	1.210	1.252	1.292	**1.329**	1.356	**1.369**	1.361	1.327	1.267	1.183
2000	**−0.079**	−0.118	−0.166	−0.223	−0.294	−0.379	−0.479	−0.589	−0.694	−0.773	−0.810
2001	**0.746**	0.643	0.530	0.407	0.274	0.129	−0.026	−0.191	−0.365	−0.545	−0.729
2002	**−0.606**	−0.675	−0.745	−0.814	−0.882	−0.946	−1.006	−1.060	−1.107	−1.147	−1.179
2003	**3.035**	3.009	2.975	2.931	2.875	2.806	2.722	2.620	2.499	2.358	2.197
2004	1.073	1.090	1.108	1.128	**1.150**	1.173	1.199	1.225	1.253	1.279	**1.300**

Table 7.4

Sharpe ratio for selected location portfolios: 1975–2004.

| | International Allocation | | | | | | | | | | |
	100%	90%	80%	70%	60%	50%	40%	30%	20%	10%	0%
1975	1.00	1.06	1.12	1.18	1.24	1.31	1.37	1.43	1.48	1.53	**1.56**
1976	-0.28	-0.14	0.00	0.16	0.33	0.50	0.66	0.83	0.98	1.12	**1.25**
1977	**1.30**	1.08	0.79	0.45	0.09	-0.25	-0.56	-0.81	-1.01	-1.16	-1.28
1978	1.24	1.25	1.24	1.19	1.09	0.94	0.74	0.53	0.34	0.18	0.04
1979	-0.68	-0.54	-0.40	-0.26	-0.11	0.02	0.16	0.28	0.40	0.51	**0.60**
1980	0.46	0.54	0.63	0.71	0.79	0.86	0.92	0.96	1.00	1.02	**1.04**
1981	**-0.97**	-1.04	-1.12	-1.19	-1.26	-1.33	-1.39	-1.43	-1.45	-1.44	-1.42
1982	-0.74	-0.63	-0.51	-0.37	-0.22	-0.07	0.09	0.23	0.36	0.48	**0.58**
1983	1.34	1.40	1.45	1.48	**1.49**	1.47	1.44	1.40	1.35	1.29	1.23
1984	**-0.15**	-0.15	-0.16	-0.17	-0.17	-0.17	-0.18	-0.18	-0.18	-0.18	-0.18
1985	4.06	4.29	**4.45**	**4.45**	4.25	3.88	3.42	2.93	2.48	2.09	1.76
1986	2.28	**2.29**	**2.29**	2.26	2.17	2.03	1.82	1.56	1.27	0.98	0.71
1987	**0.76**	0.71	0.65	0.58	0.52	0.45	0.38	0.32	0.26	0.20	0.14
1988	1.19	1.24	1.29	1.34	**1.38**	1.41	1.40	1.35	1.25	1.11	0.96
1989	0.12	0.24	0.38	0.53	0.69	. 0.87	1.05	1.23	1.39	1.53	**1.64**

continues

Table 7.4   continued

| | International Allocation | | | | | | | | | | |
	100%	90%	80%	70%	60%	50%	40%	30%	20%	10%	0%
1990	-1.05	-1.05	-1.05	-1.04	-1.02	-0.99	-0.93	-0.86	-0.75	-0.63	-0.50
1991	0.32	0.43	0.54	0.66	0.79	0.91	1.04	1.15	1.26	1.35	1.43
1992	-1.19	-1.15	-1.10	-1.02	-0.92	-0.78	-0.58	-0.32	-0.02	0.29	0.56
1993	1.43	1.46	1.49	1.53	1.57	1.60	1.64	1.64	1.59	1.43	1.14
1994	0.23	0.20	0.16	0.13	0.09	0.04	0.00	-0.05	-0.10	-0.14	-0.19
1995	0.34	0.56	0.82	1.14	1.52	1.97	2.52	3.15	3.86	4.56	5.14
1996	-0.07	0.16	0.38	0.58	0.77	0.94	1.08	1.21	1.32	1.41	1.49
1997	-0.23	-0.05	0.14	0.34	0.54	0.75	0.94	1.13	1.30	1.45	1.58
1998	0.71	0.76	0.81	0.85	0.89	0.93	0.97	1.00	1.02	1.04	1.06
1999	1.50	1.52	1.52	1.51	1.50	1.47	1.42	1.37	1.31	1.25	1.18
2000	-1.56	-1.52	-1.46	-1.39	-1.31	-1.23	-1.14	-1.06	-0.97	-0.89	-0.81
2001	-1.61	-1.52	-1.43	-1.34	-1.25	-1.16	-1.07	-0.98	-0.90	-0.81	-0.73
2002	-1.01	-1.04	-1.07	-1.10	-1.12	-1.14	-1.15	-1.16	-1.17	-1.18	-1.18
2003	2.10	2.13	2.15	2.17	2.18	2.20	2.21	2.21	2.21	2.21	2.20
2004	1.63	1.61	1.59	1.57	1.55	1.52	1.49	1.45	1.40	1.36	1.30

Based on the sample period, these results suggest an all-or-nothing strategy that would have maximized risk-adjusted returns 80 percent of the time. The problem, however, with all-or-nothing is when you miss, you miss big (on a relative basis). Risk-averse investors may not be able to live with such a bipolar strategy, and might instead find it desirable to minimize their long-run volatilities relative to their long-run average returns. The SAA does just this: It allocates funds in proportion to asset-class market weights. But, if we take the long-run result seriously, a bipolar strategy should generate an average holding closer to each asset class's market weight. This carries the promise of higher risk-adjusted returns.

In simple terms, an optimal active strategy tilts around long-run values, giving us a time-consistent active strategy. When an asset-allocation strategy tilts around the long-run solution, it takes advantage of the cyclical fluctuations in the relative returns among the different portfolio choices. Such an active allocation performs even better than the benchmark market SAA.

We know holding all the world market weights is consistent with a long-run, mean-reverting, and sensible projected outcome. We also know the *ex post* optimal result is, more often than not, a corner solution. As stated, deviating from the long-run solution carries some risk along with the promise of potential reward. So, we need to clearly see the signals able to tilt us in the proper direction.

The following is a quick review of the cyclical forecasting tools discussed so far.

A Quick Review of Cyclical Forecasting Tools

Changes to the economic environment—whether caused by taxes, regulation, or fiscal and monetary policy—impact asset prices, although market reassessments of asset prices generate distinct patterns. Identifying these patterns is fundamental to a cyclical strategy. Consensus forecasts, generated by the *Wall Street Journal* and many financial publications, are based on an average of the forecasts produced by distinguished economists and financial advisors. In Chapter 5, "Linking Up," we explored some simple models enabling us to qualitatively determine the tilts in relative performance these forecasts can generate. Another tool consists of the linkage between the economic environment and the various asset classes' relative performance. My research bears out this relationship in Figure 7.1, which is a useful thumbnail guide for cyclical investors. Taken together, these tools enable us to foresee the economic environment and take advantage of it.

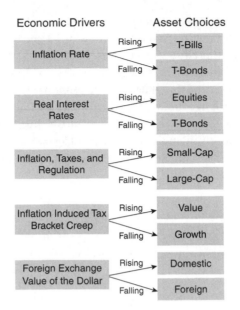

Figure 7.1 The link between economic drivers and asset choices.

To begin, Figure 7.1 shows when the inflation rate is expected to go up, a reasoned cyclical asset allocation (CAA) should tilt in shorter-maturity fixed
instruments' favor, such as Treasury bills (T-bills). The rationale is straightforward: An unexpected increase in the inflation rate has less of a negative impact
on shorter-duration fixed instruments than it has on longer-term ones.
Similarly, an expected increase in the real interest rate tilts the balance in equities' favor. Note: I take an equity approach to the equity/fixed-income choice,
whereby I look at T-bonds as stocks with constant earnings (that is, the *coupon
rate*, which is the annual interest rate payable on T-bonds) and stocks as
instruments that fluctuate in value as earnings change with economic conditions. My thinking continues that an increase in the real (or inflation-
adjusted) interest rate leads to a higher *nominal interest rate* (the interest rate
as measured in current dollars) and a higher *discount rate*. Just as higher interest rates lead to a higher discount rate and lower T-bond prices, the higher real
rate may very well lead to higher earnings, and thus higher stock prices. The
higher real rates' impact on equities is ambiguous; one can, however, unambiguously establish that T-bonds decline relative to stocks when the real interest rate is rising. Simply put, an expected higher real interest rate is a signal to
investors to increase their exposure to equities.

I have argued the small-cap effect is nothing more than a result of inflation
hedging, tax sheltering, and/or regulatory skirting. Hence, when tax rates, the

inflation rate, and/or regulations are expected to increase, my CAA recommendation is for a greater equity exposure to smaller-cap stocks. In my view, the choice between value and growth stocks is largely determined by *investor horizons*—the length of time investors plan to invest, or hold their investment positions. Because the growth companies' earnings are back-end loaded—that is, as these companies grow, their earnings also rise relative to the more steady earning streams of value companies—anything lowering investor horizons reduces the future earnings' value, tilting the balance in value stocks' favor. I maintain that uncertainty, higher tax rates, and higher interest rates all work to lower investor horizons and thus tilt the balance in value stock's favor.

Finally, I believe fluctuations in the dollar's value reflect relative returns across markets. Expectations of a rising dollar point to the increased U.S. equities' relative performance, which should lead investors to augment their exposure to U.S. equities.

This summary illustrates the way a simple outlook can be organized to develop a cyclical asset-allocation strategy.

Developing and Calculating Investors' Convictions

But our CAA toolbox is not yet complete: If we can develop a way to forecast the foreign-exchange market, that forecast's conviction can then be used to tilt a portfolio toward the asset classes favored by that forecast. How much of the potential gains are captured by this strategy depends on the forecast's quality and the investor's risk tolerance. Indeed, *investor conviction*, or the degree of certainty based on an individual investor's future view, must be incorporated into the CAA plan. For instance, the greater an investor's risk aversion, the less his or her tilt around a long-run allocation.

The economic drivers' values combined with the historical relationships identified in Figure 7.1 can be used to obtain estimates of the expected distribution of returns, or percent change in earnings, for individual stocks. The horizontal axis in Figure 7.2a measures the possible ranges of outcomes for the different asset classes in percentage points based on quarterly returns, while the vertical axis measures the possible frequency of earnings growth. For example, the vertical line at 0.3 illustrates a T-bill yield of 30 basis points per quarter, or 1.2 percent per year. This line describes the *probability density function*, which is nothing more than a point estimate of the likelihood of a return occurring during any quarter.

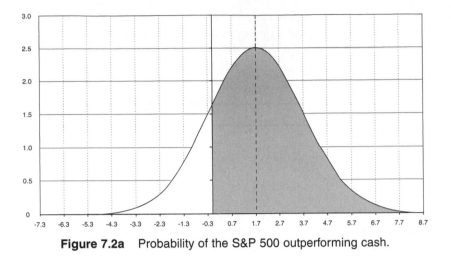

Figure 7.2a Probability of the S&P 500 outperforming cash.

The simplest way to think of the vertical distance is to imagine 100 random drawings of possible earnings. The curve's height tells us how many times one would expect to see those earnings' growth realized, and drawing a vertical line along the T-bill yield returns enables us to estimate all the possible drawings that will exceed the T-bill yields (that is, the area to the vertical line's right). The shaded area in Figure 7.2a represents all the possible outcomes under which the asset-class return exceeds the T-bill returns. The shaded area under the bell curve represents the probability the asset class will outperform cash during the coming quarter.

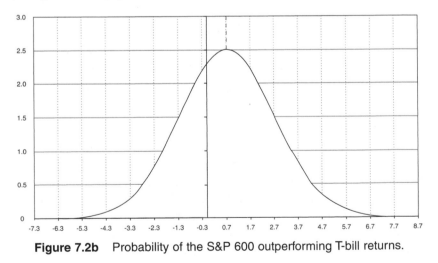

Figure 7.2b Probability of the S&P 600 outperforming T-bill returns.

The usefulness of these probability estimates is obvious. Under truly random conditions, one finds a 50 percent chance of one asset class outperforming a particular benchmark (for example, cash or the S&P indices), thus the difference between 50 percent and the probability estimates is the investor's edge, or conviction degree. The farther away the estimates are from the 50 percent random (or neutral) probability, the greater the conviction's forecast. A positive difference indicates a bullish signal for an asset class. Conversely, a negative number is indicative of a bearish sentiment. The differences' magnitude is directly related to the forecast's conviction level.

Figure 7.2c reports the expected return distributions for one asset class relative to another—that is, style, size, location, and so on. Overlaying one distribution on top of another enables one to calculate the probability an asset class will outperform another class, for example, large-caps versus small-caps. The shaded area between the two bell curves represents the probability of an asset class outperforming its benchmark.

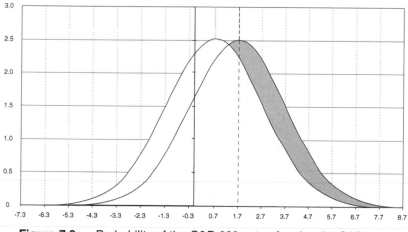

Figure 7.2c Probability of the S&P 600 outperforming the S&P 500.

I have argued that modern portfolio theory's major contributions are the concepts of diversification and risk reduction, and I have devoted a good amount of space to showing the way applications of the capital asset pricing model (CAPM) and Sharpe ratio can go a long way toward developing an efficient, well-diversified portfolio. In fact, I have argued the market SAA constructed in the previous chapter is one such portfolio. But, I have also presented evidence suggesting, from time to time, a tilt away from the SAA can be optimal. Furthermore, I have shown the tilts are not random and are, in most cases, related to changes in the economic environment. So, the challenge is finding a way to integrate economic forecasts and the risk-control measures used in modern finance into our strategy. I believe using the conviction, or likelihood, described in Figure 7.2c does just this. As stated earlier, making an allocation decision between equities and T-bonds or large- and small-cap stocks requires not just a return assumption but a conviction in the likelihood of one's success. That's why the cyclical asset-allocation process is probability based. In a formal sense, to determine a probability estimate, one needs an estimate of expected returns, standard deviations, and the correlations between the asset classes. In this way, cyclical probability estimates incorporate all the risk-control parameters used by the CAPM and the Sharpe ratio.

Alternative Approaches to Estimating Conviction Levels

I have extensive experience with two distinct alternative approaches to cyclical asset allocation. One is strictly an empirical, or quantitative, approach; the other is qualitative and based on an investment committee's experiences and views. A few well-established money managers are utilizing both approaches successfully today.

A summary of the information needed for each approach can be viewed in Table 7.5. A common thread between the empirical and qualitative approaches is the belief that historical relationships, combined with information contained in the futures markets, provide the necessary signals to develop a forward-looking world view that on average can correctly anticipate the turning points in various return cycles. More, a top-down global view focusing on policy changes at the government level and a range of geopolitical events is also useful in identifying and anticipating some secular and cyclical changes in relative performance both domestically and internationally.

Table 7.5
Investment advisory committee quarterly questionnaire.

Economic Drivers			
Inflation Rate	Rising	Stable	Falling
Real Interest Rates	Rising	Stable	Falling
Taxes and Regulation	Rising	Stable	Falling
FX Dollar Value	Rising	Stable	Falling
P/E Ratio	Expanding	Stable	Contracting
Relative Attractiveness of Asset Class			
	(10 Is Highest Likelihood)		
T-Bonds > Cash	0 1 2 3 4 5 6 7 8 9 10		
Equities > T-Bonds	0 1 2 3 4 5 6 7 8 9 10		
Value > Growth	0 1 2 3 4 5 6 7 8 9 10		
Large-Cap > Mid-Cap	0 1 2 3 4 5 6 7 8 9 10		
Mid-Cap > Small-Cap	0 1 2 3 4 5 6 7 8 9 10		
Large-Cap > Small-Cap	0 1 2 3 4 5 6 7 8 9 10		
U.S. > International	0 1 2 3 4 5 6 7 8 9 10		
Are We a Consensus?	**Yes**		**No**

The one disadvantage of the qualitative forecast is it is difficult to defend when one considers the past and asks what type of investment choice a committee would have made at a previous time. In contrast, this consideration is unnecessary in the context of the quantitative model. Because I want to illustrate the value of the cyclical approach in general, I am forced at this point to choose the probability estimates generated by the quantitative model developed by my firm, La Jolla Economics (LJE) (see Table 7.6).

Table 7.6

Historical probability estimates generated by the LJE quantitative model.

	1998.1	1998.2	1998.3	1998.4	1999.1	1999.2	1999.3	1999.4
Cash > T-Bonds	22%	20%	14%	3%	20%	16%	17%	28%
T-Bonds > Equities	44%	63%	76%	29%	11%	42%	25%	12%
International > Domestic	24%	33%	19%	42%	43%	45%	55%	46%
Large > Small	54%	74%	54%	62%	52%	53%	53%	42%
Large > Mid	54%	74%	54%	62%	52%	53%	53%	42%
Mid > Small	50%	50%	50%	50%	50%	50%	50%	50%
Value > Growth	38%	47%	38%	45%	23%	47%	57%	36%
Large Value > Growth	38%	47%	38%	45%	23%	47%	57%	36%
Mid Value > Growth	38%	47%	38%	45%	23%	47%	57%	36%
Small Value > Growth	38%	47%	38%	45%	23%	47%	57%	36%

	2000.1	2000.2	2000.3	2000.4	2001.1	2001.2	2001.3	2001.4
Cash > T-Bonds	39%	57%	62%	72%	59%	38%	32%	28%
T-Bonds > Equities	26%	31%	54%	53%	73%	49%	48%	44%
International > Domestic	54%	72%	38%	27%	45%	35%	39%	32%

	2000.1	2000.2	2000.3	2000.4	2001.1	2001.2	2001.3	2001.4
Large > Small	56%	56%	52%	57%	52%	56%	46%	55%
Large > Mid	56%	56%	52%	57%	52%	56%	46%	55%
Mid > Small	50%	50%	50%	50%	50%	50%	50%	50%
Value > Growth	45%	51%	63%	49%	55%	44%	37%	33%
Large Value > Growth	45%	51%	63%	49%	55%	44%	37%	33%
Mid Value > Growth	45%	51%	63%	49%	55%	44%	37%	33%
Small Value > Growth	45%	51%	63%	49%	55%	44%	37%	33%

	2000.1	2000.2	2000.3	2000.4	2001.1	2001.2	2001.3	2001.4
Cash > T-Bonds	21%	45%	52%	60%	46%	46%	40%	29%
T-Bonds > Equities	53%	53%	50%	50%	52%	52%	34%	35%
International > Domestic	41%	46%	44%	36%	49%	38%	45%	48%
Large > Small	55%	42%	48%	53%	60%	46%	44%	58%
Large > Mid	55%	42%	48%	53%	60%	45%	35%	56%
Mid > Small	50%	50%	50%	50%	50%	49%	54%	60%
Value > Growth	49%	50%	53%	49%	48%	37%	56%	50%

continues

Table 7.6 continued

	1998.1	1998.2	1998.3	1998.4	1999.1	1999.2	1999.3	1999.4
Large Value > Growth	49%	50%	53%	49%	48%	36%	56%	49%
Mid Value > Growth	49%	50%	53%	49%	48%	48%	56%	41%
Small Value > Growth	49%	50%	53%	49%	48%	21%	56%	73%

	2004.1	2004.2	2004.3	2004.4
Cash > T-Bonds	58%	38%	69%	60%
T-Bonds > Equities	46%	41%	47%	42%
International > Domestic	46%	38%	40%	49%
Large > Small	43%	23%	47%	43%
Large > Mid	47%	22%	45%	47%
Mid > Small	55%	77%	54%	41%
Value > Growth	51%	51%	39%	54%
Large Value > Growth	51%	51%	36%	55%
Mid Value > Growth	49%	51%	39%	49%
Small Value > Growth	55%	53%	59%	56%

Source: La Jolla Economics

Equipped with probability information, investors and financial advisors can develop decision rules for determining how and when to choose an investment's style, location, and/or size, and whether to do so in a passive or active mode. This process can be called the value-timing approach to asset allocation. An initial decision in this approach's implementation has to do with whether an investor or advisor has any preconceived opinions about any asset classes. If one does not feel any strong attachment or aversion to any asset class, the LJE model can return a 50 percent probability in the pair-wise comparison of the asset classes. In other words, a 50 percent probability suggests there is an equal chance one asset class will outperform the other, so there is no reason to change the existing, or default, allocation. Hence, when we have no strong opinion about the economy's future, we should buy the market, and we should only deviate from the SAA when we have strong convictions about the economy's future.

As I have argued, that conviction's degree is represented by the probabilities. Here's one example of a strong conviction: If one is 100 percent certain large-caps are going to outperform small-caps, the size allocation in one's portfolio should be 100 percent large-caps and 0 percent small-caps. A 0 percent or 100 percent allocation conveys certainty in a conviction while a 50 percent allocation conveys an absence of conviction. All this suggests it is the deviation from the 50 percent probability telling us how much we should deviate from the normal allocation. This is a precise application of the cyclical strategy: One should deviate from the basic allocation in direct proportion to how much the probabilities deviate from the 50 percent mark.

Using a factor of two produces a familiar result. If an asset-class probability is 100 percent, the difference between that probability and 50 percent multiplied by two gives us the new allocation for the asset class: 100 percent. It is nice to see this simple allocation procedure enables one to deviate from the long-run SAA and produce tilts in an allocation designed to take advantage of a changing economic environment.

The Cyclical Allocation Tilts: A Value-Timing Story

I'd like to stress once again that a cyclical asset-allocation framework is not a black box that processes all the statistical variables and spits out an investment plan. Rather, the framework is a logical one that sets out choices for investors. Stocks versus T-bonds, domestic equities versus international equities, large-caps versus small-caps, and on down the line. Figure 7.3 illustrates the culmination of the CAA process, where the quantitative model estimated the probability one asset class would outperform another, and where the benchmark allocation was then tilted for the asset classes in direct proportion to the probability estimates. The second line of the probability estimates, summarized in Table 7.6, shows the likelihood fixed-income instruments would outperform or underperform U.S. equities for the sample period. The LJE model put that probability at 42 percent for 2004's fourth quarter. Hence, the model prescribed an increase in equity exposure at the fixed-income component's expense. Figure 7.3, second column, shows for 2004's fourth quarter, the T-bill allocation was increased to 4.7 percent while the T-bond allocation was reduced to 27.9 percent. Overall, the fixed-income allocation was reduced to 32.6 percent from its 40 percent benchmark.

The difference between columns one and two in Figure 7.3 reveals the overall asset-allocation tilts produced by the model. (Column one shows the benchmark weight used.) The tilts can be easily described: The strategy increased the exposure to U.S. equities at the fixed-income instruments' expense. Despite the lower allocation to fixed income, the CAA process also increased the allocation to cash. A way of interpreting this result is that the CAA process called for a reduction in the duration of the fixed-income portfolio. Within the style allocation, the tilts favored value stocks, and within the size allocation, the tilts favored mid- and small-cap stocks. The sole domestic underweighting came with large-cap growth stocks.

By combining the overweights and underweights in Figure 7.3 with the links between the economic drivers and asset choices in Figure 7.1, one can reverse-engineer the process and make inferences about the implicit forecast in the CAA strategy sample. The message is quite simple: The allocations were bearish on fixed income and bullish on all equities except large-cap growth stocks, to which there was an almost neutral allocation.

Behind these results, the fourth-quarter 2004 outlook called for a slight rise in T-bond yields, no significant increase in the underlying inflation rate, a continuation of the economic recovery (albeit at a slower pace), and a bottoming and strengthening of the foreign-exchange dollar value. So, the expected rise in the real interest rate led to an increase of the portfolio's equity exposure. The U.S. dollar's expected bottoming led to a neutral allocation between domestic and international stocks. Within the U.S. equity market, the LJE model favored value and small-cap stocks.

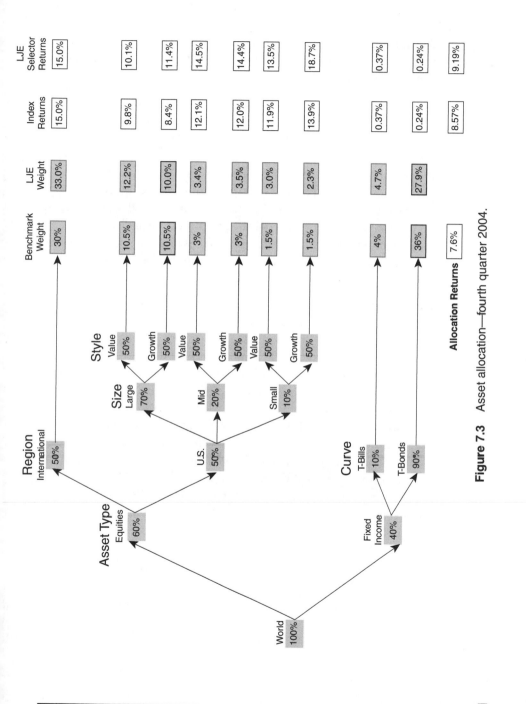

Figure 7.3 Asset allocation—fourth quarter 2004.

The probability estimates reported in Table 7.6 formalize the precision of these convictions. Comparing the benchmark allocation (column one) and the CAA allocation (column two) reported in Figure 7.3, one can discern the tilts produced by the quantitative process: an increase in the exposure to U.S. stocks at the fixed income's expense. Within the domestic stocks, the tilt favored value and small-cap stocks.

Figure 7.3 also reports the returns of the MSCI and S&P/BARRA indices (column three) as well as the individual stock portfolios' performance generated by the LJE selector process (column four). The performances of the benchmark allocation using the various indices and the allocation using the LJE selector portfolios are reported in Figure 7.3 (last row). The numbers show that during 2004's fourth quarter, the benchmark increased 7.6 percent while the LJE asset allocation gained 8.57 percent. So, the LJE allocation outperformed the benchmark by 97 basis points. Substituting the indices (that is, the S&P 500, and so on) with the LJE selector portfolios increased the strategy performance to 9.19 percent. During the quarter, the full-fledged LJE strategy outperformed the benchmark by 259 basis points.

The CAA forecast embodied in the probabilities easily explains the CAA allocation process's performance during 2004's fourth quarter. The LJE model expected T-bond yields to rise slightly, and they did. The model looked for economic activity to continue at a healthy pace, and it did. Based on that forecast, the major tilts were away from T-bonds and into growth stocks, small-cap stocks, and international stocks. A detailed attribution analysis of the fourth-quarter sample shows there were two major allocation calls: one was to underweight T-bonds and the other was to overweight stocks. Underweighting T-bonds added 62 basis points to the result. The equity allocation added 35 basis points. The stock selection added approximately 62 basis points to the excess performance generated by the CAA allocation. The LJE forecast was pretty much on target: The index allocation outperformed the benchmark by 97 basis points during the quarter.

Table 7.7

Annual return of the market weight strategic asset allocation and the cyclical asset-allocation strategies.

	SAA Benchmark	CAA Index Return
1998	16.8%	32.3%
1999	17.1%	19.2%
2000	−1.1%	.3%
2001	−7.4%	−2.3%
2002	−5.4%	−6.0%
2003	17.3%	18.1%
2004	10.0%	10.8%
Sharpe Ratio	.33	.59
Beta	.49	.51
Alpha	1.6%	4.8%
T-Stat	1.08%	2.16%

Of course, one quarter does not a successful strategy make. Using the probability history reported in Table 7.7, I have calculated both CAA strategy performance and SAA benchmark performance for the last seven years ending in 2004. Not surprisingly, the CAA strategy beat the SAA strategy in each and every year, outperforming the SAA strategy by an 83 basis points average per quarter. The data also show the CAA strategy produced a slight increase in the returns' volatility. Comparing the risk-adjusted returns ratio, however, to the returns' standard deviation (the Sharpe ratio), it is apparent the increased returns more than compensated for the increased volatility. Comparing the average return and the series' standard deviation, one finds the SAA and S&P 500 generate approximately the same quarterly rate of return. The S&P 500's volatility, however, is about twice that of the SAA strategy. This is consistent with my earlier finding that the SAA strategy's major contribution is in the risk-reduction area. Also, the SAA and CAA strategies have almost identical volatilities, the major difference between them being the higher rate of return produced by the CAA strategy. Again, this result is consistent with my view that the value-timing strategy increases returns without adversely affecting volatility. In fact, the data show the CAA strategy's Sharpe ratio is about twice that of the SAA strategy, which is in turn about twice the Sharpe ratio for the S&P 500 during the same period.

A cyclical asset-allocation strategy that tilts around benchmark weights in direct proportion to an outlook's conviction is superior to a strategic asset-allocation strategy based on the market-capitalization weights of the different asset classes' market-capitalization weights. In the CAA scheme, the investor's performance quality is obviously dependent on the probability estimates' quality, whether derived qualitatively (such as the consensus estimates of experts) from black-box quantitative models. This process is flexible enough to accommodate a number of probability estimates. But the important point to remember is this approach reduces the chance of unintended consequences and forces investors to make choices consistent with their world views—as expressed in the probability estimates they rely on. If a probability estimate does not match an investor's outlook, revisions are in order: Either the outlook or the probability estimate must change.

8

THE CYCLICAL ASSET ALLOCATION STRATEGY'S VERSATILITY

Many asset-allocation approaches drive home the point that there should never be any unintended bets made in a portfolio. This is correct. But, in making this point, many financial advisors argue—given the same expected returns combination—the different market variables' variance–covariance matrix produce the same allocation each and every time. The cyclical asset allocation (CAA) approach differentiates itself in important ways. The probabilities for CAA are derived from (and related to) the overall economic environment and the investor's outlook. If probabilities and/or allocations do not match an investor's outlook, either the allocations or the outlook must change to align the two, and more than likely, the allocations are changed to fit an outlook. This is an important CAA strategy characteristic. It says CAAs are intuitive and investors can see the adjustments they need to make to their portfolios. In other words, investors do not need to rely on black-box results before making their allocation decisions—nor do investors need to know advanced statistics and matrix algebra.

The CAA approach minimizes the caches of unintended bets in the asset-allocation process. Although it does not guard against undesirable outcomes, it does protect investors from being wrong due to unintended outcomes. Although all investors would prefer not to be wrong, I would rather be wrong because I made the wrong choice and not because an unintended bet blindsided me.

As with a traditional strategic asset allocation (SAA), the CAA approach is flexible and robust enough to accommodate differences in risk tolerances, investment objectives, and other investor constraints. But, it's also flexible and robust enough to merge with, enhance, or outright revolutionize the approaches of various asset management firm types. In what follows, I summarize some investment advisors' (with whom I am close friends) experiences to illustrate the CAA's versatile approach.

Case Study: An Asset Management Firm for High-Net-Worth Individuals

A financial-management firm based in Hawaii is our first case study. This firm's investment philosophy is fairly straightforward, using a focused approach to produce consistent and rewarding performance for clients. Although this group offers a variety of portfolio-management approaches—including equity, balanced, fixed-income, and aggressive-growth options—it is best known for its balanced approach to meeting client objectives.

The firm's investment style can be described as *top-down*, meaning it places a big emphasis on the economic outlook as it sees it. This outlook is a major influence on the tilts or swings the firm incorporates into its asset-allocation and stock-selection process. Investment professionals at the firm meet daily to identify and monitor economic and market changes to recognize future trends and their implications for asset values. Constantly monitoring the economic environment enables the asset managers to determine portfolio tilts early on.

In past years, once the managers collectively perceived a change in the economic environment, they would make a change to the firm's asset allocation. This approach as practiced, however, had some shortcomings. Once the investment committee adopted a particular view, there was no guarantee the derived allocation would be the same as others made in the past when the committee perceived the same change. This led the firm to question some of its investment decisions' time consistencies. Another problem, potentially, concerned the way the firm translated its forecasts into its actual investment decisions. The question was: Do the investment choices made reflect the committee's intentions? Another issue had to do with how frequently revisions to the outlook were done. How often can a firm revise its forecasts without getting whipsawed? The firm developed some interesting procedures to address most of these concerns.

Over the years, there have also been some leaks in the Hawaii firm's investment process. Although the firm has developed a reputation for protecting its clients' assets against downswings in the market, along the way—although it made the correct macro forecasts—the vehicle selections the firm prescribed have sometimes produced unintended bets. The firm has also been concerned with finding a way to ensure identical outlooks produce identical allocations.

These bumps led the firm to experiment with alternative approaches that gradually brought it to formally adopt a CAA strategy. Two features distinguish the Hawaii firm's strategy as it is practiced today: It now has a customized benchmark and determines the probabilities used to tilt portfolios over cycles.

Given the firm's the balanced-fund approach and its desire to maximize the allocation swings between fixed income and equities based on its macro outlook, the firm chose a neutral, or base, allocation of 50 percent equities and 50 percent income for its benchmark. The equities are allocated to size and style choices using the approximate Russell index size allocation (that is, 70 percent large-cap, 20 percent mid-cap, and 10 percent small-cap). The value/growth choice is based on the BARRA index allocation, whereby each style receives an approximate 50 percent allocation within the size category. The benchmark's fixed-income portion is allocated equally among cash, short-term, intermediate, and long-term instruments. The firm's benchmark allocation and the exchange-traded funds (ETFs) used to fill each asset-allocation bucket are shown in Figure 8.1.

The firm subjectively generates the custom benchmark set, probability estimates, and the likelihood of outcomes, and reviews monthly or as dictated by economic events. (The sample questionnaire used to generate the probability estimates is shown again in Table 8.1.) Based on experience and the information gathered, each investment committee member ranks his or her probability choices and the averages are computed. Some subjectively arrive at these probabilities while others quantitatively arrive at them, depending on the models and decision rules each committee member has developed over the years. The outliers on the committee have to defend their positions and the discussion leads to a consensus view used to determine the final allocations. For example, if someone on the committee forecasts a higher probability of equities outperforming Treasury bonds (T-bonds) over the next quarter, a viewpoint not held by most on the committee, she is asked to explain the rationale leading to her conclusion. In the process, if she convinces the committee of the outlying forecast's likelihood, the probabilities are revised accordingly.

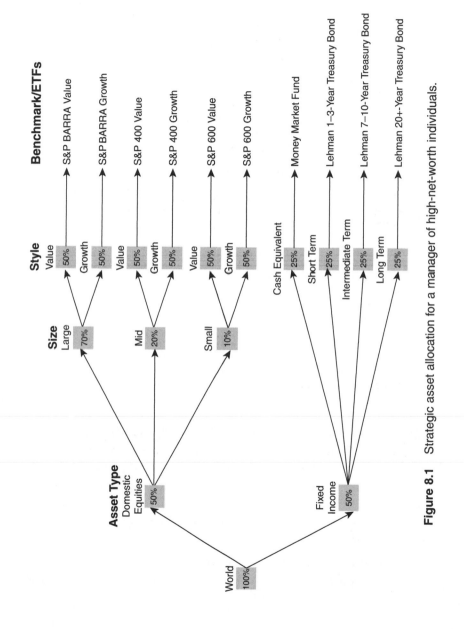

Figure 8.1 Strategic asset allocation for a manager of high-net-worth individuals.

Table 8.1

Investment advisory committee quarterly questionnaire.

Economic Drivers			
Inflation Rate	Rising	Stable	Falling
Real Interest Rates	Rising	Stable	Falling
Taxes and Regulation	Rising	Stable	Falling
FX Dollar Value	Rising	Stable	Falling
P/E Ratio	Expanding	Stable	Contracting

Relative Attractiveness of Asset Class											
	(10 Is Highest Likelihood)										
T-Bonds > Cash	0	1	2	3	4	5	6	7	8	9	10
Equities > T-Bonds	0	1	2	3	4	5	6	7	8	9	10
Value > Growth	0	1	2	3	4	5	6	7	8	9	10
Large-Cap > Mid-Cap	0	1	2	3	4	5	6	7	8	9	10
Mid-Cap > Small-Cap	0	1	2	3	4	5	6	7	8	9	10
Large-Cap > Small-Cap	0	1	2	3	4	5	6	7	8	9	10
U.S. > International	0	1	2	3	4	5	6	7	8	9	10

Are We a Consensus?	Yes	No

The investment committee also discusses the overall economic environment's consistency and the way that macro environment translates into the probability estimates. If the committee's outlook, for example, calls for a rising inflation rate, the firm's allocation should produce a lower exposure to cash. (See the discussion in the Chapter 7, "Taking It to the Tilt," related to Figure 7.1.) If this is not the case, either the outlook or the probability must be revised until the two converge.

Adopting the CAA approach has worked. By establishing a customized market benchmark the firm has reduced the unintended bets within its asset-allocation process, although the discussion leading to formulating probability estimates has improved the firm's consistency in asset-allocation choices. These improvements should help further solidify the firm's reputation as a consistent manager with great skill at protecting against the downside.

Case Study: A Global Financial Management Plan

This Hong Kong manager's needs are fairly unique and interesting. This firm offers a service whereby it selects and monitors individual outside managers to ensure they remain ranked among the top in their categories, or replaced when they do not do so. In addition to this service, the firm also offers an asset-allocation program with some fairly interesting characteristics. Largely due to the client base's geographic location, the firm's managers have tried to provide less U.S.-centric allocations than ones guided by market-capitalization weights. To this end, the firm's strategy has been to reallocate some funds away from the U.S. and into other areas of the world, specifically the Pacific region. Transaction costs, taxes, and other considerations have dictated that portfolio allocations be revisited only once a year, with exceptions made for extraordinary events. Finally, the firm's portfolio revisions are designed to take advantage of a changing economic environment; a top-down approach is used to tilt portfolios toward perceived changes in the macro environment. The firm's benchmark selection, along with the tilts in the annual revision of asset allocations, generates a conservative portfolio, a balanced portfolio, and a growth portfolio. Clients can select from these based on their risk tolerances and preferences.

The firm's allocations are based on the coming year's economic outlook. (The outlooks, or forecasts, are similar to those the *Wall Street Journal*'s economist panel generated. Using the *Journal*'s forecasts, one can qualitatively surmise the asset-allocation tilts the firm's model produces. These are discussed in Chapter 5, "Linking Up.") Based on its forecasts' historical variability, the Hong Kong firm develops probability estimates for the likelihood the different asset classes will outperform each other. Table 8.2 displays sample allocations for each firm's portfolios.

Table 8.2
Far East global manager's conservative, balanced, and aggressive asset allocation: 2005.

	Conservative	Normal	Aggressive
Asia Equities	8%	16%	20%
Asia T-Bonds	18%	6%	4%
Europe Equities	6%	11%	15%
Europe T-Bonds	20%	8%	6%
Emerging	5%	7%	10%
U.S.			
Cash	6%	4%	2%
T-Bonds	21%	14%	7%
Growth	6%	15%	18%
Value	10%	19%	18%
	100%	100%	100%

The Hong Kong firm has had some concern regarding the path of worldwide monetary and fiscal policies. But, despite these reservations, its global outlook has remained bullish. It currently believes a large upside for regions outside the U.S. remains a real possibility, although this forecast is less certain today than it has been in the past. As a result, the firm has come to view various world regions as equally attractive (more or less) in terms of the risk/reward tradeoffs. This view has resulted in an essentially equal allocation among the major world regions, with portfolios remaining less U.S.-centric than strict market-weighted portfolios.

In the firm's conservative 2005 portfolio, Asia commanded 34 percent of allocations, a 16 percentage-point increase over 2004. A 26 percent allocation to European equities represented an 8 percent increase over 2004, although the allocation to emerging markets remained unchanged at 5 percent. The U.S. allocation dropped to 35 percent, a 24 percentage-point decrease from 2004.

In the 2005 portfolio, the regional fixed-income portion was allocated in inverse proportion to the firm's assessment of regional central banks sticking to inflation targets. Europe led the way in this respect, with a 77 percent fixed-income allocation in the conservative portfolio. This allocation was virtually unchanged from 2004. Reflecting increased uncertainty regarding monetary policy and risk/reward tradeoffs, however, the firm reduced the fixed-income allocations for the portfolio's two remaining regions: the U.S. and Asia. At 63 percent, the U.S. allocation came in 12 percentage points lower than it did in 2004, while Asia's fixed-income allocation was reduced to 68 percent for 2005 from 82 percent in 2004.

The main change in the growth portfolio was a 14 percent increase in the emerging-market allocation at the remaining world regions' expense. The equity allocation increased to 76 percent for Asia, 68 percent for the European region, and 62 percent for the U.S. For 2005, the Hong Kong firm viewed the various world regions pretty much as equally attractive in terms of the risk/reward tradeoff. An increased equity exposure is the way the firm moved along the expected returns and the risk/return tradeoff's volatility. There were two components to this. First, as the firm moved from the conservative portfolio to the growth portfolio, it increased the equity exposure within each region without affecting the global allocation. Second, it increased the riskier assets' exposure with the highest expected returns at the equity region's expense with the lowest expected return. Increased uncertainty reduced the firm's allocation to variables with the greatest expected returns. The greater-expected-returns dispersion forced the firm's risk/return tradeoff to mute increases in equities and regional exposures for all the portfolios. This new allocation was aimed to protect the conservative portfolio against a downside and enabled the growth portfolio to increase its upside by taking into consideration the expected risk/return tradeoff.

The company's global strategy performance is reported in Table 8.3. In addition to the conservative, balanced, and growth portfolios, some reference portfolios—using the Morgan Stanley Capital Index (MSCI) as a proxy for global equity performance and the Merrill Lynch Global Broad Market Plus index as a proxy for global fixed-income performance—are reported as well. Using these two proxies, I constructed the following equity/fixed-income benchmark portfolios: 30/70 conservative, 60/40 balanced, and 70/30 growth. The results in Table 8.3 show the Hong Kong firm's asset-allocation strategy fared quite well when compared to the reference portfolios over one- and two-year time horizons. The excess performance over the two-year horizon illustrates once again that CAA is a value-adding strategy.

Table 8.3

Performance of the Far East global manager asset-allocation strategy.

	2003	**2004**	**2003–2004**
Global Conservative Portfolio	18%	7.86%	28.14%
Global Balanced Portfolio	23.7%	9.39%	35.36%
Global Growth Portfolio	27%	10.67%	40.56%
Equity Benchmark			
MSCI	30.81%	12.84%	47.61%
Fixed Income Benchmark			
Global T-Bonds	5.1%	3.5%	8.78%
Fixed Income/Equity Combinations			
30/70 Conservative	12.81%	6.3%	19.92%
60/40 Balanced	20.53%	9.1%	31.5%
70/30 Growth	23.1%	10.03%	35.45%

Source: Fund literature, MSCI, and Merrill Lynch

Case Study: A Lifecycle-Fund Family

Lifecycle funds offer a very simple way for individual investors to select the right portfolios for their situations. All an investor has to do is choose the fund, or combination of funds, matching the point in time for which he is saving. Each fund is managed to give an investor a broad and diversified asset allocation. Following is an array of five different lifecycle options: a capital preservation fund invested solely in fixed-income instruments, a 2010 fund (40/60 equities to fixed income), a 2020 fund (60/40 equities to fixed income), a 2030 fund (70/30 equities to fixed income), and a 2040 fund (85/15 equities to fixed income). The asset allocations in these funds automatically adjust over time so portfolios remain appropriate for investment horizons. Figure 8.2 shows a graphical representation of the lifecycle allocation.

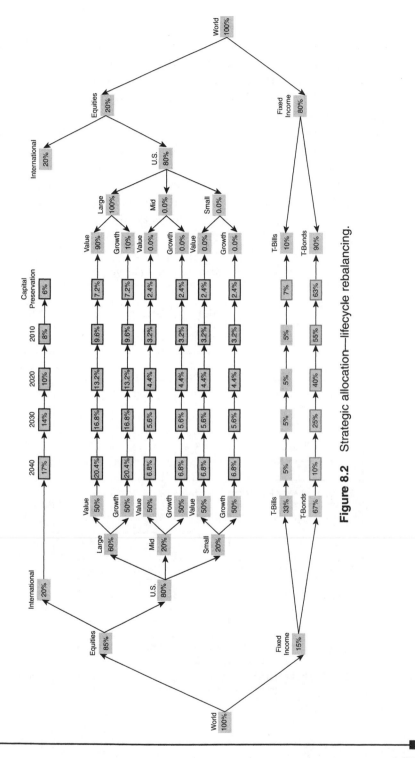

Figure 8.2 Strategic allocation—lifecycle rebalancing.

One lifecycle-fund family based in the Midwest invested its portfolios in unaffiliated mutual fund shares (including index funds, money-market funds, and ETFs) representing broad classes of assets (namely stocks, T-bonds, and money-market instruments). Early on, this fund family hired a consultant to provide it with an asset-allocation strategy. The consultant used a traditional quantitative approach to asset allocation, and the outcome produced was not altogether a happy one. For the most part, the family's lifecycle portfolios underperformed their benchmarks during 2001 and 2002 (see Table 8.4). The 2040 portfolio declined 13.9 percent during 2001 and another 18.9 percent during 2002. In general, this performance lagged behind that of a blended, or benchmark, portfolio consisting of a 15 percent allocation to the Merrill Lynch U.S. fixed-income index and an 85 percent allocation to the S&P 500 index.

Table 8.4
Performance of the Midwest lifecycle fund.

Returns				
Funds	2001	2002	2003	2004
Capital Preservation	3.1%	−2.2%	11.6%	6.1%
Lifecycle 2010	−1.3%	−7.8%	14.4%	7.2%
Lifecycle 2020	−6.9%	−12.4%	19.3%	8.6%
Lifecycle 2030	−10.5%	−15.7%	23.9%	10.2%
Lifecycle 2040	−13.9%	−18.9%	29.3%	11.7%
Equity and Fixed–Income Benchmarks				
Merry Lynch Master	8.4%	12.0%	4.5%	4.2%
S&P 500	11.9%	−22.1%	28.6%	10.9%
Combination of the Fixed Income and Equity Benchmarks				
40/60 (2010 Benchmark)	9.8%	−1.7%	14.2%	6.9%
60/40 (2020 Benchmark)	10.5%	−8.5%	19.0%	8.2%
70/30 (2030 Benchmark)	10.9%	−11.9%	21.4%	8.9%
85/15 (2040 Benchmark)	11.4%	−17.0%	25.0%	9.9%

Source: Morningstar

Perhaps resulting from the underperformance, the fund family began to look for alternatives, and among the approaches considered was one not only focused on backward-looking historical relationships, but also on forward-looking measures taking into account changes in the political and economic environment. The fund family switched to a CAA strategy beginning in 2003, and the new strategy featured some interesting twists.

The fund family kept the equity/fixed-income allocation a strict SAA, considering it an invariant to the overall economic outlook. A second modification was making automatic adjustments to the equity/fixed-income allocation over a participant's lifetime linear adjustments. For example, because a 2040 portfolio began with an 85/15 equity to fixed-income allocation and a 2030 portfolio started with a 70/30 split, over the ten-year difference in horizons, it would take a hearty 1.5 percent reduction per year in the equity allocation for the 2040 portfolio to converge into the 2030 portfolio.

The CAA strategy modifications tilted the equity funds allocation based on the economic outlook and the historical relationships between the economic environment and the size, style, and location effects outlined in Table 8.5.

The tilts, however, were moderated because the tilts' major objective was to generate, if possible, enough added value to cover the expense ratios. Nevertheless, the funds' relative performance dramatically improved. During the 2001–2002 period, the funds lagged the 85/15 benchmark by a 13.09 percent average per year (see Table 8.4). Yet, after the adoption of the CAA strategy, the funds led the benchmark by a 2.55 percent average per year. All this was accomplished without any significant change in the funds' risk profile. In fact, as shown in Table 8.6, at 0.92, the beta (or systematic risk) for the 2040 portfolio is slightly less than the actual market (because a beta of one is considered in sync with the market). To put this in perspective, a portfolio with 85 percent S&P 500 stocks and 15 percent Treasury bills (T-bills) would have a beta of 0.85 (or a price volatility below the market). The fund family's reallocated 2040, with almost no allotment to T-bills, produced essentially the same beta. The other capital asset pricing model (CAPM) measure also points to good news. The alpha (that is, the excess return over required to compensate for systematic risk) delivered by the new 2040 portfolio was a robust 1.96 percent—almost the same excess return amount the 2040 portfolio delivered against the 85/15 benchmark.

Table 8.5

Historical probability estimates generated by the
La Jolla Economics quantitative model.

Probabilities	2003.1	2003.2	2003.3	2003.4	2004.1	2004.2	2004.3	2004.4
Cash > T-Bonds	46%	46%	40%	29%	58%	38%	69%	60%
T-Bonds > Equities	52%	52%	34%	35%	46%	41%	47%	42%
International > Domestic	49%	38%	45%	48%	46%	38%	40%	49%
Large > Small	60%	46%	44%	58%	43%	23%	47%	43%
Large > Mid	60%	45%	35%	56%	47%	22%	45%	47%
Mid > Small	50%	49%	54%	60%	55%	77%	54%	41%
Value > Growth	48%	37%	56%	50%	51%	51%	39%	54%
Large Value > Growth	48%	36%	56%	49%	51%	51%	36%	55%
Mid Value > Growth	48%	48%	56%	41%	49%	51%	39%	49%
Small Value > Growth	48%	21%	56%	73%	55%	55%	59%	56%

Source: La Jolla Economics

Table 8.6
Lifecycle performance relative to the S&P 500 and risk characteristics.

Lifecycle Fund	Annualized 2001–2002	Excess Returns 2002–2003	Risk Measures Beta	Alpha	Sharpe Ratio
2010	−8.20%	0.27%	0.45	1.51	0.47
2020	−10.20%	0.32%	0.63	1.34	0.41
2030	−12.11%	1.65%	0.77	1.51	0.4
2040	−13.09%	2.55%	0.92	1.96	0.42

Source: Morningstar

Case Study: A Hedge Fund

We have not yet considered a CAA approach to hedge funds, an investment vehicle that has gained much popularity in recent years. The case for hedge funds is straightforward: They're highly flexible. Hedge funds can incorporate one or many alternative investment strategies, such as hedging against market downturns, investing in asset classes (such as currencies or distressed securities), or utilizing return-enhancing tools (such as leverage, derivatives, and arbitrage). The funds' added flexibility is a great allure to investors.

The CAA strategy is well suited to the top-down macro strategies employed by hedge-fund managers. The reason for this is the mandate of macro hedge-fund managers is to roam the world in search of returns. In doing so, they can focus on particular regions, asset sizes (that is, large-, mid-, and small-cap stocks), and asset styles (that is, value or growth stocks), as well as the various fixed-income instruments.

Incorporating the CAA strategy with a hedge-fund strategy requires only a few steps, which we can investigate by looking at the experiences of a hedge fund, like our lifecycle-fund family based in the Midwest. As with the CAA strategy, the program for this hedge fund is to begin by defining the world in terms of the various asset classes and locations. Borrowing a page from the efficient-market theory, this hedge fund argues the world market should be on the efficient frontier, meaning a portfolio constituting the world market would have to be market-efficient. I used this argument in Chapter 6, "To Start, a Benchmark," to develop my version of the global market benchmark, and in what follows, I retain my version of the benchmark allocation, which I report in Figure 8.3.

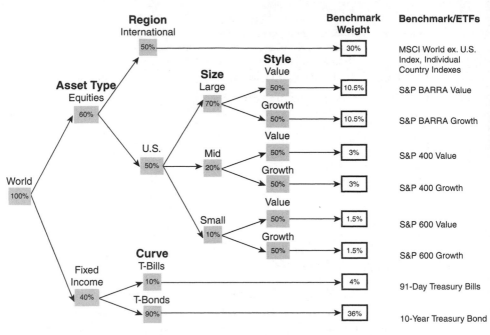

Figure 8.3 Strategic asset allocation.

To quickly review this benchmark allocation process, the asset-class returns' probabilities are formulated and applied to an investor's long-term goals. This produces a recommended asset allocation. Just as with a CAA, historical relationships combined with the information contained in the futures markets provides our Midwest hedge fund with the signals necessary to tilt its benchmark allocations to take advantage of cyclical fluctuations. Armed with this probability information, the hedge fund develops decision rules for determining how and when to choose an investment's style, location, and/or size. It also determines whether to allocate in an active or passive mode.

A summary of the probability estimates for 2004's fourth quarter is presented in Table 8.5. (This is the same CAA sample used in Chapter 7, Figure 7.3.) The likelihood of fixed-income instruments outperforming U.S. equities was 42 percent for the sample—a prescription for an increased equity exposure. Overall, the fixed-income allocation was reduced to 32.6 percent from its 40 percent benchmark (although inside this allocation, the exposure to cash was increased, representing a call for a reduction in the fixed-income portfolio's duration). The style allocation tilted toward value stocks while mid- and small-cap stocks were favored within the size allocation. The sole domestic underweighting was for large-cap growth stocks.

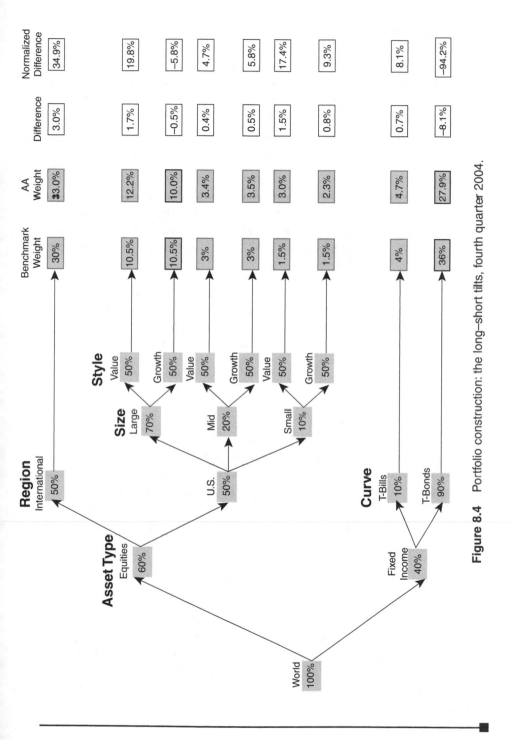

Figure 8.4 Portfolio construction: the long–short tilts, fourth quarter 2004.

The overweights and underweights shown in Figure 8.4 point to a bearish position for fixed-income instruments and a bullish stance for equities (excepting the neutral-rated large-cap growth stocks). These underweights and overweights constitute the core strategic elements for the Midwest hedge fund. Its process is quite simple. All the overweights are added together and normalized to 100. For the sample in question, the overweights and underweights added up to 8.6 percent each. In turn, the international allocation was overweighted by 3 percent. By dividing the 3 percent by the 8.6 percent, one can view the hedge fund's net long-position for international.

As one can guess, this whole process generates both a long and a short portfolio. At a quarter's beginning, the long match the short and, over time, they drift apart. If the tilts are correct, the long part of the investment strategy increases in value (that is, it gets longer) while the short part—the part being bet against will lose value—gets shorter. The difference between the two represents the hedge-fund strategy's gain.

This long–short construction provides some interesting insights. In a way, one can look at the whole process as a long-only portfolio strategy, where the investor tilts around long-run benchmarks based on the probabilities (or the outlook). This allocation, however, can be broken into two separate portfolios (see Figure 8.4, first column): one consisting of the benchmark allocations (second column), and one consisting of a long–short portfolio comprised of the tilts (third column). Viewed this way, the long-only allocation can be separated into an SAA as well as a long–short position.

The long–short strategy is directly related to the difference between CAA and SAA, so we can infer the long–short hedge-fund strategy is solely focused on capturing the value-added the CAA produces. In previous chapters, I discussed the SAAs' performance that buy the market allocations and showed the way the diversification this allocation produces significantly reduces portfolio risk. I have also shown the tilt strategy combined with quantitative probability estimates—that is, the CAA strategy—is an improvement over the SAA strategy. It then follows the returns realized by the Midwest hedge fund are directly related to the value added by the long-only strategy.

The hedge fund's performance is summarized in Figure 8.5 and Tables 8.7 and 8.8. The reported results are subject to the usual caveats. They are based on forecasts for relative asset-class performance prior to the sample period. Transaction fees are not included in the results and the hypothetical trades are initiated at each quarter's beginning while the positions are not changed until the next quarter. Table 8.7 suggests, by most any modern financial matrix, the cyclical hedge-fund strategy delivers. Take the CAPM metrics: The Midwest hedge-fund strategy produces a low 0.13 percent beta with a significantly positive 12.5 percent alpha. The Sharpe ratio produces equally impressive statistics. Finally, the hedge fund's annual returns compare quite favorably to most equity indices, such as the S&P 500.

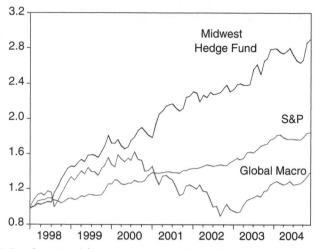

Figure 8.5 Growth of $1 Invested In the S&P 500, the Global Macro Index, and the Midwest hedge-fund strategy.

Table 8.7
Midwest hedge-fund global macro strategy.

Benchmark	Beta	Alpha	T-Stat
S&P 500	0.13	12.50%	3.71
Global Macro Index	0.13	12.20%	3.26

Table 8.8
Midwest hedge-fund global macro strategy: Sharpe ratio.

S&P 500	0.17
Global Macro Hedge Fund Index	0.99
Midwest Hedge Fund	1.17

Summary

These case studies illustrate the CAA approach's versatility. The results are robust enough to withstand and accommodate the many idiosyncratic demands the managers and participants employing the CAA strategy make, although the strategy itself can be easily adjusted to accommodate a variety of investment horizons and lifecycle constraints, a multitude of asset classes, and a wide range of risk tolerances.

9

ACTIVE VERSUS PASSIVE MANAGEMENT

The debate over whether to actively or passively manage occurs with frequency in the investment profession.[1] Although the two terms mean different things to different people, *active management* is generally considered a strategy incorporating active stock picking and market timing. In contrast, *passive management* usually refers to buy-and-hold strategies applied to individual stocks and/or asset classes. Passive management proponents argue active management does not perform any better than the market over the long run. They also argue, because index-like portfolios have lower expense ratios, passive portfolios deliver higher net-of-fee returns. Active managers counter with the argument it is possible to consistently outperform benchmarks.[2]

At different points in market cycles, either the active or passive manager has more real-time ammunition with which to argue his position. But what I set forth in this chapter is investors do not need to put all their eggs in either an active or passive basket. Rather, a third possibility exists—the possibility there is a time for active management and a time for passive management.[3] From a strategic asset allocation (SAA) view, an active- and passive-management combination is in fact superior to either a purely passive or purely active strategy.

The Case for Passive Management

While searching for an elegant description of the case for passive management, I came upon a statement by Rex A. Sinquefield, Dimensional Fund Advisors, Inc.'s cofounder and an index-fund investing pioneer. His statement—which was his volley in an active versus passive management debate held in San Francisco in the mid-1990s—was exactly what I was looking for.[4] Sinquefield argued,

> With respect to market behavior there are, at the extremes, two views. At one extreme is the well-known efficient market hypothesis, which says that the prices are always fair and quickly reflective of information. In such a world neither professional investors nor the proverbial "little investors" will be able to systematically pick winners...or losers. At the other extreme is what I'll call the market failure hypothesis. According to

this view, prices react to information slowly enough to allow some investors, presumably professionals, to systematically outperform markets and most other investors.

At the level of investor behavior, this discussion deals with how a financial advisor should handle his or her clients' money. It is my contention that active management does not make sense theoretically and isn't justified empirically. Other than that, it's okay. But it's easy to understand the allure, the seductive power of active management. After all, it's exciting, fun to dip and dart, pick stocks and time markets; to get paid high fees for this, and to do it all with someone else's money.

Passive management, on the other hand, stands on solid theoretical grounds, has enormous empirical support, and works very well for investors.

His bias is quite obvious. But markets certainly do work, and this point is where Sinquefield and his passive-management position stand strong. Perhaps what he doesn't consider is one can be both active and passive, believing in market efficiency over the long-run while making reasoned adjustments to a portfolio along the way to maximize return.

Let's use the S&P 500 to illustrate this. We know the S&P 500 return is a capitalization-weighted average of the individual stock returns making up the index. The index construction's constraints require, on a cap-weighted basis, 50 percent of the stocks in the index to outperform the index while 50 percent underperform. The same constraints hold for active managers. The math is very precise on this and one cannot escape the index construction's budget constraints. Armed with this conclusion, we can now interpret numerous studies' results showing the way actively managed portfolios underperformed their passive benchmarks. Let's have Rex Sinquefield help illustrate this last point. During the debate in San Francisco, he said,

> In the most recent and comprehensive study done to date, a dissertation at the University of Chicago, Mark Carhart studies a total of 1,892 funds that existed any time between 1961 and 1993. After adjusting for the common factors in returns an equal-weighted portfolio of the funds underperformed by 1.8% per year.

Notice how carefully and precisely Sinquefield made this statement, which he claimed as more proof "the beat-the-market efforts of professionals are impressively and overwhelmingly negative." He mentioned the study's results are based on the equal-weighted returns of the different funds in the sample.

Assuming the list of funds is exhaustive, once the funds' market-cap is taken into consideration, one can safely conclude (on a cap-weighted basis) 50 percent of managers would have outperformed during the sample period and 50 percent would have underperformed. In other words, the debate over active and passive management is only meaningful in the context of a weighting scheme different from the cap-weighted average. Only then can the number of managers outperforming or underperforming deviate from the 50 percent mark.

Active and Passive Management: Some Testable Hypotheses

A couple of testable implications are derived from the passive management hypothesis. First, the index benchmark should be an above-average performer among active managers. Second, the benchmark ranking's deviation among active managers should be random and mean-reverting. A companion argument commonly made by some active-management proponents is it is easier for small-cap managers to beat small-cap benchmarks than it is for large-cap managers to beat large-cap benchmarks. One logical conclusion is large-cap stock portfolios should be indexed while small-cap portfolios should be the active managers' domain.

I tested these implications using data supplied to me by a well-known East Coast pension consultant and discovered a sample universe of active managers who could consistently outperform their benchmarks (see Figures 9.1 and 9.2). The results would clearly have been devastating to the active-management hypothesis if the managers selected underperformed their benchmarks. Fortunately, this was not the case. It is possible the pension consultant who supplied me the data knows his business well and was able to identify superior managers. Unfortunately, the results, although damaging to the indexing hypothesis, are not conclusive. For example, when consultants know their business, they can pick winners while the majority of active managers underperform. The criteria for selecting a consultant include (among other things) style consistency, longevity, and proven above-average performance. But, the selection process is fraught with sample selection and survivor bias. As a result, I am unable to definitively conclude active management produces superior returns. So, one should take the conclusions from this one sample with a grain of salt. I can say with confidence, however, the data does not rule out the possibility active management can indeed outperform indexing.

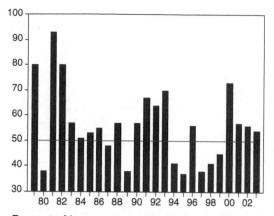

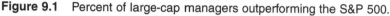

Figure 9.1 Percent of large-cap managers outperforming the S&P 500.

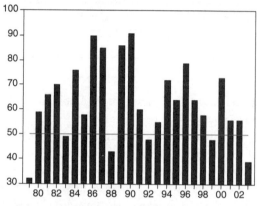

Figure 9.2 Percent of small-cap managers outperforming the Russell 2000.

Survivor bias does not necessarily have a systematic affect on the large-cap and small-cap managers' relative performance. I tested this hypothesis by again using the data my consultant friend supplied. Table 9.1 shows the excess returns for small-cap managers were greater than those for large-cap managers during the 1994–2003 period. Given my misgivings about survivor bias, all I can safely conclude at this point is small-cap managers are more likely to generate excess returns than large-cap managers. But, this statement feels incomplete. The data in Figure 9.1 show the number of managers outperforming the S&P 500 was well above the 50 percent mark for the 1978–1983 and 1989–1993 periods. In contrast, the number of managers outperforming the S&P 500 during the 1993–1999 period was well below the 50 percent mark. Figures 9.1 and 9.2 also show the existence of periods when the percentage of outperforming small-cap managers was lower than the percentage of outperforming large-cap managers.

Table 9.1
Active versus passive management: size effects.

	Returns
Large	**1994–2003**
Average of Active Managers	12.63%
Index (S&P 500)	11.06%
Excess Returns	1.57%
Small	
Average of Active Managers	13.74%
Index (Russell 2000)	9.48%
Excess Returns	4.26%

Source: Pension Consultant

The data damage the view active management should be left to only small-cap managers. But, the data also open up the range of possibilities. The existence of market cycles suggests there are times when active large-cap managers perform better than small-cap managers relative to each benchmark. There are cycles when active management adds a great deal of value and cycles when it does not, and if a manager finds a way to anticipate these cycles, he can devise rules determining when to pursue an active strategy and when to pursue a passive one. Doing so not only brings higher returns to the portfolios he oversees, but it also enables him to maximize his performance ranking within the universe of active managers.

Size Cycles and Market Breadth

In what follows, I illustrate the way active- and passive-management cycles are related to the interaction between the benchmark indices' weighting schemes and the size effect, which is visible when the market tilts toward either small-caps or large-caps. Because a weighting scheme is known in advance, all one needs to do to implement a strategy that takes advantage of active/passive cycles is to forecast the size effect. In earlier chapters, I developed the size effect theory, arguing the small-cap effect is nothing more than the result of inflation hedging, tax avoidance, and regulatory skirting. When taxes, inflation, and regulations increase, small-cap companies tend to outperform because they can adjust more quickly to changing economic conditions than less-flexible large-cap companies. Thus, by tracking changes in these variables, one can identify size cycles. My firm's track record suggests one can do a pretty good job of this.

The case for active management does not rest on a market inefficiency concept. It rests on stock indices' weighting schemes and small-cap cycles' existence. The theoretical argument regarding market efficiency is, however, very compelling. Some time ago, Rex Sinquefield made the case that the efficient market theory—which, in brief, states consistently "beating the market" is improbable because existing stock prices are the result of all current information—is simply an application of Adam Smith's invisible-hand theory to financial markets. I share this efficient market world view. More, although it is true market inefficiency is a sufficient condition for justifying active management, it is not a necessary condition. In this sense, I again part ways with Sinquefield's passive-investing-only mandate.

A broad market can be defined as a majority of stocks outperforming a benchmark index. This is a good way for an active manager to envision market breadth. To illustrate why, let's borrow an analogy from the efficient market theory: Assume a number of people are throwing darts at a blackboard containing the names of all the stocks in the S&P 500. The chance of one dart thrower picking a winning stock is equal to the number of stocks outperforming the benchmark index at any point in time. If 60 percent are outperforming, the dart thrower has a 60 percent chance of hitting a winner. Hence, the broader the market breadth, the greater the chance an active portfolio manager outperforms a benchmark.

Now, let's add weighting schemes to the market breadth concept. For an index where all stocks have the same market capitalization, the cap-weighted return and the average gain of the stocks in the index are identical. At any point in time, if the returns are randomly distributed, half the stocks in the index will outperform the benchmark and half will underperform. Going back to the efficient market analogy, our dart thrower in this sense only has a 50/50 chance of hitting an outperformer.

But consider the case of a cap-weighted index where there is some variation in the stocks' market-cap. By ranking stocks by market capitalization in descending order and dividing them into groups accounting for 50 percent of the index's market-cap, one can show the following: the greater the larger-cap stocks' weight in the index, the smaller the number of stocks in the market-cap's top half and the greater the number of stocks in the market-cap's bottom half. It follows, during small-cap cycles, more than 50 percent of stocks in an index outperform the index. Hence, during small-cap cycles, the odds favor active managers.

The constraints imposed by an index's construction require, on a cap-weighted basis, 50 percent of the stocks' market value in the index to outperform while 50 percent to underperform. The half of an index holding the larger market-cap stocks hold a smaller number of stocks than the other half. Conversely stated, the half of an index holding the smaller market-cap stocks have a larger number of stocks than the other half. Thus, a top-heavy index has more than 50 percent of its stocks in the lower market-cap half. The math is very precise here and one cannot escape the constraints imposed by index construction. This is a powerful insight. The implication is the weighting scheme inexorably link small-cap cycles and active management together.

Comparing small- and large-cap indices, a small-cap index's weighting scheme is closer to an equal weight than a large-cap index's scheme. This explains why it is easier for smaller-cap managers to consistently outperform their benchmarks than it is for larger-cap managers. As the percentage of stock names outperforming benchmarks reliably remains in the 50 percent neighborhood, small-cap managers only need a small edge to outperform the market and steadily rank above average.

As the market switches from a small-cap to a large-cap cycle, the percent of stock names outperforming an index like the S&P 500 substantially declines, so large-cap managers face a tough hurdle during large-cap cycles. During small-cap cycles, large-cap managers need an edge significant enough to overcome the adverse size effect if they hope to produce excess returns relative to their index. This is possible. But from a dart-throwing perspective, the odds of hitting the winners large-cap managers face can be too low during large-cap cycles. Hence, indexing can be the superior strategy during such cycles.

So, let's link the market breadth and weighting scheme once and for all. Holding the weighting scheme constant, the greater the size cycle's strength, the greater the difference between the equal- and cap-weighted returns and the greater the number of stocks that outperform their benchmark indices. Thus, the stronger the size effect, the greater the market breadth.

Small-Cap Cycles Favor Active Managers

Before we look at some size effect examples, I'll make a note on my data service: It does not keep track of the returns of companies deleted from stock indices. Therefore, as we go back in time, my data suffers from some survivor bias. I have tried to take care of this by tracking the deleted companies' earnings, but this data is incomplete. Still, the small number of missing companies does not alter the results reported in this section in any significant way.

Table 9.2 reports the percent of stocks in the S&P indices that outperformed their benchmarks during recent periods. By putting this data into the framework of size cycles, we can empirically test much of what was stated previously in this chapter and come to some conclusions. I again use the dart-thrower analogy to help readers visualize performance over size cycles.

Table 9.2
Percent of stocks outperforming their index.

	1998	1999	2000	2001	2002	2003
S&P 500	33%	31%	63%	69%	64%	55%
S&P 400	33%	30%	46%	61%	59%	44%
S&P 600	48%	36%	47%	54%	54%	47%

Source: Research Insight

A dart thrower has a better chance of outperforming any index during a small-cap cycle. We know a large-cap cycle existed during the 1998–1999 period and a small-cap cycle occurred during the 2000–2004 period. The data show, on average, the percentage of stocks that outperformed their benchmarks was higher during the small-cap market than during the large-cap market. Sixty-three percent of large-cap stocks outperformed the S&P 500 index during the large-cap cycle, while only 32 percent of the large-cap stocks outperformed during the small-cap cycle. For small-caps, the variation was less pronounced. Forty-eight percent of small-cap stocks outperformed the S&P 600 index during the large-cap cycle and only 44 percent of the small-cap stocks outperformed during the small-cap cycle.

The odds of a dart thrower outperforming an index systematically change over the course of a cycle, and the odds of a larger-cap dart thrower change the most. The data reported in Table 9.2 enable us to show 32 percent of the largest-cap stocks outperformed during the small-cap cycle while 63 percent outperformed during the large-cap cycle, a significant change. As for small-caps, 44 percent outperformed during the small-cap cycle while 48 percent outperformed during the large-cap cycle, a very small change. It follows the number of large-cap stocks outperforming greatly improved as we moved from the small-cap cycle to the large-cap cycle.

During a small-cap cycle, a large-cap dart thrower has a better chance of beating a large-cap benchmark than a small-cap dart thrower has of beating a small-cap benchmark. During the 2000–2004 small-cap cycle, 63 percent of large-cap stocks outperformed the S&P 500, on average. Meanwhile, only 48 percent of small-cap stocks outperformed the S&P 400 during the small-cap cycle.

During a large-cap cycle, a small-cap dart thrower has a better chance of outperforming a small-cap benchmark than a large-cap dart thrower has of beating a large-cap benchmark. During the 1998–1999 large-cap cycle, 44 percent of small-cap stocks outperformed the small-cap index, on average, while only 32 percent of large-cap stocks outperformed the large-cap index.

Generally, a dart thrower throws better during small-cap cycles. During large-cap markets, it is more difficult for active managers to outperform their benchmarks. Table 9.3 reports the performance of a sample of large-cap managers provided by our friendly pension consultant. The numbers clearly support the original dart-throwing analogy, leading to the conclusion the number of active managers outperforming an index increase and exceed the 50 percent mark during small-cap cycles.

Table 9.3
S&P 500 ranking among the active manager universe.

	1998	1999	2000	2001	2002	2003
Average of all Managers	41%	45%	73%	57%	56%	54%
S&P 500	59%	55%	27%	43%	44%	46%

Using the sample indices' excess return, I can also test the hypothesis that the greater the disparity in cap-weighting, the greater the size effects' impact on the active managers' relative performances (that is, the likelihood active managers will succeed in beating their benchmarks). I chose the S&P 500 for the large-cap data and the Russell 2000 for the small-cap data, as these exhibit the possible benchmarks' longest time series. A below-the-line (negative) number for the return bar in Figure 9.3 indicates when the S&P 500 underperformed the Russell 2000. A small-cap market is identified in this case. An above-the-line (positive) number for the rank bar occurs when more than 50 percent of the sample of managers beat the S&P 500. Notice most pairs of observations are on opposite sides of the line. The negative correlation between the two variables shows large-cap managers tended to beat the S&P 500 consistently during small-cap periods. Conversely, when the S&P 500 outperformed the Russell 2000 (that is, during large-cap markets), active managers did poorly, with less than 50 percent outperforming the S&P 500.

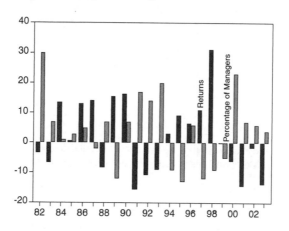

Figure 9.3   S&P 500 returns net of the Russell 2000 returns versus the percent of large-cap managers above the S&P 500 benchmark.

The percent of active managers who outperform their benchmarks increases during small-cap cycles (see Figure 9.4), but the size effect also acts differentially on the large- and small-cap managers' relative ranking. As the percent of stocks outperforming an index fluctuates more for larger-cap stocks (see Table 9.4), we know improvements in performance are greater for larger-cap managers. Symmetrically, during large-cap markets, it is tougher for all managers to outperform their indices, although the task is perhaps hardest for larger-cap managers. During the large-cap cycles surveyed, the percent of large-cap managers who outperformed the large-cap benchmark (indicated when the relative excess-return bar is above the zero line) is less than the percent of small-cap managers who outperformed the small-cap benchmark (indicated when the relative rank bar is below the zero line). In contrast, during small-cap cycles, the excess returns are below the zero line while the relative rank is above the zero line. This negative correlation supports the hypothesis that the fluctuations in the percent of large-cap active managers outperforming their benchmarks is larger in both absolute and relative terms.

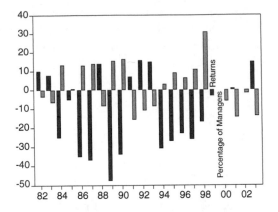

Figure 9.4 S&P 500 returns net of the Russell 200 returns versus the percent of small cap managers above the Russell 2000 returns.

Table 9.4
Active versus passive management during size-related cycles.

	Returns	
Large	**1994–1999**	**2000–2003**
Average of Active Managers	22.62%	−0.84%
Index (S&P 500)	20.92%	−5.33%
Excess Returns	1.70%	4.49%
Small		
Average of Active Managers	14.90%	12.01%
Index (Russell 2000)	13.39%	3.86%
Excess Returns	1.51%	8.15%

Source: Pension Consultant

When the large-cap effect dominates and market breadth narrows, it is harder to beat a benchmark and indexing becomes a much more attractive strategy. The results reported in Table 9.4 confirm this. But, looking again at Table 9.2, an above-average number of stocks obviously outperform when the small-cap effect dominates. Importantly, the greater the difference between the equal-weighted returns and a benchmark's cap-weighted returns (that is, the S&P

500), the easier it is to identify and select the appropriate stocks combination to beat a cap-weighted index.

The implication for a portfolio strategy is straightforward: During small-cap cycles, the odds of beating an index rise. Portfolio managers should be active at such times. During large-cap cycles, the odds of beating the market decline. Portfolio managers should quasi-index in this environment. For consultants and investors in general, size cycles should guide the process of deciding between an active or passive allocation style.

The Potential Benefits of Size-Related Active/Passive Strategy

There's also the question of timing cycles. Consistency over cycles is harder to achieve for large-cap managers than small-cap managers, although a strategy based on the size effect—whereby any manager shifts between an active and passive mode—offers potential benefits. Table 9.5 reports such a switching strategy's viability based on the size effect.

Table 9.5
Strategy based on active/passive selection.

	1998 Large Cycle	1999 Large Cycle	2000 Large Cycle	2001 Small Cycle	2002 Small Cycle	2003 Small Cycle
Return/Rank						
Active	25%	20%	–4%	–11%	–21%	29%
Rank	41%	45%	73%	57%	56%	54%
S&P 500	28.6%	21.0%	–9.1%	–11.9%	–22.1%	28.7%
Rank	59%	55%	27%	43%	44%	46%
Active/ Passive	28.6%	21.0%	–4%	–11%	–21%	29%
Rank	59%	55%	73%	57%	56%	54%

Source: Pension Consultant

The first two rows show the percentages of managers who outperformed the S&P 500 during the 1998–2003 period and represent the median returns for active managers. The third and fourth rows report the S&P 500's returns and the rank among the active managers. The fifth row specifically reports the switching strategy's performance. During the 1998 and 1999 large-cap markets, the active/passive switching strategy dictated indexing. During the 2000–2003 small-cap market, the strategy dictated active management. As shown, during the five-year period, the switching strategy would have improved both portfolio returns and the managers' relative rankings. The magnitude of the improvements is marginal at best. In terms of consultant rankings, however, it is a very significant development. The switching strategy would have outperformed both the benchmark and the median active manager in each five years. Choosing the switching strategy would have done wonders for a consultant's relative ranking.

Standard & Poor's recently began publishing an equal-weighted S&P 500 index to go along with its cap-weighted index. This has become an important tool for developing an optimal strategic passive/active allocation. The equal-weighted index's returns represent a proxy for the average return achievable by "throwing darts" at the S&P 500 board of stocks, and thus can be used as a proxy for the equal-weighted returns active managers can achieve on average. In contrast, the cap-weighted S&P 500 constitutes the index, or benchmark, for passive strategy performance. Table 9.6 shows there are prolonged time periods when the equal-weighted S&P 500 outperforms the cap-weighted index. I contend during these time periods (that is, 2000–2003) that active management outperforms. The data also show there are long time periods when large-cap stocks outperform. Again, I contend during these periods (that is, 1994–1999) that passive management outperforms.

Table 9.6
Annual returns of the equal-weighted
and cap-weighted S&P 500.

	Cap-Weighted	Equal-Weighted
1989	6.7%	7.4%
1990	3.9%	−4.9%
1991	30.5%	35.5%
1992	7.6%	15.6%
1993	10.1%	12.5%
1994	1.3%	1.6%
1995	37.6%	32.2%
1996	23.0%	23.1%
1997	33.4%	24.6%
1998	28.6%	11.0%
1999	21.0%	10.2%
2000	−9.1%	8.2%
2001	−11.9%	2.3%
2002	−22.1%	−10.2%
2003	28.7%	26.0%
2004	10.9%	23.0%

Source: Standard and Poor's

Using the traditional S&P 500's monthly returns and the equal-weighted S&P 500, I constructed 11 portfolios. The first portfolio allocates 100 percent of assets to the cap-weighted stocks. Each additional portfolio reduces the cap-weighted exposure by 10 percentage points. The process continues until 100 percent is allocated to the equal-weighted index. In Table 9.7, I report the summary statistics for the 11 portfolios (along with a twelfth "Best" portfolio, constructed using 20/20 hindsight).

Table 9.7

Average annual returns and standard deviation of alternative combinations of the cap- and equal-weighted S&P 500 equity portfolios: 1990–2004.

	100%	90%	80%	70%	60%	50%
Average Annual Return over the Risk Free Rate	9.16%	8.99%	8.81%	8.63%	8.46%	**8.28%**
Standard Deviation	15.74%	14.51%	13.45%	12.60%	12.01%	**11.71%**
Sharpe Ratio	0.582	0.619	0.655	0.685	0.704	**0.707**
	40%	**30%**	**20%**	**10%**	**0%**	**Best**
Average Annual Return over the Risk Free Rate	8.10%	7.93%	7.75%	7.57%	7.40%	11.03%
Standard Deviation	11.73%	12.06%	12.68%	13.56%	14.64%	14.23%
Sharpe Ratio	0.691	0.657	0.611	0.559	0.505	0.775

Source: Research Insight

The numbers show a portfolio consisting solely of the equal-weighted stocks generated an average of 9.16 percent risk-adjusted excess returns per year (Table 9.7, first row, "100%"), while the cap-weighted portfolio returned 7.40 percent per year. But, as I have stated, common sense suggests returns alone should not be the sole criteria for an investor's allocation decision. Risk must also be taken into account. The second row in Table 9.7 shows the estimated standard deviation of the returns for each portfolio. At 14.64 percent, the cap-weighted stocks' volatility is a bit lower than the equal-weighted portfolio's 15.74 percent standard deviation. For the third row, I simply calculated the ratio of the portfolio returns to their standard deviation, the idea being the portfolio with the highest return-to-standard-deviation ratio offers the highest reward-to-risk ratio. The data show the portfolio consisting of 50 percent cap-weighted stocks generates the highest reward-to-risk ratio. Looking at the average monthly returns for each year, it is also apparent there are runs in the data. Some simple tests put to rest the hypothesis that the runs are randomly generated.

Table 9.8 shows in eight of the 15 sample years, a corner solution (in this case, a 100 percent allocation to one asset class) would have constituted the optimal allocation. (The optimal choices are indicated in bold, with seven corner solutions in the all-equal-weighted "100%" portfolio and one corner solution in the all-cap-weighted "0%" portfolio.) In all the cases, a corner solution matches the equal- and cap-weighted indices' relative performance (see Table 9.6). Visually analyzing the ratio of the cap-weighted to the equal-weighted S&P 500 also points to the existence of clear cycles in the data (see Figure 9.5).

Table 9.8

Sharpe ratio for selected equal- and cap-weighted portfolios: 1990–2004.

	0%	10%	20%	30%	40%	50%	60%	70%	80%	90%	Equal Weighted 100%
1990	-0.498	-0.535	-0.571	-0.605	-0.638	-0.669	-0.698	-0.726	-0.753	-0.779	-0.803
1991	1.427	1.437	1.447	1.455	1.463	1.470	1.476	1.481	1.485	1.489	1.492
1992	0.557	0.660	0.761	0.860	0.954	1.043	1.127	1.204	1.274	1.338	1.394
1993	1.140	1.419	1.814	2.373	3.044	3.406	3.084	2.511	2.036	1.693	1.448
1994	-0.191	-0.214	-0.240	-0.264	-0.281	-0.282	-0.266	-0.239	-0.209	-0.181	-0.157
1995	5.145	5.990	7.017	8.078	8.710	8.403	7.336	6.110	5.054	4.222	3.579
1996	1.495	1.649	1.810	1.960	2.074	2.124	2.095	1.995	1.853	1.695	1.540
1997	1.581	1.786	2.043	2.345	2.641	2.788	2.643	2.276	1.868	1.519	1.245
1998	1.061	1.068	1.060	1.032	0.978	0.898	0.797	0.685	0.570	0.460	0.360
1999	1.183	1.278	1.383	1.475	1.513	1.442	1.254	1.014	0.786	0.596	0.446
2000	-0.810	-0.826	-0.835	-0.820	-0.753	-0.603	-0.387	-0.173	-0.004	0.118	0.205
2001	-0.729	-0.714	-0.684	-0.632	-0.557	-0.459	-0.349	-0.238	-0.136	-0.046	0.029
2002	-1.179	-1.265	-1.345	-1.393	-1.370	-1.253	-1.067	-0.864	-0.679	-0.526	-0.402
2003	2.197	2.308	2.362	2.345	2.260	2.124	1.961	1.794	1.634	1.487	1.356
2004	1.300	1.393	1.476	1.549	1.613	1.669	1.719	1.763	1.802	1.837	1.867

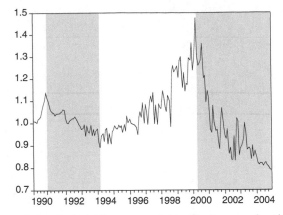

Figure 9.5   Ratio of the cap-weighted to the equal-weighted cumulative returns.

What Does the Data Tell Us?

Under the assumption of perfect foresight, I calculated the potential gains gen-erated by a strategy taking advantage of the cycles. Such a strategy produced an 11.03 percent risk-adjusted return per year, well in excess of the 9.16 percent per year generated by the equal-weighted S&P strategy and much greater than the 7.40 percent per year generated by the cap-weighted S&P 500 on a risk-adjusted basis. The switching strategy produced an excess return of 353 basis points per year over the cap-weighted S&P 500's returns. It is apparent a tac-tical switching-strategy allocation would have been superior to a traditional strategic allocation and/or any pure strategies, passive or active.

The results presented in Table 9.8 are at odds with the various findings in the academic literature used to advocate the passive strategy. But, the results also don't support a 100 percent active strategy. In fact, the results suggest a mix-ture of the two. The practical question an asset allocator might ask is whether 15 years is long enough to generate a long-run result. If 15 years is long enough, the optimal long-run asset allocation would be either 40 percent to the index strategy and 60 percent to the active strategy, or 50 percent to each strategy. That would have generated the highest reward-to-risk ratio in our sample (see Table 9.7). Nevertheless, the data suggest the ideal SAA is a blend of the passive and active strategies.

The size effect and the relative performance between active and passive management are directly related—they are two sides of the same coin. The interaction between the index's weighting scheme and the size effect is a powerful insight because it tells active managers when their portfolios should be "index-like" and when they should pursue an active strategy with gusto. By taking advantage of the correspondence between the size effect and market breadth, we can make inferences regarding the conditions under which active management prevails over passive management.

The results reported in Table 9.4 show active managers beat their benchmarks during both large- and small-cap cycles. As a result of the sample-selection and survivor biases, however, the active managers' returns overestimate the true average (that is, the average of all active managers). Therefore, I cannot state with assurance active management is superior to passive management. Because the excess returns are larger during small-cap cycles, I can only say with confidence the odds of active management outperforming passive management are much higher during small-cap cycles.

A problem with specific mandates managers face (that is, they must allocate to large-caps, to value stocks, and so on) is they can be constrained from taking advantage of the size effect. There are solutions to this. During the times when large-cap stocks are out of favor, managers should rank by market capitalization all the stocks their style would normally buy (relative to dividend yields, momentum, value, and so on). Choosing the stocks with smaller capitalizations within the buy lists enables managers to capture the size effect while remaining true to their styles. Another solution is to use a linear cap- and equal-weighted scheme combination, where the weighting factors are used to tilt a portfolio to capture a size effect.

Consultants do not look kindly on managers who drift too far from their styles. So, style consistency's constraints and the economic environment's impact on a particular style can decimate a manager whose style goes out of favor. Ironically, those who follow the purest strategies tend to have the most volatile performance rankings. The same holds for SAA managers who do not take into account size cycles. Their performance rankings also suffer some volatility.

For strategic managers, I have in mind a very simple cyclical portfolio strategy: During small-cap cycles, the odds of beating an index rise; therefore, the cyclical asset allocation (CAA) strategy should choose actively managed funds to fill the allocation buckets. During large-cap cycles, the odds of beating the market decline, so the CAA strategy should choose index funds, such as exchange-traded funds (ETFs). For consultants and investors in general, size cycles should be used to determine when to choose either the active and passive style.

Of course, a potential problem with a strategy switching between active and passive management is plan sponsors are reluctant to pay "active" management fees during periods of index-like performance. An alternative for plan managers is to hazard their SAA benchmark's underperformance during large-cap cycles by filling their asset-class buckets with actively managed funds, even though this stacks the odds against the managers. In this case, if the asset-allocation strategies do underperform their benchmarks, the asset allocators can only hope their clients stay on. Only then do they collect the higher management fees.

But there's an alternative to this: Asset-allocation managers must educate their clients about the cyclical nature of active/passive relative performance. In doing so, they are able to explain why switching between active and passive strategies maximizes a client's long-run return, and thus why a passive/active strategy deserves a higher management fee.

10

LOCATION, LOCATION, LOCATION?

I have already unveiled my view that regulatory increases and changing tax laws tend to tilt the economic environment in favor of small-cap stocks, as smaller companies are more nimble and thus can react much more quickly to economic changes. In financial parlance, smaller-caps exhibit a lot more "elasticity" than larger-caps—or, put another way, these companies have a greater ability to substitute. Nevertheless, as economic time goes by and scheduled tax and regulatory changes take effect, the need to be nimble to take advantage of these changes disappears. Hence, over the longer term, my analysis points to a market where larger-caps dominate. Again, the rationale is straightforward: As uncertainty regarding the tax code and regulations is reduced, the impact of tax and regulatory burdens becomes smaller and more predictable. As larger-cap companies have the resources to hire the best lawyers and accountants, they thus have the greater ability to chip away at the day's defined tax and regulatory burdens. The concept of elasticity—as it applies to both larger- and smaller-cap companies, as well as global locations—is the subject of this chapter.

To the extent that one views the regulatory burden as a fixed cost, larger corporations have an advantage over smaller ones. Regulatory fixed costs amount to a lower increase in per-unit costs for the bigger firms. One example of this came when the federal government mandated that America's big-three automakers develop catalytic converters to reduce emissions. Absent this new antitrust provision (that is, regulatory fixed costs), the automakers could have joined forces and developed a single converter they all could have shared. Needless to say, the federal provision forced the development of two catalytic converters too many, and the higher costs associated with this reduced the attractiveness of domestic cars relative to foreign cars not subject to the antitrust provision. The extra costs associated with the converters' development were born in part by shareholders with lower profits and by domestic workers with lower employment. But, that's not all. This new regulation had a disproportionate impact on the domestic car producers. If the converters' development costs were roughly the same for the three automakers, the development costs' amortization increased the unit costs the most for the smallest of the three. In other words, the regulation put the smallest company at a competitive disadvantage to the larger ones.

The catalytic converter example has clear investment implications. After the economic environment becomes predictable, the regulatory burden becomes a fixed cost. This condition tends to favor larger-cap companies as they can amortize costs over a larger base. It follows a simple way to reduce the regulatory burden's effect is to get bigger, and thus companies have an incentive to grow. Whether this growth is through direct investment or acquisitions is irrelevant to the argument. As long as companies get bigger, they can minimize the regulatory burden's impact. One can make a similar argument regarding technology: the greater the gains related to technology-driven productivity growth, the greater the ensuing output volume. The cost-amortization argument points to a consolidation of businesses where a few large companies will dominate their industries.

Free Trade Leads to Market Returns Convergence

International trends are also inadvertently pushing the world toward consolidation. More specifically, the removal of trade barriers is bringing world markets into a single market. To see this, consider an extreme case of a world made up of two identical countries that have trade restrictions so high they do not trade with each other at all. In this case, two identical economies develop and the world has two of everything. What happens, however, if the two economies merge with the elimination of all trade barriers between the countries? The answer depends on whether the per-unit costs decline as the production volume increases (that is, whether economies of scale exist). If economies of scale exist, it is in each country's best interest to grow. In addition, the country that grows first has the cost advantage over the other country, and thus eventually dominates the world market.

In real life, however, we do not start with countries or companies of equal size. But, freer trade still gives an advantage to the more efficient entities. As the world does indeed move toward freer trade, some consolidation can occur to take advantage of economies of scale in the production process. Yet the consolidation argument I am advancing goes beyond this. The economies of scale I focus on are a direct result of the regulatory burden and its costs' amortization.

The quest for consolidation arises because the per-unit regulatory cost burden lowers as volume grows. Because regulations generally tend to be national in scope, it follows that a prudent company tends to have a well-diversified portfolio of production facilities. Diversification's advantages in the event of a local shock are significant.[1] A recent article in the *Wall Street Journal* made the point that international investing is not producing as much diversification as it used to. The reason for this, the author writes, is the strong correlation various markets have shown in recent years. The correlation's source, according to the article, is industries seem to be moving in harmony around the world.[2] My interpretation of the author's conclusion is people who aim at diversifying their portfolios must pay as much attention to industry groups as they do to global locations. I have been making this point for the past few years; such a correlation trend is entirely predictable.

The high correlation among industry returns across countries is easily explained in terms of the "law of one price," or purchasing power parity (PPP). Putting these similar concepts together, the high correlation is explainable because identical things' prices across countries tend to be equal when expressed in the same currency. To the extent the correlation among industries is not perfect, however, one must conclude PPP is not perfect and PPP violations occur. In fact, these violations are what give rise to location effects, which include entire global regions, specific countries, and smaller localities. I offer a very simple framework for the location effect.[3] When PPP holds—that is to say, when there is exchange-rate parity between currencies—the value added for a top-down investment strategist is in large part derived from industry selection. When PPP violations are observed, however, location matters a great deal. The reason for this is fairly obvious: Mobility is not perfect across countries or production factors. The levels and types of government expenditures and the manner in which revenue is raised differ across countries. This means that, across countries, the burden of taxation disproportionately falls among the least mobile factors, which are those production factors literally cemented to their localities, such as single-plant factories. This is important because it suggests country-specific effects do indeed exist. Thus, I contend changes in national economic policies produce systematic deviations from PPP. To the extent these deviations can be anticipated, I also contend investors and portfolio managers who are tuned in to location effects can sail with the wind at their backs.

In a frictionless world, production factors and the mobility of goods and services guarantee differences in rates of return are arbitraged away. In such an idealized world, PPP holds. This means, as long as there is no deviation from PPP, rates of return are identical across national markets. This is a potent insight and it has two distinct implications. First, if the regulatory burden is of a fixed-cost nature, corporations have an incentive to increase their operations' scale to minimize the regulatory burden's impact. Yet a second and perhaps more important implication is if a domestic equity market is reasonably diversified, one does not need to invest abroad when PPP holds. All markets in this second case are perfectly correlated with each other, and their synchronization means one can achieve full diversification by investing in one's own national market.

Fixed Factors Give Rise to Location Effects

The trend toward freer trade and the accompanying regulations uniformity in fact turn the regulatory burden into a constant cost. This makes a compelling case for large public companies, or large-cap stocks, in the long run. Does this mean small-caps have no future? Nothing could be further from the truth. But, the case for small-caps is a bit different.

A few global companies dominating markets does not eliminate the little guy's role. Although the concept of an integrated economy with a single global market is a great theoretical construct, it is a chimera in real life. Local and country effects are here to stay. Special interest groups are always creating artificial barriers partially segmenting some markets. In other cases, a local effect could be due to immobile natural resources (for example, those that bring on tourism) or explicit economic policies (for example, those that brought on the California energy crisis). Regional and country effects can also create market segmentations representing market shares simply too small for larger global companies to go after. Given a market's size in relation to that of a company, it cannot be worth it for a larger company to alter its overall plans to capture a small market. Larger companies can very well decide to bypass or ignore some markets altogether, ceding these markets to other players—in particular to the smaller players.

Fiscal policy differences among national economies affect the national economies' relative performance.[4] Rates of return and the valuations of production's immobile factors within the borders of national economies also change in direct proportion to national economic performance. To see this, consider a perfectly mobile factor of a company located in Country A. If rates of return are higher in Country B, the mobile factor in Country A moves, or relocates, to arbitrage the difference. Generalizing this mechanism, I conclude the after-tax returns for mobile factors will be equalized across countries. That's what I mean when I say a factor is priced in the world market; local returns for a factor equal the world's after-tax return grossed up by local taxes.

The tax's initial net effect on the mobile factor is an increase in the production costs of the domestically produced goods and services using the factor in question. If a country in question, however, is a price taker in the world market—that is to say, it must take the price the market offers as it faces a perfectly elastic demand curve for its product—it has no pricing power and, as a result, has to eat the higher production costs. In this case, either profitability declines or the amount of money paid to production factors goes down by the tax's amount. The important point in this example is a tax on a mobile factor—a production aspect that can literally move, or the situation whereby a company can strategically place production in one of several places most advantageous to the company—hurts some of the local factors in the form of either lower profits for domestic producers or lower prices paid to the immobile factors. In short, a tax's incidence is totally different from a tax's burden. Whether a tax falls on the factor upon which it is levied depends on the supply-and-demand elasticities of the production factors. This is the key point of this discussion. Elasticities determine whether a tax can be passed on to consumers, backward to suppliers, or laterally to other production factors.

The calculus for immobile production factors is a little different.[5] Because, by definition, an immobile factor cannot move across national boundaries, it cannot escape local taxes. So, the rate of return for a fixed factor depends on world demand for the factor's product less domestic taxes. It's possible, through international goods trade, the before-tax returns to the immobile factor can be equalized, but it is clear that the after-tax return cannot. For immobile factors—again, those productions factors physically tied to localities—the after-tax return need not be the same across countries. I can say even more than that: Changes in a country's fiscal policies affect the immobile factors' after-tax return. The important point is the immobile factor acts like a shock absorber. Because a mobile factor has to be compensated at world levels, it follows an immobile factor suffers the burden of all adverse economic shocks. This reality, however, has its side benefit: An immobile factor also captures the complete upside of good economic policy, something a mobile factor cannot do. The perfectly elastic supply curve tells us competition in the world market dissipates any excess rent the mobile-factor army tries to garner. Because the elastic factor is priced in the world market, any attempt to pay this factor a lower salary is met by an outflow, or out-migration, of the factor. Hence, in equilibrium, the local payment to the elastic factor is always the world price grossed up by any local taxes. In contrast, the inelastic factor faces no such competition from the rest of the world. Inelastic factors capture and feel the consequences of both good and bad local-policy actions while mobile factors are affected by neither.

The supply side is not the only source affecting the final equilibrium's elasticity. Substitution effects also occur on the demand side. Take the case of the perfectly elastic demand curve. Assuming an industry producing export goods, increases in domestic tax rates lower the after-tax price local producers receive. If local companies, however, have production facilities outside a taxing jurisdiction, they can completely avoid a tax. As production is shifted outside a country, domestic production unambiguously declines. The question is who pays the local tax. If free trade exists, a good's domestic price has to be the same as the world's price. Because a producer gives a price and the producer's profit margin cannot decline (lest he produce elsewhere), it follows domestic production factors absorb a local tax in the form of lower wages. This is another example of the difference between the taxation's incidence and burden. The producer in this example is able to shift the tax burden backward to domestic production factors.

A final situation in the immediate discussion is one where the demand for a product is perfectly inelastic. The best way to understand this is to visualize a consumer who must have a certain good, and in a certain amount, or else the consumer will die, so to speak. If the consumer receives any less than the minimum required amount of the good, it's all over for the consumer. The consumer in this situation, however, is willing to pay anything for the required amount of the inelastic product. This example helps illustrate the fallacy of conservation as some people espouse it. Suppose you do conserve a product and purchase only the bare minimum needed to survive. Demand in this case is very inelastic. That conservation, however, increases the economy's susceptibility to being exploited by the demanded good's suppliers. Hence, when demand for a product becomes more inelastic, the suppliers' monopoly power increases. This power, in turn, can easily be exploited. I believe this is precisely what happened during the 1970s. The U.S. energy policy increased the demand for foreign oil, although regulations made that demand very inelastic. That gave the monopoly power to OPEC and OPEC went on to exploit it.[6]

In summary, the various supply-and-demand examples suggest small-cap and location (or country) effects are directly connected to the relevant response of reduced elasticities to different policy and regulatory shocks. A related insight has to do with whether companies are able to shift the economic shocks' impact forward or backward.

Global, Regional, and National Companies

Differences in fiscal policies give rise to different real economic performances across countries. In turn, different economic performances can give rise to different real rates of return at the corporate level. The U.S. analogy is quite useful here. Federal fiscal and monetary policy tends to have a common influence on the individual states' economic performances. The dispersion of economic performance among the states, however, is best explained by differences in state fiscal policies as well as the mobility of goods, services, and production factors across states. Looking at investment choices in this context, three types of companies can be identified: truly global, regional, and national.

To classify companies in this way, we need to think of them not only in terms of their relative abundance, but also in terms of the way their total returns are determined. For example, I believe truly global companies are those with sales and production facilities all over the world; profits or production facilities of any one particular region do not dominate such companies. General Electric (GE) is a good fit for this category. GE produces and sells its products all over the world. Thus, one is hard pressed to identify GE strictly as a U.S. company. Looked at from the investor's perspective, when GE is included in a portfolio, some degree of global diversification is being achieved. Taken further, when an investor apportions the sales and production facilities of companies to the various world regions, he can get a handle on how well companies are internationally diversified and exposed before adding them to a portfolio.

Regional companies are those that have placed the bulk of their production facilities within a fiscal or monetary union. For these companies, a region's harmonized fiscal and monetary apparatus has a larger impact on the corporate bottom line than the rest of the world's apparatuses. Such companies either have most of their production and/or sales facilities located within the U.S., the European Monetary Union (EMU) countries, or (to a lesser extent) the Mercosur countries (the southern common market consisting of Argentina, Brazil, Paraguay, and Uruguay).

There are differences within the regional trading blocks as well. A local company is one where an individual state's fiscal policy has a larger impact on corporate valuations than the union's fiscal policies. (In the EMU's case, the individual country is the entity with the greater impact; in the U.S.'s case, state fiscal policies weigh more than federal fiscal policies). In the national company's case, either the bulk of the production or sales facilities are within state borders.[7]

With these three company sets identified, we now have three new factors:

- **The Global Factor**—Some forms of capital, some classes of highly skilled labor, and many aspects of the Internet information-technology phenomenon can be considered truly mobile or capable of highly elastic responses. But companies, often fixed in our minds, can also exhibit a great amount of elasticity. A corporation can have multiple plants and facilities and, as such, can take advantage of the differences in tax and regulation policies across countries. These multinationals, by changing their production plans, can arbitrage tax and regulatory differences across the globe. Meanwhile, prices for these companies are determined in the global economy—that is, prices are determined by world supply-and-demand conditions. National and local conditions can indirectly enter the global company equation, but only if they affect global demand and supply.

- **The Regional Factor**—The development of regional trading blocks has led to the identification of regional factors moving freely within those regional blocks' boundaries. Examples of these blocks include the U.S. and the EMU countries. Currently, the U.S. has total mobility as well as free trade among the states. Euroland also has clear free mobility. For example, European Community passport holders are free to move and relocate within any of the member countries. In addition, trade barriers within the EMU are rapidly coming down with the harmonization of trade policies.

- **The National Factor**—When goods and services are free to move within national economic boundaries, but face some restrictions in the form of transportation costs and/or regulations, the national factor kicks in. The national factor can affect companies large and small, global or local. This can be viewed in terms of immobile production factors. Immobile factors cannot move across national boundaries and thus cannot escape local taxes. Although it's possible that through international trade the before-tax returns to immobile factors can get equalized, the after-tax returns will not.

Before we get to the investment implications of the location effect, we need to set ground rules regarding real rates of return across countries and PPP violations. These are intertwined. As markets are not perfectly correlated, PPP is not complete and international investing produces some additional diversification. As trade barriers come down, however, and the world moves to a global price rule, integrations increase and the diversification effect of international investment declines. We're, of course, not at this point. So, to take advantage of diversification and understand the correlation trends among markets, we must develop a PPP violation theory. The framework of the real exchange rate gets us there. At the macro level, differences in rates of return reflect a violation of PPP, or what some of us call a real-exchange-rate change.

Although it's true the different monetary unions put in place some guidelines that tend to have a common influence on the fiscal policies of member countries (or states), the coordination is not exact. So, the difference in fiscal and monetary policies gives rise to different real economic performances.[8] In turn, the different economic performances can give rise to different real rates of return. Thus, countries adopting pro-growth policies—such as lower or flatter taxation—experience higher levels of economic activity and higher real rates of return. As one country's rates of return increase relative to neighboring countries, the real exchange rate improves and a PPP violation is observed. The country with the higher rate of return then attracts capital and, in time, higher rates of return are eliminated and PPP restored. The simple theory is fiscal or other real economic shocks cause a temporary deviation from PPP, after which capital-flows change to eventually bring about equilibrium. Thus, this framework suggests a simple strategy for taking advantage of changes in real rates of return across countries: Use real exchange rates as the appropriate framework of analysis during a fixed-exchange-rate period.

Viewed this way, a simple and clear portfolio strategy emerges—a strategy that is couched in terms of size and captures the three location factors.

Let's look at larger companies first. For the location strategy, larger companies are to be considered either global or regional. These companies are so large and are located in so many places the impacts of any one country's policies are relatively unimportant. This suggests national issues are less significant for larger companies at the margin. Instead, global shifts impact these companies. I've argued a reduction in trade barriers, lower tax rates, and improved monetary conditions are bullish for both the world economy and larger companies, and competition increases the degree of integration within the world economy. But, larger companies are also best positioned to arbitrage the differences in regulations and/or taxation. The example of DaimlerChrysler helps illustrate this point. If German regulations increase, this company can produce more cars in the U.S. If, on the other hand, U.S. regulations increase, this company can shift production to Europe. GE, General Motors (GM), and other such global companies can put similar tax-and-regulation arbitrage strategies into action. In this way, global companies are best positioned to take advantage of the many changes in the global economy and thus provide the investor some international diversification.

Because larger companies are literally all over the map, a portfolio strategy based on fiscal-policy actions and/or location effects at the national or regional level cannot be fruitful. A more advantageous portfolio strategy for larger corporations can be to focus on the global economic environment and then attempt to identify which industry sectors will benefit from that environment. With this insight in mind, the following should be observable: When a particular large-cap stock shows up on an analyst's value screen, other large-cap stocks in the same industry but located in other countries should also show up. At the same time, some of the domestic large-cap companies in unrelated industries should not show up. This is something value players know all to well. It also suggests value players can have a comparative advantage during the transition to freer trade and a more integrated world economy. International value players have already developed ways to compare profit, income statements, and cash flows across countries. Therefore, they are able to react much more quickly than their competitors during the move to freer trade. It is also fair to point out, however, their advantage diminishes over time: Global competition and freer trade brings about uniform accounting standards, which erodes some of the information edge value players have gathered over the years.

The fact that companies in a particular industry tend to pop up on value screens at the same time all over the world yields another interesting insight. These companies can effectively insulate themselves from the impact of fiscal policies on their relative performance by growing—that is, becoming more global. In so doing, they reduce the potential impact that any one nation or government can have on their bottom lines. Their only exposure is to the economic environment. Viewed this way, the recent transnational merger mania among larger companies within the same industries is easily understood. Market forces are at work. The larger companies that are only getting larger are achieving a degree of location independence helping to insulate them from local economic policies and regulations.

Small-Cap Companies and the Location Effect

Given the world outlook of freer trade, reduced regulation, lower taxes, and stable monetary policies, the forecast for large-cap global companies is quite bullish. As the location (or country) effect is reduced, however, the potential big play at this level is to select the right industry. Today's financial press talks about the phenomenon of a high correlation in industry performance across national borders. So, it follows those investors able to identify correct industry groups are able to increase their returns well above the large-cap average. This strategy, it must be pointed out, is not without risk. If the wrong industry is selected, performance suffers accordingly. But, large-cap international investors and portfolio managers can shift the direction of their analysis to reduce risk: In the current pro-growth global environment, rather than worrying about exchange-rate risk, investors and managers have to compare industries across countries to ascertain both the country effect and whether or not a company is a good candidate for a takeover or merger. For investors and managers who have invested resources in acquiring knowledge on the way to compare companies in different countries, the transition to a freer global economy is a big opportunity to capitalize on this expertise. (Note again this expertise's importance will diminish in coming years, so such investors and managers should make hay while the sun shines.)

For small-cap investors and managers, location will remain a big issue. Unlike large-cap investors and managers, the small-cap group will have to keep track of changes in the fiscal and monetary policies of national economies in relation to regions or the rest of the world. Although pro-growth global trends also benefit smaller companies, the fact that these companies have concentrated production and sales arms suggests there are country-specific effects in addition to the global/regional effect.

I have argued the global/regional effect is the average response to the joint actions of member countries. I have also stated, however, there will be a dispersion of returns around the mean depending on the dispersion of fiscal-policy changes. Thus, by identifying these changes, one can identify the countries that will provide companies with above-average gains. Through careful analysis of the unification of regulations and tax rates, one can identify the proper regions or countries that will outperform. Care must be exercised in stock selection here as there can be some industries that are inexorably linked to a region. This strategy is in fact best played on companies in industries that are abundant across countries.

An Application of the Location-Based Strategy

As a California resident, I have been very close to a situation that serves as a perfect example of the location effect. A few years back, temperatures unexpectedly rose in Southern California. As the heat intensified, people turned on their air conditioners. Combined with the extra energy needed to keep refrigerators cool, the added demand for power outpaced the suppliers' ability to suppliers to deliver. The result was the first in what became a series of rolling blackouts in Southern California.

At the time, I asked: What will the impact of the energy crisis be? How will California companies be affected? I analyzed the situation from the viewpoint that California is an integrated economy and represents one of the largest world economies. This integrated-economy framework enabled me to derive some interesting insights and investment implications.

In an ideal world, absent transportation costs, mobility ensures the equalization of factor-returns across regions. For example, if the return on capital is higher outside California, capital flows out of the state. In the course of leaving the state, the return on capital inside California increases (with less supply) and the differential return between capital in the state and the rest of the world narrows. This process continues until the differential is arbitraged away.

Because the world is not frictionless, however, and transportation and transaction costs do exist, the complete equalization of factor-prices across regions does not materialize. For example, if it costs five cents to transport an orange from California to New York, price differentials in excess of five cents will be arbitraged through the importation and exportation of oranges between the two regions. Differences of less than five cents persist, however, so the arbitrage is not worth the effort. Viewed this way, we can use persistent price differentials as an approximation for transportation costs between localities. Furthermore, these price differentials can also be interpreted as the degree of protection a local economy has against foreign competition. That is, as long as a price charged in-state is below the out-of-state price plus the transportation cost, it is not profitable to arbitrage the difference in prices and no foreign competition (supply) is forthcoming.

This analysis plays into the California example. Looking back, it is apparent environmental regulations were a significant contributor to the California energy crisis. For instance, the focus on clean fuels made it difficult to build plants burning anything other than natural gas. The impact of these policies was to increase demand for natural gas to the point where, on the basis of the British thermal unit (BTU), a standard energy measure, natural gas became a premium fuel. Historically, however, natural gas had sold at a discount to light crude oil.

The good news for California was arbitrage happened and more power came to the state. The high rate of return for energy mobilized market forces in a way that reduced transportation costs. More, easing environmental regulations going forward allow for the burning of fuels other than natural gas. This obviously helps on the equation's supply side, with the long-run implication being natural gas will return to its historical status and the demand for coal and nuclear fuels will rise. In this, we have an initial investment implication: Given the lead time for building power plants, it is likely coal will fare better in the medium-term, although nuclear power will be the longer-term play.

In the short run, a focus on arbitraging regional differences is of critical importance when applying the location effect to an investment strategy. In the case of the California crisis, delivery mechanisms represented the regional difference. There were simply two ways of acquiring the needed energy. One way was to import the energy itself. The other way was to import fuel to generate the energy. The problem in California was that the pipelines transporting natural gas were running at full capacity. Hence, it was virtually impossible to increase that supply. Energy itself needed to be imported.

Now, let's take the California example a few steps farther. So far, I have focused on the direct arbitrage of the differences in energy costs across regions. One can indirectly arbitrage these differences, however, through trade in goods. For example, companies with multiple plant facilities can take advantage of the differences in energy prices across regions if they have facilities located in lower energy-priced areas. All they need to do is shift their production facilities to those lower-cost areas and in so doing avoid the areas where energy costs are higher—or worse, an area suffering through an energy crisis. Obviously, the ultimate step in shifting facilities is to leave a state altogether. For companies unable to relocate, the impact of higher energy prices can be measured by taking an integrated-economy view. Let's assume California is not large enough to alter the prices of goods and services in the world economy. In this case, the prices received for California's goods and services outside the state are a given. Meanwhile, the mobile factors in the economy—capital, for instance, or highly skilled labor— migrate to arbitrage differences in prices and are paid at the national rate. Given that the prices of final products and the rewards to mobile factors are determined in the national economy, neither will be affected by local market conditions. Hence, a rise in energy prices reduces the returns to the immobile production factors—one for one. What constitutes an immobile factor depends on the situation. In California, real estate is one such factor. Inner-city labor, it can be strongly argued, is also quite immobile. It follows, due to the circumstances in California, real estate and lower-skilled workers underperform in the state. To the extent that government assistance to lower-income people must increase, one can project the financial health of the state will deteriorate and taxes will increase.

In addition to immobile production factors, there are also immobile production facilities. For whatever reason, some companies cannot shift their production outside a state when it would be beneficial for them to do so. The simplest reason why is they do not already have production facilities outside their home states. The most direct way to identify companies in this category is to classify those with single-plant facilities. Ideally, an investor should do this for all the stocks in the S&P 1500 universe. That's an arduous task, however, and for the sake of the California example, I used a short cut.

I began the process of ascertaining corporate immobility in California by identifying the headquarter locations of all the stocks in the S&P 1500, the underlying assumption being these are most likely the companies to be most affected by the economic environment in California. I identified 247 companies with headquarters in California—77 large-cap companies, 64 mid-caps, and 106 small-caps. The cap-weighted returns of the three portfolios for a sample period in 2001 are reported in Table 10.1. As expected, each portfolio underperformed its respective benchmark. Because California has a large concentration of high-tech companies, and because the blackouts occurred around the time the tech bubble burst, a high-tech effect had to be taken into account. To control this effect, I excluded computer and electronic companies and the remaining companies' returns. As expected, tech stocks underperformed and exhibited a disproportionate effect—especially on the large-cap portfolio. Once the tech stocks were excluded, however, the relative performance of the remaining California-based large-cap companies was reversed. In fact, the performance of the portfolio consisting of nontech large-cap California companies was virtually identical to that of the benchmark (that is, the S&P 500). As I mentioned earlier, larger corporations, or large-capitalization stocks, are more likely than not to have production facilities outside of their home states. Hence, the California effect has been much weaker for California's large-caps.

Table 10.1

Performance of size-related portfolios of California-headquartered companies during the California energy crisis: January 2001–April 2001.

	All	Nontech	Benchmark
Large	−26.14%	−9.53%	−9.73%
Mid	−8.58%	−11.12%	−7.99%
Small	−10.54%	−12.52%	−5.69%

Source: Research Insight

But to truly identify the California factor, one needs to apportion some part of production to California. To do this, one needs to make a simple generalization: The smaller the company, the greater the likelihood it is a true state-specific company. Hence, a down and dirty way to identify the true California companies is to focus on smaller-cap stocks. The data confirm the underperformance of nontech California companies increases as one moves down the size scale. The California-based large-caps were even with the S&P 500 for our sample period. The California mid-caps lagged the S&P 400 by 3.13 percent. The California small-caps lagged the S&P 600 by 6.93 percent. Based on the evidence presented here, I conclude looking at the location of production facilities is a sound way to begin isolating the effect of the California energy crisis on the state's companies—or, for that matter, to begin isolating location effects for any company.

The results are fairly conclusive. Large-caps are able to ensure against localized shocks. A corollary is that large-caps are not able to fully capture the impact of beneficial localized shocks unless they shift all their production to the locality. If they can't do that, the small-caps located in a region undergoing beneficial shocks outperform. This small-cap effect shows the exact way to take advantage of location/country effects. It also raises a concern regarding large-caps trying to become location-independent. If we again assume the various world markets will consolidate so they are dominated by a few global companies, it follows location will become irrelevant for large-cap managers. Large-caps will become truly global concerns, and to some extent, they will become location/country independent. At this point, the concept of global investment will become meaningless at the large-company level and the relevant framework for company selection will be sectoral or industry-specific.

The Location Strategy: A Global Perspective

The financial pages of most newspapers and magazines gave almost no hints developed markets would post high single-digit gains for the 2004 calendar year, according to the Morgan Stanley Capital Index (MSCI), while emerging-market gains would reach the high teens (see Table 10.2). Concerns about high energy prices, a weaker dollar, twin deficits in the U.S., and terrorism in different parts of the world were not strong enough to overwhelm the positive developments taking place in the world economy. Viewing economic expansion, the spike in oil prices, terrorism, and the effect of the weaker dollar as different economic shocks, it follows the impact of each on the various world economies depended on the differences in regional supply-and-demand elasticities.

Table 10.2
Global stock markets or national stock markets 2004 returns in dollars.*

Developed Markets	Percent	Emerging Markets	Percent
Europe	17.8	Asia	12.2
Far East	15.2	Europe and Middle East	28.8
Nordic Countries	25.0	Far East	11.7
North America	9.4	Latin America	34.8
Pacific	17.2	Emerging Markets	22.4
World	12.8		
U.S.	8.8	China	−0.001
Japan	14.7	India	16.4
Germany	14.3		
Norway	49.6	Indonesia	44.5
		Mexico	45.0
		Venezuela	45.4
		Russia	4.1
Canada	20.5	Chile	24.5
Australia	26.6	South Africa	40.7
New Zealand	29.8		
Ireland	39.2	Czech Republic	76.6
Greece	41.2	Poland	58.6
Hong Kong	20.8	Taiwan	6.5

continues

* The figures included in this table are percentages.

Table 10.2 continued

Developed Markets	Percent	Emerging Markets	Percent
Finland	3.9	Pakistan	8.6
		Philippines	24.1
		Thailand	−4.0
		Sri Lanka	7.8
		Colombia	125.6
		Israel	18.4

Source: Morgan Stanley Capital Index

For 2004, all the regional stock indices—both developed- and emerging-market—posted positive returns in U.S. dollars. The global economic expansion produced higher worldwide profits and equity values. Country-specific actions in China and Thailand played a big part in this. China's central bank, trying to engineer a soft economic landing for the country, imposed a 100 percent reserve requirement on all its banks (in other words, it forced the banks to stop lending). That measure alone clearly slowed China's economic growth below levels it would have otherwise reached in 2004. Thailand, meanwhile, followed an appeasement policy toward terrorism that paralyzed private-sector initiatives. Not all the developments in 2004, however, were negative. There was no inflation and the world economy appeared to be on its way to higher real gross domestic product (GDP) growth. Both were bullish factors.

Absent regional barriers, trade and migration arbitrages regional differences across countries, producing a tendency for regional stock markets to move together. Yet one peculiar feature of the regional indices' performance and the individual country stock markets reported in Table 10.2 is in each region, the anchor country underperformed its respective regional indices. That was the case for the U.S., Germany, and Japan in the developed-market regional indices, and for China in the emerging-market regional indices. The story for 2004 seems to have been peripheral countries outperformed their centers.

Let's look at the individual global shocks for 2004 and measure the impact of each on regional stock-index performance.

OIL

All the regional anchor countries—the U.S., Japan, Germany, and China—are oil importers. Hence, it is safe to argue an abrupt rise in oil prices has a negative impact on these economies vis-à-vis their regional counterparts. A corollary to this line of reasoning is the oil-producing countries within the different regions should be stellar performers. This was the case for the developed countries in 2004, as per the regional indices. For instance, Norway, with a 49.6 percent gain, clearly outperformed the 25 percent gain of the Nordic Countries index. The story repeated itself in the emerging-market regional indices. Indonesia (+44.5 percent) outperformed Asia (+12.2 percent). Mexico (+45 percent) and Venezuela (+45.4 percent) outperformed the Latin American regional index (+34.8 percent). Russia, with a 4.1 percent rise, was the sole exception—it lagged the 28.8 percent gain of the European, Middle Eastern, and African index. In large part, the decline in the Russian market was due to the government's attempt to nationalize Yukos, the giant oil producer. In addition, the signals the Putin government sent have been neither pro-market nor pro-democracy, so it's no wonder the Russian stock market has responded negatively.

There are two distinct arguments in the financial press regarding the origins of the surge in oil prices. One combines the belief that the oil supply is dwindling with the notion of a terrorist risk-premium. The other holds a rise in oil consumption is due to a growing world economy. Those who believe oil supplies are drying up argue there will be a secular increase in oil prices, and would be hard pressed to argue for an abrupt increase in the price of oil unless there was an unexpected surge in consumption due to a growing economy. If they took this latter position, they would be caught in a bit of a trap. They'd have to argue the rising price of oil would choke the world economy. From there, they'd have to admit once the economy slowed down, oil prices would fall, stimulating growth once again. At that point, their low-supply position would have fully unraveled. No, the increase in oil prices has been due to higher growth. It is a bullish story, and one explaining the rise in world equity markets with the oil-producing nations rising more than the oil-consuming nations.

COMMODITIES

A surge in world economic growth is the only explanation for the rise in oil prices, and this reasoning applies to higher commodity prices in general. Commodity-based economies, such as Canada, New Zealand, and Australia in the developed-market category, and Chile and South Africa in the emerging-market category, all outperformed their regional-market indices in 2004 (see Table 10.2). Simply put, growth goes a long way toward explaining the surge in commodity prices and the relative performance of regional and national stock markets.

The markets have been sending a clear message: Countries that succeed in the battle against terror will be handsomely rewarded, and those that perpetuate the problem through appeasement will be punished. The data clearly point to areas where the rewards are being handed out. In Colombia, where one might say the war on drugs has met the war on terror, terrific strides have been made in restoring order. In response, Colombia's stock exchange has posted gains beyond expectations: It more than doubled during calendar 2004. In the Philippines, the government has shown some backbone against resident terrorists and the market has responded with gains well above the region's average (that is, 24.1 percent versus 12.2 percent). In contrast, countries following the appeasement route, such as Thailand, have seen their stock markets post large negative declines. Such relative performance could be a good guide for some of the hot spots in the Middle East.

TAX RATES

New European countries, such as Ireland and Greece, have outperformed Europe's developed-market index (see Table 10.2) for good reason—they lowered tax rates. For the same reason, the Czech Republic and Poland have outperformed Europe's emerging-market index. The largest and slowest-growing countries in Old Europe have been pushing for tax harmonization as a way to force New Europe to raise tax rates and erode any advantage New Europe countries may have. But, the New Europeans have taken a cue from Ireland and haven't budged. The financial markets, on the climb in New Europe, are sending a clear message: Flexibility and low tax rates are the way to economic growth.

The Elements of Location-Based Strategies

The performance of the different regional stock markets suggests democracy, well-defined property rights, and market-oriented government policies combine to bring about economic well-being. Many world regions are clearly moving in this direction, which is a bullish story for the world economy. So, paying attention to political and economic developments worldwide is a perfunctory step in a global asset-allocation strategy.

Reductions in trade barriers, lower tax rates, and improved monetary conditions are bullish for the world economy in the sense that they increase competition and thus increase the degree of the individual world economies' integration. For a cyclical asset allocation (CAA) strategy to capture this global effect, it must be couched in terms of size and take into account both location and industry effects. As larger companies tend to be located in so many places, any one country's policies' impact is relatively unimportant. Thus, national issues are less significant at the margin for larger companies. Rather, global shifts impact larger companies. In this way, global companies are best positioned to capture many of the changes going on in the global economy, thus providing a portfolio with some international diversification. This insight has an interesting application where size can be used to offset location effects without having to significantly alter a country's overall portfolio allocation. Take Japan's case during the last decade. The unambiguous consensus among investors and most wire houses was the Japanese market would underperform the world market. This forecast's obvious asset-allocation implication was to underweight Japan in a global portfolio. If one looks at the global portfolios of the wire houses over the last decade, however, the allocation to Japan was always in the neighborhood of the Japanese global weight. In other words, the global allocation to Japan was a neutral allocation—not an underweight. But, I contend these allocations were effectively underweighting the Japanese exposure. The reason for this is most recommended Japanese stocks were the larger blue-chips. If one looks back at these companies, a large portion of their sales and production facilities were located outside Japan. In short, the Japan exposure of the wire-house portfolios was much less than the allocations to the large Japanese companies.

Companies with multi-plant facilities are able to take advantage of the differences in operating prices across regions if they have facilities located in lower-priced areas. All they need to do is shift their production facilities to those areas when those areas will provide greater returns to the bottom line. Obviously, the ultimate step in shifting facilities is leaving a country. Companies that cannot do this suffer the full brunt of policy mistakes, but also enjoy favorable policy actions' full impact. In practice, the easiest way to identify these companies is to mark those with single-plant facilities. But, an even easier method is to identify small companies in general; smaller companies are simply less likely to have production facilities outside of a state or a country.

One conclusion we can draw at this point is small-cap international investors and portfolio managers have the potential to earn higher rates of return than their large-cap counterparts, and small-cap investors and managers with regional focuses or biases are positioned to generate the best performance. More specifically, the small-cap strategy with the greatest return potential is the one focusing on location and attempts to maintain a neutral industry focus. We can go back to Japan for an example of this. In a paper written a few years back, I pointed out Japan was planning a reduction in marginal tax rates, from about 65 percent to about 50 percent.[9] This meant a profitable company in Japan, without changing its behavior or production plans, would increase its after-tax cash flow on production from 35 cents to 50 cents, a 42 percent increase. The story, however, does not end here. Dynamic effects would also occur: The behavior of Japanese companies would also change to take advantage of higher after-tax cash flows. As both production and profits would increase, the impact on a particular company's cash flow would depend on its share of Japanese operations. Thus, the Japanese tax-rate cuts would have a larger impact on the after-tax cash flows of smaller (that is, national) companies. At the time, the investment implication was straightforward. All Japanese-based companies would rise in value, with smaller-caps gaining the most. Looking at the performance of the Japanese stock market during 1999, the overall market climbed about 50 percent while the Japanese small-cap index rocketed well over 100 percent. It's abundantly clear, although the larger Japanese global companies did well, the smaller Japanese companies did even better. Investing in smaller companies is the way to play the country effect.

My own native Dominican Republic (D.R.) offers another illustration of this. With the opening of trade in the D.R., it became clear many of the Dominican agricultural operations would not be able to compete with the U.S., as the D.R. would be much better off importing rice and many other staples. The early question was: What would the Dominican farmers produce? Some smart producers answered this. They recognized instead of going toe-to-toe with U.S. producers by growing the usual staples, they would be better off specializing in niche markets. But which ones? They quickly discovered developed countries are quite interested in organically grown products. More important, they learned organically grown products sell at a premium.

The organic market continues to be a great opportunity for D.R. farmers. It enables local growers to save on chemical fertilizers, which are very expensive, while the decline in production has been proven to be much less than that of U.S. farmers who have switched to organic methods. Historically, D.R. farmers have used chemicals less intensively than U.S. farmers, so they enjoyed a clear competitive advantage over U.S. organic growers coming out of the gate.

Summary

Natural endowments, government regulations, and many other variables combine to create pockets of market segmentation and product differentiation. It is in these markets smaller-cap stocks have the greatest advantage. They are nimble and can adjust faster than large-caps to changing market conditions. In the global perspective, it is in fact at the small-cap level democratic capitalism flourishes, giving competitive opportunities to emerging nations. Local entrepreneurs develop products for niche markets. As they become successful over time, they expand the scale of their operations and move into more conventional markets. In the process, these companies can even join the large-cap universe. So, it is at the niche level smart investors must isolate regional differences due to government regulations and other country-specific factors. Alternatively stated, it is at the small-cap level the country effect is most pronounced.

11

EYE ON ELASTICITY

W hether national economic polices affect a company depends, in large part, on the company's supply-and-demand elasticities. In the previous chapter, I argued some companies are so large and located in so many places the impact of any one country's fiscal, monetary, or regulatory policies is relatively unimportant. Thus, when national issues are less significant at the margin, only by global shifts (to a great extent) impact a company. Because larger companies are literally all over the map, a portfolio strategy based on policy actions and/or corporate locations at the national or regional level may not be fruitful, although a more advantageous strategy may be to focus on the global economic environment and attempt to identify which sectors benefit from that environment. Although the size analysis is an appropriate and simple way to identity companies for which national economic concerns are not as important as global economic concerns, it is not the only way to capture this effect. Identifying the international mobility of production factors within industries, along with the mobility of goods and services across national boundaries, is important as well. The greater this mobility, the more a local industry can insulate itself from local economic shocks.[1]

Elasticity and Profitability: Airlines

Industries unable to easily alter production plans (for example, industries with inelastic supply) change their prices to accommodate fluctuations in demand (see Figure 11.1). A classic example of an inelastic industry was the airline industry before it was deregulated in 1978. Largely due to government restrictions, airlines were unable to easily expand their supply when there was increased demand. As a consequence, when more people wanted to travel, ticket prices rose. For inelastic industries, profitability and share prices primarily reflect changes in demand. Generally, forecasting changes in the level of economic activity or economic conditions to predict aggregate demand is critically important to the cyclical investor. A close look at the airline industry's experience demonstrates this point.

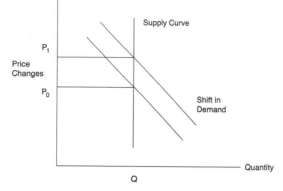

Figure 11.1   Inelastic industry: price changes in response to a shift in demand.

Deregulation, as per the U.S. Airline Deregulation Act of 1978, changed the shape of the airline industry's supply curve. New carriers' entry almost instantly increased competition and industry prices became more elastic. Demand, in short, was largely met with the new airlines' arrival. Once a scheduled flight was operational, independent of which airline was flying it, empty seats drove the market. With an occupancy rate below 100 percent, the marginal cost of filling the extra seat was very low. So, competition for the marginal, elastic passengers pushed coach tickets' marginal price down. The industry lost most—if not all—of its pricing power in the mass market. Fluctuations in demand following deregulation were satisfied primarily by altering production levels without the industry experiencing significant changes in profitability (see Figure 11.2).

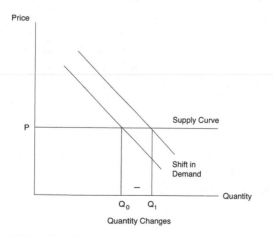

Figure 11.2   Elastic industry: quantity changes in response to a shift in demand.

To its credit, the airline industry didn't stand still. Over time, and with the aid of computers, airlines have learned to predict almost to the person the demand for each flight by passenger class. Armed with this knowledge, airlines are now able to alter the different classes' availability (that is, fares) on each flight to maximize revenues. They charge a higher price to the inelastic traveler (for example, the business traveler, who must be in a specific place at a specific time) and a lower price to the elastic traveler (for example, the leisure traveler, who is typically flexible as to destination and timeframe, and often adjusts travel plans to keep expenses as low as possible). In so doing, airlines effectively move along their demand curve; they have altered the price structure in such a way as to fill each flight.

Unfortunately, however, the airlines have not been able to escape demand function realities. An elastic demand means little or no opportunity is available for excess profit unless you are the low-cost provider. Older airlines with unionized workforces have not been able to lower their cost structures, and thus the newer airlines with younger and less-costly structures have gained significant market share. The older established airlines have been teetering on the edge of bankruptcy while the low-cost airlines seem to thrive.

The moral of the story, at least for investors, is clear: To identify industries likely to outperform the market in general, we must first decide whether demand for an industry's product will rise or fall and then whether an industry has pricing power (be it on the demand or supply side).

The airline industry tells us elasticity depends in part on government regulation and in part on industry-specific innovation. I've used this approach over the years while conducting numerous industry-specific analyses.[2] By focusing on an industry's ability to react to economic shocks (technological advances, regulatory changes, and so on), I have witnessed the way changes in elasticity have generally been gradual and predictable. I've also seen, almost without exception, similar shocks cause similar industry results and stock-price performance varies with industry elasticity. As I mentioned, inelastic industries initially adjust to demand shifts by varying prices while keeping output levels roughly constant. Consequently, inelastic industries' profits are very sensitive to demand shifts in the short run. Investors and portfolio managers would obviously prefer to hold inelastic industries facing rising demand and elastic industries experiencing declining market conditions.

Elasticity and Profitability: Tax Rate Changes

Indeed, investors and financial managers need to watch elasticities at all times. Before the enactment of the Tax Reform Act of 1986, which eliminated the investment tax credit, lengthened depreciation schedules, and made other changes to business taxation, most financial analysts focused on the different industries' capital intensity. They reasoned if an industry was capital intensive, that industry's tax payments would rise. As a result, stock prices in that sector would be depressed. Similarly, if an industry was labor intensive, tax payments would fall and stock prices would rise. At the time, I argued this reasoning was flawed because it ignored the difference between the initial incidence and the final tax burden. The person (or company) upon whom a tax is levied can well experience no loss in net income if he passes the tax forward onto consumers or backward onto suppliers. Likewise, a person upon whom no tax has been levied can well suffer large net income losses as a consequence of taxes levied on others. (This analysis was correct, and I will soon get to the results.) In the words of Noble Laureate Paul Samuelson,

> Even if the electorate has made up its mind about how the tax burden shall be borne by individuals, the following difficult problems remain: Who ultimately pays a particular tax? Does its burden stay on the person on whom it is first levied? One cannot assume that the person Congress says a tax is levied on will end up paying that tax. He may be able to shift the tax; He may be able to shift it "forward" on his costumers by raising his price as much as the tax; or shift it "backwards" on his suppliers (wage earners, rent and interest receivers) who end up being able to charge him less than they would have done had there been no tax. Economists therefore say: We must study the final incidence of the tax totality of its effect on commodity prices, factor-prices, resource allocations, efforts, and composition of production and consumption. Tax incidence, thus, is no easy problem and requires all the advanced tools of economics to help towards its solution.[3]

The Relationship Between Elasticity and Beta

As inelastic industries are not able to quickly adjust their production schedules during demand shocks, it follows inelastic industries' profitability fluctuate along with demand shocks. During rising demand periods, industry profits go through the roof—although during below-average demand cycles, industries

---

unambiguously underperform. The airline example, in particular, shows the way government regulation can significantly alter an industry's response functions to changing demand conditions. But, in the same way, technological innovations and other variables can affect an industry's supply and/or aggregate demand functions.

The supply-and-demand analysis sheds light on the beta and alpha concepts, where the beta coefficient measures a portfolio's systematic risk in relation to the market overall, and the alpha coefficient measures excess return, or the return over that required to compensate for systematic risk. Inelastic industries generate excess return. Excess return, however, can be fairly volatile for most industries (a high beta situation). Excess return is large and positive during rising excess demand periods, and large and negative during declining excess demand periods. Positive alpha industries can be characterized as both inelastic and experiencing secular aggregate demand, which can come as the result of technological innovation, government regulation, or a number of other factors. In a positive alpha situation, demand increases for an industry, although (due to supply constraints) the industry cannot accommodate all the increase in demand. Hence, prices ration the available output.

Investors who pay attention to government regulations and technological innovations are able to anticipate industry responses to aggregate demand shocks. In doing so, they are able to anticipate changes in the various industries' alpha and beta coefficients and, from there, implement a successful industry-selection strategy.

A clear application of this comes at the country level. Government regulations and economic policies determine, in part, supply-and-demand elasticities for countries, just as for industries. In a world economy, the countries' sum of monetary and fiscal policies determines, to some degree, the demand for a country. Trade policy partly determines the mobility of goods and services along with production factors across national borders. In short, regulatory and tax polices partially determine the elasticity of responses to changing economic conditions.

Investment Implications

To complete this analysis, I focus on the economic environment to determine when there are relative increases in demand for a country's goods and services. When this is the case, I expect to see a higher rate of return for the industries producing inelastic goods and services—which I contend are nontraded goods. In any event, the degree of inelasticity is reflected as a deviation from purchasing power parity (in other words, when there is a deviation from the exchange-rate equivalence between currencies) or, alternatively stated, a real-exchange-rate appreciation.

I have argued selecting small companies with markets consisting solely of the local market is a very simple and efficient way to capture the country effect. Although it is true the proper way to focus on the country effect is to analyze company responsiveness to changing economic conditions, choosing small-caps as a way of capturing the country effect is a first-order approximation that works well. In this way, we can identify inelastic companies based on their locations and their products' tradability. Finally, in the context of the traditional financial literature, I have produced a simple explanation as to why international small-cap stocks are high beta stocks that produce high returns during rising aggregate demand periods and underperform during economic slowdown periods.

An Elasticity-Based Portfolio Strategy

To develop and implement a successful industry portfolio strategy, we need to identify changing market conditions (that is, industry demand) as well as different industries' ability to capture shocks or pass on the impact to consumers. The methodology for industry selection is fairly straightforward. Given a future economic environment's forecast, I set out to find previous instances where either similar or directly opposite shocks occurred. The rationale is industry groups respond to shocks in the same manner. Put another way, industries behave in a similar way when experiencing comparable shocks. Opposite events also contain information as they provide an inverse ranking of the relative performance expected under a forecast scenario.

Since the early 1980s, my research has focused on economic policy's impact on industry performance. I first outlined this strategy's basic elements in a series of papers published in the *Financial Analyst Journal* (*FAJ*).[4] At the time, I argued industry elasticities needed to be taken into account by analysts and the easiest way to determine elasticity responses was to look at the way the combination of profits and employment reacted to economic shocks. In the *FAJ*, I outlined a methodology for measuring *capital tax sensitivity* (CATS). I argued an industry's sensitivity to tax changes depends on the elasticities (that is, the industries' ability to alter production and shift taxes forward to consumers or backward to suppliers) and not capital intensity (or the concentration of capital in an industry). I argued this was the best way to select the industry groups that would benefit from the Reagan tax-rate cuts, which landed in 1986 and became fully effective by 1988. For 1987, I predicted low-CATS industries would be top performers and high-CATS industries would perform poorly as a result of the changes in the tax laws. If substitution effects were important, as I anticipated, low-CATS industries would be outstanding performers even if they were capital intensive (that is, even if the taxes paid by these industries increased more than average corporate tax payments as a result of the tax reform). High-CATS industries, meanwhile, would be relative laggards even if they were labor intensive (that is, even if their tax payments declined or increased below the average).

High-CATS industries provided the test for the two approaches. The evidence presented in Table 11.1 clearly supports the CATS approach. Low-capital-intensive, high-CATS industries, which—according to the conventional wisdom—were expected to benefit from the Reagan tax reform, gained an average of only 3.74 percent. Capital-intensive, low-CATS industries, which were expected to be hurt by the tax reform, gained an average of 15.36 percent. The elasticities' significant impact is undeniable. Following the Reagan tax-rate cuts, low-CATS industries underperformed the market while high-CATS industries outperformed. Investors and portfolio managers choosing to ignore the substitution effects resulting from elastic responses do so at their peril.

Table 11.1
Capital tax sensitivity versus capital intensity: 1987 performance of Standard & Poor's stock indexes.*

High-CATS/ Low-Capital-Intensive Industries	Percent	Low-CATS/ High-Capital-Intensive Industries	Percent
Beverages/Brewers	24.24	Agricultural Machinery	53.90*
Beverages/Soft Drinks	8.43	Aluminum	9.09
Computer and Business	7.52	Banks/NYC	−29.15
Computer Services	7.31	Banks/Outside NYC	−21.89
Department Stores	−16.55	Coal/Bituminous	−14.15
Entertainment	19.69	Containers/Paper	9.30**
Foods	2.94	Copper	−0.48
Hospital Management	−1.22	Gold Mining	55.68

High-CATS/ Low-Capital-Intensive Industries	Percent	Low-CATS/ High-Capital-Intensive Industries	Percent
Hospital Supplies	4.55	Machine Tools	0.61
Leisure	−13.11	Machinery/Specialty	35.03
Publishing	9.34	Metals/Miscellaneous	19.70**
Radio/TV Broadcasters	35.97	Metals/Nonferrous	43.90**
Restaurants	−3.22	Oil Well and Service	−0.48
Retail Food Chains	2.94	Oil/Offshore Drilling	26.98
Tobacco	6.93	Paper	6.98
Toy Manufacturers	−35.93	Railroads	9.09
		Steel	56.99
Average	3.74	Average	15.36
S&P 500	2.01		

* The figures included in this table are percentages.

** Investor's Daily stock index performance

Source: Financial Analyst Journal, September/October 1988

Over the years, I have updated and improved my approach to identify those industries that would see increased demand for their products under changing economic parameters. But just as important to the investor is how well an industry can respond to changing demand. I have watched this, too, and I believe the any macroeconomic shock's ultimate burden depends on an industry's supply-and-demand elasticities as well as the nature of the shock itself.

Using historical evidence, I have developed a classification for identifying the way each industry performs under different economic conditions. In particular, I have examined the different industries' output, employment, and price responses over time. Industries that respond to shocks with above-average employment increases and below-average profit gains are identified in my classification as elastic industries. In turn, industries that respond to shocks with below-average employment increases and above-average profitability gains are classified as inelastic. The implications for industry selection are obvious. Investors will love to identify inelastic industries experiencing positive demand shocks. By a positive demand shock, I mean demand is increasing, and by inelastic, I mean output is not increasing that much. Hence, inelastic industries undergoing demand shocks have to eliminate excess demand through price increases (see Figure 11.1). In short, inelastic industries have pricing power and an increase in demand means higher profits. (People often argue such pricing power is analogous to a taxing power, but more on that later.) Conversely, investors will want to avoid inelastic industries—the stocks of companies in inelastic industries are what the financial literature call high beta stocks—undergoing or projected to undergo adverse or negative shocks, such as a falloff in demand. When an industry is inelastic, it is difficult for its companies to adjust production; when there is a decline in demand, that decline has to be eliminated through lower prices.

Unlike investors, governments love elastic industries (that is, industries with a beta in the neighborhood of one, the same as the market) witnessing an increase in demand. The reason for this is, although there are little or no additional profits in this scenario, employment can be increased in very short order. The *maquiladoras* in the emerging markets are a perfect example of this. These elastic manufacturing and assembly plants number in the thousands—having greatly increased in number over the last decade—and employ a large number of laborers.

An Application: The Oil Price Hike

It is apparent investors have to acquire two pieces of information to develop a successful industry-selection strategy: They need to know the shift in aggregate demand for industry goods and services. They also need to figure out the nature of the supply response (that is, elastic or inelastic). Once these two variables are known, one can make inferences as to an industry's beta (that is, systematic risk compared to that of the overall market) and determine whether it will experience rising or falling demand as the result of the economic environment. From all this, a common-sense strategy emerges: Buy inelastic (high-beta) industries undergoing positive shocks and short inelastic (high-beta) industries undergoing negative shocks. Elastic industries (with a beta of one) will always be market performers. They play an important role, however, in this strategy: They provide insurance against an aggregate-demand forecast's accuracy, as an incorrect forecast could lead one to select the worst-performing industries.

To illustrate the sort of thinking that goes into producing an accurate aggregate-demand forecast, I look to a recent case of an inaccurate forecast. Coming off repeated record highs, a barrel of oil's price shot up more than 5 percent during May 2004. Early the next month, the barrel price shattered the $42 mark, prompting concerns high-and-rising oil prices would jeopardize the economic recovery. The bearish reasoning featured the following: If consumers and companies pay more for energy, they will buy less of something else; oil-price increases are like a tax on business; oil's higher price reduce the economy's aggregate demand, which in turn produces lower gross domestic product (GDP).

The Equivalence Between a Supply Shift and a Tax on Oil

Let's investigate the extent to which an oil price increase has on added-tax effect on the economy. A tax increase drives a wedge between the price consumers paid and the price suppliers received. Graphically, a tax increase's effect can be depicted as a supply curve's upward shift, where the vertical distance between the two supply curves is the tax's amount (see Figure 11.3a). Consumers facing a higher price (P^*) move upward along the demand curve and cut back on their purchases. Consumption of the taxed commodity falls to Q_1 from Q_0. Suppliers facing a lower price (P_1) reduce the quantity delivered to the market place. Because consumers want to buy a lower quantity and suppliers want to sell a lower quantity, the new equilibrium requires that a lower quantity is transacted. The difference between the price the consumer paid (P^*) and the price the suppliers paid (P_1) denotes the marginal tax rate while the new quantity transacted denotes the tax base. The product of the two denotes the tax revenues collected (the rectangle P^*–B–D–P_1). Finally, the triangle e–D–P_1 denotes the profits the suppliers generated.

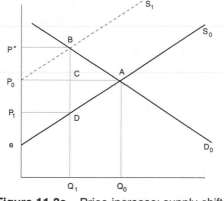

Figure 11.3a   Price increase: supply shift.

Figure 11.3a shows a leftward shift of the supply curve is equivalent, in effect, to a tax increase. So, in both cases, the price consumers paid increases and output decreases. A monopolist, or a cartel, exploits its market power by curtailing the quantity of the good it supplies. Graphically, the monopolist gets to collect tax revenues (the rectangle P^*–B–D–P1) and the production profits (the triangle e–D–P_1). One can see the incentive: By curtailing output, the monopolist gets to collect a higher profit.

Graphically, one can also show a price decline resulting from a supply shift is analogous to a subsidy (see Figure 11.3b). A new equilibrium produces a higher quantity transacted (Q_1) with consumers paying a lower price (P_1). The triangle f–B–P_1 denotes the profits the supplier generated and the rectangle P^*–D–B–P_1 denotes the subsidy's cost.

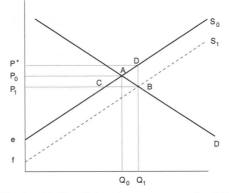

Figure 11.3b   Price decrease: supply shift.

Price hikes that the supply shifts generate are indeed analogous to tax increases and result in lower output and lower overall profits (see Figure 11.3a). But those who argue a price hike acts like a tax hike are implicitly assuming the disturbance that causes the new equilibrium is a supply shift. Supply shifts, however, are not the only disturbances in a market. Demand shifts can be equally important. Figures 11.3c and 11.3d show demand shifts produce a positive relationship between the change in equilibrium price and quantity. More important, under a demand shift (see Figure 11.3c), one can show the higher price leads to higher output (Q_1) and higher profits. The trapezoid P_0–A–B–P_1 denotes the increment in profits the new equilibrium produces.

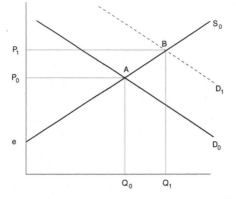

Figure 11.3c Price increase: demand shift.

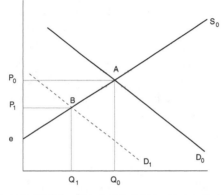

Figure 11.3d Price decrease: demand shift.

Demand and Supply Shifts: Their Different Investment Implications

The moral of the story so far is price changes alone do not provide sufficient evidence of an equivalence between prices and tax changes. The nature of a price shift is an important piece of information. If a demand shift generates a price change, one gets a very different outlook than if a supply shift generates a price change. Some supply/demand shifts are quite bullish while others are quite bearish. For example, the recent increase in the price of oil and other commodities has a bearish slant if interpreted as a supply shift and a quite bullish slant if interpreted as a demand shift. On the other hand, a tech price decline is quite bullish when interpreted as a supply shift and quite bearish when the result of a demand shift.

Recent arguments point to the idea that supply shifts were the source of increased oil prices and were in part based on short-term fluctuations—such as strife in oil-rich Venezuela and production shortfalls in Iraq. They were also based in part on more permanent factors, such as geologist Marion King Hubbert's belief that the life of any oil well resembles a bell-shaped curve; that production increases to a peak by the time half the oil is pumped—and, after that, production inexorably declines. The supply-shift argument was also grounded in the idea the Organization of the Petroleum Exporting Countries (OPEC) is an effective cartel. All these factors (went the reasoning) contributed to an inward shift in the world oil supply and (all else being the same) higher prices followed (see Figure 11.3a).

Although it makes sense to assume normal oil-producing conditions will return to Venezuela and Iraq, the global outlook is very grim if one buys into Hubbert's theory. Applying the theory, the secular trend is for the oil supply to decline and for the supply curve to become less elastic, which would thus increase OPEC's monopoly power. At the margin, OPEC's incentive will always be to curtail output. But, a totally different interpretation of events is produced by the belief high energy prices are due to a demand shift. The argument is simple: World prosperity has led to an increase in the demand for oil. New players on the world scene, such as China and India, have shifted the world demand for oil farther out (see Figure 11.3c). Adding in the fact technology is less efficient in emerging economies than in developed countries, it is easy to see why the new players will incrementally use more British thermal units (BTUs) per unit of GDP than developed countries use.

The fact commodity prices have risen and remained strong during the period of increased oil prices is more evidence of a demand shift. Finally, for those who still believe in the OPEC cartel's power, I have a simple question: Why is the price of oil in constant dollars about a third to a half of what it was during the heyday of the cartel—and why has the price remained there for the last 20 years? My answer is market forces determine the oil price. President Reagan's decontrol of energy prices in the 1980s broke the cartel's back.[5]

The high price of oil is a demand-driven phenomenon, and the price will remain high as long as the world economy is growing. Making this forecast early on requires one to see that the supply side of the oil market is at best only half the story. Thus, for an aggregate-demand forecast to have a hope of being accurate, it must take into account both supply and demand shifts.

I have already shown price increases supply shifts induce generate effects similar to those tax increases elicit. Thus, symmetry suggests a supply-side induced price reduction should produce effects similar to a tax-rate cut. It does, and (as I have shown) under these conditions, total supplier profits increase while the price consumers pay declines (see Figure 11.3b). The computer sector is a prime example here: Computing power has increased enormously in recent years while the price of such computing power has declined. At the same time, technological innovations have led to huge increases in productivity.

Clearly, price declines induced by supply shifts are quite bullish for the world economy. On the other hand, price declines induced by demand shifts are quite bearish (see Figure 11.3d). A lack of demand induces a doubly negative effect on profits. Not only do producers collect less money per unit sold, they also sell fewer units. The quintessential example of this is Japan during its deflation years—a stock market bubble that burst in the early 1990s reduced the net worth of individuals and corporations alike. In turn, the credit worthiness of companies was reduced, forcing banks to curtail their loans. The decline in asset prices also reduced the net capital and capital adequacy of the banks, forcing them to further curtail their loan operations. These conditions created what some called a *liquidity trap*. As the Japan central bank printed money to stimulate the economy, the commercial banks did not lend the extra money. Instead, the money was held as excess reserves. The abundance of bank reserves reduced short-term interest rates, while stagnation lowered long-term rates. Worse, the yield curve flattened to near zero levels, hence the liquidity trap. The Japanese economy remained stagnant for several years following this turn of events. Eventually, most of the bad loans were worked out and the banks began lending again, once their capital had increased. Rising asset prices started to generate a virtuous cycle, and climbing net worth in the Japanese private sector made the sector's credit worthy once more.

A reduction in supply leads to a movement along the demand curve that results in a higher equilibrium price and lower output. Supply shifts, however, are not the only source of a price increase. A demand shift can also produce a higher price of a good, yet the effect on equilibrium output is very different. A shift in demand leads to a movement along the supply curve, producing higher output and higher prices. This simple analysis shows the correlation between prices and the economy depends on the nature of economic shocks.

Price changes alone are not enough to determine whether society is better or worse off. My analysis illustrates there are good price increases (that is, demand-led) and good price decreases (that is, supply-led). Symmetrically, there are bad price increases (that is, supply-led) and bad price decreases (that is, demand-led). To make inferences about the state of the economy, we need to determine the direction of price changes and the nature or source of the changes. As for the latter, we need to be able to tell a demand shift from a supply shift.

Looking at current global conditions, I believe the surge in basic commodity prices is demand-led, the result of a growing world economy. I also believe the decline in technology-related prices is supply-led, the result of incredible productivity increases and technological innovation in the U.S. and elsewhere. As long as these trends continue, there is no reason to be bearish on the world economy.

Looking at the data presented in Figure 11.4a, there has been a positive correlation between oil-price levels and the growth of real U.S. GDP in recent quarters. The timing of this double surge is yet more evidence recent oil-price hikes have been demand-driven. Figure 11.4b shows the correlation extends to real GDP and the spot index of the Commodity Research Bureau (CRB). These price increases are demand-driven and growth-driven. Compare the growth rate of China, Japan, and Germany (Figures 11.5a, b, and c). A direct corollary exists between high-growth nations (China) and high-oil-use nations (China).

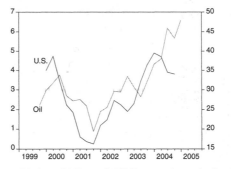

Figure 11.4a　U.S. real GDP growth and oil prices.

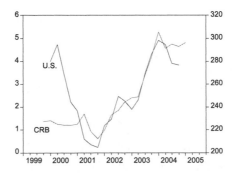

Figure 11.4b　U.S. real GDP growth and the Commodity Research Bureau commodity spot index.

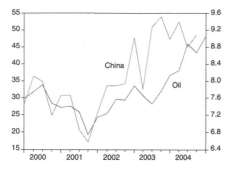

Figure 11.5a China real GDP growth and oil prices.

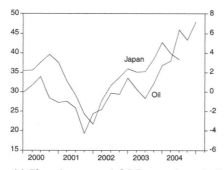

Figure 11.5b Japan real GDP growth and oil prices.

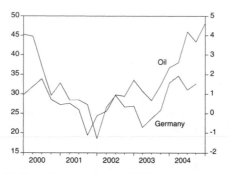

Figure 11.5c Germany real GDP growth and oil prices.

Higher oil prices produce several effects. They increase the incentives to produce more energy, be it from oil-related or alternative sources. They also crowd out slower-growing countries from the energy markets. For these countries, demand is not growing as fast, so higher energy prices lead to a movement along the aggregate demand curve. Making a tough situation even worse, higher energy prices have a negative impact on the real GDP growth rate of the slower-growing countries. Countries such as Japan are among those at risk today. So far, Japan has not fared well in the high-energy-price, high-commodity-price environment (see Figure 11.5b).

All these arguments lead me to conclude rising oil prices are the result of world economic expansion. An important implication of this conclusion is rising oil prices caused by an increase in demand cannot cause a recession. Rather, a recession leads to lower oil prices. In the context of the analysis presented so far, oil is an inelastic industry experiencing an increase in aggregate demand. This high-beta situation is bullish not only for the oil industry, but also for the world economy, as the high oil price is a result of rising aggregate demand.

There's one last way I'd like to look at the industry effect, and we can stick with the oil example to do so. An argument many have made is a rising oil price and a weaker dollar leads to an increase in the underlying inflation rate. At the risk of sounding like a two-handed economist, my response to this depends on the different reasons behind higher oil prices and a lower dollar.

First, let me state I believe inflation to be a monetary phenomenon and the Federal Reserve (the Fed), through its open-market operations, can (in principle) control the underlying inflation rate. With this being the case, the inflation potential of an economy depends on the monetary system's organization. Put simply, inflation depends on the way the monetary authorities respond to changing economic conditions.

So, let's consider the case of a relative price change. Let's say on top of a price change, we overlay the argument the Fed follows a price rule of 2 percent. Any increase in the price of a group of commodities can be matched by a reduction in the price of the other commodities, such that the two percent target rate can be achieved. Under this scenario, inflation is not a problem. The industry groups behind rising import prices and higher commodity prices can have some pricing power, while groups behind services and certain domestic goods cannot. This can be the case if, as I believe, stronger growth leads to a rise in basic commodity prices relative to other goods and services, and the weaker dollar reflects a change in the U.S. terms of trade. In this circumstance, I would expect to see a barrel of oil buy more goods and services than it did previously, although energy substitutes and competing import goods can all benefit. By estimating each industry sector's elasticity, a clear strategy designed to take advantage of oil- and commodity-price changes emerges.

12

KEEPING THE WHEELS ON THE HEDGE-FUND ATV

Financial publications love to discuss the proliferation of hedge funds, with much ink devoted to the negatives these days. But the positive case for hedge funds is straightforward: Hedge funds have several alternative investment strategies at their disposal, such as hedging against market downturns, investing in asset classes (such as currencies or distressed securities), and utilizing return-enhancing tools (such as leverage, derivatives, and arbitrage). The hedge fund's added flexibility as an investment vehicle is a great allure adding to their popularity, with alternative investments representing nearly $700 billion in today's managed assets.

On the supply side, the arguments for hedge funds are fairly clear. Intellectually, hedge-fund strategies (different strategy definitions are presented in Table 12.1) offer investment managers the highest fees—2 percent of assets under management plus 20 percent of the returns over some benchmark. In contrast, traditional money managers charge a 1 percent fee. Although discounts are common for both manager types, until now, there has been a clear fee-difference between the two investment approaches. Hedge fund economics, as they currently stand, are such that a mildly successful hedge fund can make a lot more money than even the hottest traditionally managed fund. The prospect of huge profits creates a great temptation to enter the business. So, not surprisingly, hedge funds have proliferated. A combination of ease of entry and competition in the hedge-fund sector inevitably creates downward pressure on management fees. Whether competition among hedge-fund managers drives average fees closer to traditional managers' fees depends on whether hedge funds deliver higher returns after fees than the traditional long-only investment options. In the long run, the only way hedge-fund establishments are going to survive while charging higher fees is if they deliver higher net-of-fee returns and/or much lower volatility. This is an empirical issue.

Table 12.1
Hedge-fund strategy definition.

Convertible Arbitrage strategies consist of convertible bond investments. The idea is to buy a company's convertible bond and sell the same company short the common stock.

CTA Global or Commodity Trading Advisor funds invest in listed financial and commodity markets as well as currency markets all over the world. They can follow systematic or discretionary strategies.

Distressed Securities involve buying back, at a low price, the securities of companies experiencing financial difficulties. Securities range from the lowest to highest risk (that is, senior secured debt to common stock).

Emerging Market Strategies, as the name implies, invest in the emerging markets' bonds and equities.

Event Driven strategies try to exploit price movements related to anticipating events affecting companies (for example, mergers, acquisitions, bankruptcies, and so on).

Fixed-Income Arbitrage strategies try to exploit price anomalies related to interest rate instruments.

Long-Short Equity strategies invest mainly in equities and derivative instruments. The manager uses short selling, but maintains a position in the neutral stock.

Equity Market Neutral strategies attempt to exploit inefficiencies in the market through balanced overvalued securities buying and selling so that either a neutral-beta (that is, risk) or a neutral-dollar (that is, amounts invested) approach is obtained.

Merger Arbitrage funds invest in companies involved in the mergers-and-acquisitions process. Typically, they go long on targeted companies and sell short the acquiring companies.

Relative Value strategies look to take advantage of the relative price differentials between related instruments.

Short Selling strategies maintain a net or simple short exposure relative to the market.

The potential downside of hedge-fund strategies is, if misapplied, they can bring disastrous results. The Long-Term Capital Management (LTCM) debacle is such an example. John Meriwether, a bond trader from Salomon Brothers with a well-known and favorable track record, founded LTCM in 1993. Investment banks quickly poured more than $1 billion into the fund, yet in only a few years the fund was well overexposed to risk and near belly-up. Many consider LTCM to be a worst-case scenario—the hedge-fund ghost haunting the sector to this day. Without getting into the specifics of the LTCM demise, I want to point out what is a continuing contributing factor to the downside of many hedge funds: The compensation schemes many employ have all the makings of one-sided bets when the funds underperform. The schemes induce managers to take on more risk in the hope of turning around performance and rising above their high watermarks. When performance does not improve, managers have an incentive to close their funds down and start new ones. In this way, they get rid of the drag of being underwater.

If we apply this analysis to our cyclical asset allocation (CAA) strategy, the hedge fund's flaw seems obvious: If managers have no other incentive than to be active all the time, they miss out on the cyclical passive opportunities. To be fair, let's investigate hedge-fund performance to see if this is in fact the case.

Do Hedge Funds Offer Higher Returns, Lower Risks, or Both?

Hedge Fund Research, Inc., (HFRI) publishes data on several hedge-fund strategies on a regular basis. The data are net of fees and presumably not subject to survivor bias—although it is fairly obvious a hedge fund about to close may not be compelled to provide performance information to institutions such as HFRI.[1] To be sure, many survivor-bias issues should concern investors who are investigating hedge-fund performance. In general, the quality of past information varies greatly across indices, depending on the dates when individual indices began their activities. Adding hedge funds to indices, the deletion of funds that cease reporting results, and the missing data that occurs when fund managers opt not to report results (what is known as the self-reporting bias) all combine to affect the numbers within indices. In addition, hedge-fund indices may suffer from selection bias. For example, some indices exclude managed funds while others do not. Then, there's the question of the sample's length. Current hedge-fund data span only 14 years. Many consider this period too short to generate meaningful statistical inferences. That may be the case; this is, however, the only historical information at our disposal.

Although 14 years may not enable one to form definitive conclusions, it certainly points one in the right direction. Investors really have no choice. They're not going to sit around for 30 or 40 years until there's enough data to begin hedge-fund performance analysis. Neither will I.

The conventional wisdom is that hedge-fund investors are more comfortable with a lot more risk, and so expect a higher return. Given this view, the summary statistics (using HFRI data) for the different hedge-fund strategies reported in Table 12.2 are somewhat unexpected. When compared to the S&P 500, the bulk of the hedge-fund strategies do not deliver higher returns than those of the broad-based market index. In fact, one can make the case that for the few strategies with higher monthly returns than the S&P 500, the differences do not appear to be statistically significant.

Table 12.2

Average monthly returns and standard deviation for selected hedge-fund strategies: January 1990 to December 2004.

	Monthly Returns	Standard Deviation	Sharpe Ratio
HFRI Fixed Income : Arbitrage Index	0.69%	1.25%	0.95
HFRI Equity Market Neutral Index: Statistical Arbitrage	0.71%	1.14%	1.14
HFRI Equity Market Neutral Index	0.75%	0.92%	1.61
HFRI Fixed Income: High Yield Index	0.80%	1.84%	0.85
HFRI Fixed Income (Total)	0.86%	1.00%	1.79
HFRI Convertible Arbitrage Index	0.86%	0.98%	1.86
S&P 500	0.96%	4.23%	0.51
S&P 500 Equal Weighted	1.11%	4.53%	0.58
HFRI Event-Driven Index	1.19%	1.91%	1.53
HFRI Distressed Securities Index	1.23%	1.77%	1.71
HFRI Emerging Markets (Total)	1.29%	4.31%	0.76
HFRI Macro Index	1.29%	2.44%	1.35

continues

Table 12.2   continued

	Monthly Returns	Standard Deviation	Sharpe Ratio
HFRI Equity Hedge Index	1.39%	2.58%	1.42
HFRI Market Timing Index	1.03%	1.95%	1.23
HFRI Composite Index	1.15%	2.00%	1.40

Source: Hedge Fund Research, Inc.

The surprising result is that, with the exception of emerging-market strategies, the reported hedge-fund strategies produce a lower standard deviation than the S&P 500 monthly returns. In other words, the reduction in the returns' volatility appears to be the great contribution of the various hedge-fund strategies to investor well-being. Who would have thought?

The third column in Table 12.2 reports the ratios of the return strategies to their standard deviations. The ratios enable one to easily identify the strategies offering the highest reward-to-risk ratio. Looking at the results, it is apparent, with the exception of emerging-market strategies, all other hedge-fund strategies produce a higher reward-to-risk ratio than the S&P 500 or the equal-weighted S&P 500.

The question now is whether hedge funds experience return cycles. Many hedge-fund investors and managers have a goal to find the *12 percent T-bill*, or a lot of gain over a short period of time. Unfortunately, as the data in Table 12.2 show, this is an elusive goal. The hedge fund's general inability to find the 12 percent T-bill is a strike against the sector's big-gain aura. But, it also causes one to question whether hedge-fund returns exhibit any cyclicality: Do they move in relation to macroeconomic conditions over cycles or do they behave randomly over time, with the best bet being they tend to return to their historical averages after diverting from their means? If they do act cyclically, an active strategy that chooses among hedge funds and/or the S&P 500 can produce returns superior to a plan of investing exclusively in hedge funds. Looking at the ratio of the hedge-fund strategies' cumulative returns to the S&P 500, it is apparent there are runs in the data. As a cycle-minded investor can guess, some simple tests reject the hypothesis that the runs in the data are randomly generated.

Five of the six hedge-fund strategies reported in Figures 12.1a through 12.1f—market neutral (see Figure 12.1a), fixed-income arbitrage (see Figure 12.1b), fixed-income high-yield (see Figure 12.1c), equity market neutral statistical arbitrage (see Figure 12.1e), and fixed-income (total) (see Figure 12.f)—underperformed the S&P 500 during the 1990–2004 period. The sixth strategy, convertible arbitrage (see Figure 12.1d), barely outperformed the S&P 500. The data also show most of the strategies were keeping up with the S&P 500 prior to 1994, as evidenced by the flat or rising relative performance line in Figures 12.1a, b, d, and e. This is an interesting result. All six hedge-fund strategies underperformed the S&P 500 during the 1994–2000 period. Then, from 2000 to 2003, these strategies outperformed the S&P 500.

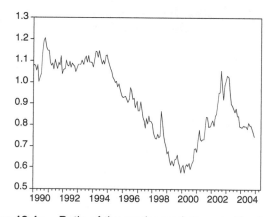

Figure 12.1a   Ratio of the equity market neutral hedge-fund index to the S&P 500.

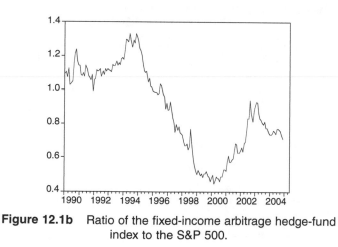

Figure 12.1b   Ratio of the fixed-income arbitrage hedge-fund index to the S&P 500.

Figure 12.1c Ratio of the fixed-income, high-yield hedge-fund index to the S&P 500.

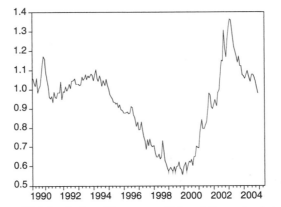

Figure 12.1d Ratio of the convertible arbitrage hedge-fund index to the S&P 500.

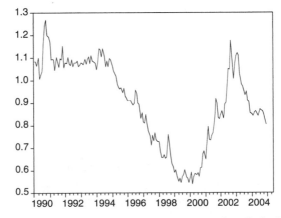

Figure 12.1e Ratio of the equity market neutral statistical arbitrage hedge-fund index to the S&P 500.

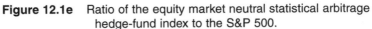

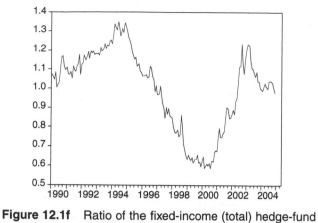

Figure 12.1f Ratio of the fixed-income (total) hedge-fund index to the S&P 500.

There's a clear pattern of relative underperformance and outperformance for the hedge-fund strategies. Another six strategies—macro (see Figure 12.2a), distressed securities (see Figure 12.2b), event driven (see Figure 12.2c), emerging markets (see Figure 12.2d), market timing (see Figure 12.2e), and hedge-fund composite (see Figure 12.2f)—outperformed the S&P 500 during the 1990–1994 and 1999–2004 time periods.

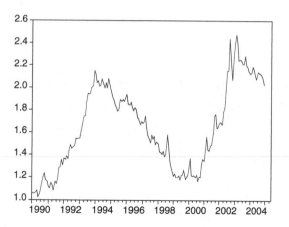

Figure 12.2a Ratio of the global macro hedge-fund index to the S&P 500.

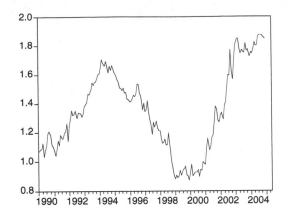

Figure 12.2b   Ratio of the distressed securities hedge-fund index to the S&P 500.

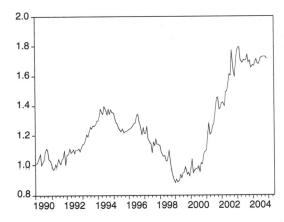

Figure 12.2c   Ratio of the event-driven hedge-fund index to the S&P 500.

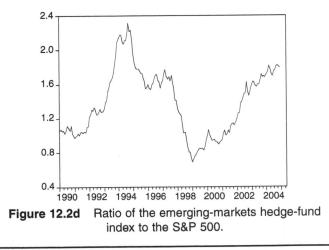

Figure 12.2d   Ratio of the emerging-markets hedge-fund index to the S&P 500.

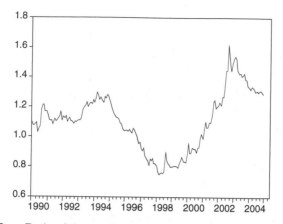

Figure 12.2e   Ratio of the market-timing hedge-fund index to the S&P 500.

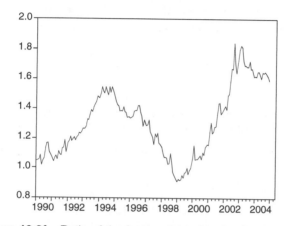

Figure 12.2f   Ratio of the fund-weighted hedge-fund composite index to the S&P 500.

The Size Effect and the Hedge Fund's Performance

Why did some hedge-fund strategies outperform during periods when other hedge-fund strategies underperformed? The pattern went as follows: hedge funds did well when large-cap stocks did not and vice versa. The results' empirical regularity suggests cycles exist during which hedge funds outperform the market (that is, the S&P 500) as well as cycles during which hedge funds underperform the market. The data in Figures 12.1 and 12.2 show fairly robust and uniform cycles across the various strategies. In short, the data reinforce the idea that there is a time for active management (in this case, hedge-fund investing) and a time for passive management (that is, indexing).

Again, under the assumption of perfect foresight, I calculate the potential gains generated by a strategy taking advantage of such cycles. The summary results of the perfect-foresight strategy are reported in Table 12.3. Comparing the results in Tables 12.2 and 12.3, one can see the active/passive strategy that switches between hedge funds and the S&P 500 produces more volatility and higher monthly returns. For most strategies, the reward-to-risk ratio increases, which suggests the increased returns are more than enough to compensate for the increased risks of most strategies. It is apparent, at least to me, a strategy that switches between hedge funds and the S&P 500 (that is, the active/passive strategy) is desirable for many investors. If one could anticipate these cycles, one could develop a simple strategy that would determine the optimal times to be invested in hedge funds and the optimal times to index to the market. Once again, this is the value-timing strategy, which takes advantage of the cyclical patterns in the relative performance of the different asset classes.

Table 12.3
Average monthly returns and standard deviation for selected active/passive hedge-fund strategies: January 1990 to December 2004.

	Monthly Returns	Standard Deviation	Sharpe Ratio
HFRI Market Timing Index	1.35%	2.77%	1.27
HFRI Macro Index	1.71%	3.02%	1.57
HFRI Fixed Income: High Yield Index	1.43%	2.86%	1.32
HFRI Fixed Income: Arbitrage Index	1.40%	2.52%	1.46
HFRI Fixed Income (Total)	1.44%	2.49%	1.54
HFRI Event-Driven Index	1.51%	2.77%	1.46
HFRI Equity Market Neutral Index: Statistical Arbitrage	1.19%	2.60%	1.14
HFRI Equity Market Neutral Index	1.21%	2.52%	1.21

	Monthly Returns	Standard Deviation	Sharpe Ratio
HFRI Equity Hedge Index	1.51%	2.90%	1.41
HFRI Emerging Markets (Total)	1.91%	3.65%	1.48
HFRI Distressed Securities Index	1.71%	2.71%	1.75
HFRI Fund Weighted Composite Index	1.49%	2.69%	1.49
HFRI Convertible Arbitrage Index	1.28%	2.54%	1.29

The odds of active managers outperforming passive managers rise as the number of stocks outperforming their benchmarks increases. A favorite analogy from the efficient-market theory best makes this point. Again, assume a number of people throwing darts at a blackboard containing the names of the stocks in the benchmark S&P 500. The chance of a dart thrower picking a winning stock is equal to the percentage of stocks outperforming the benchmark at any point in time. Hence, the broader the market breadth, the greater the chance an active portfolio manager outperforms his benchmark.

In Chapter 9, "Active Versus Passive Management," I demonstrated the way the size effect and the relative performance between active and passive strategies are directly related. They are two sides of the same coin. The interaction between the weighting scheme of an index and the size effect is a powerful insight as it tells active managers when their portfolios should be index-like and when to pursue an active strategy with gusto. By taking advantage of the one-to-one correspondence between the size effect and market breadth (that is, the odds of beating a benchmark by randomly selecting stocks), one can make inferences regarding the conditions under which active management prevails over passive management. All that's required is for the average return of an equal-weighted index to beat its cap-weighted counterpart—or, more specifically, for small-cap stocks to beat large-caps stocks at all times. Under these circumstances, on average, active management beats passive management.

I mentioned earlier that Standard & Poor's began publishing an equal-weighted S&P 500 to go along with its cap-weighted index. The equal-weighted returns represent a proxy of the average return that can be achieved by throwing darts at the board of S&P 500 stocks, so it can be used as a proxy for the equal-weighted returns active managers can achieve on average. In contrast, the cap-weighted

S&P 500 constitutes the index, or benchmark, for passive-strategy performance. The results reported in Figure 12.3 show periods when the cap-weighted S&P 500 outperformed the equal-weighted index and vice versa.

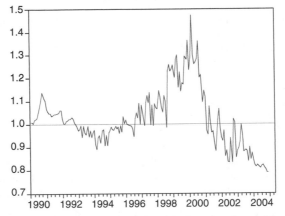

Figure 12.3   Ratio of the cap-weighted to the equal-weighted S&P 500.

Size Cycles and Passive/Active Cycles in Hedge Funds

The performance of the equal-weighted S&P 500 relative to the cap-weighted index is a tailor-made empirical indicator of the desirability of a pure-passive strategy, a pure-active strategy, and a strategic and tactical allocation to active and passive strategies. Notice that small-caps in Figure 12.3 outperformed larger-cap stocks during the 1990–1994 and 2000–2004 periods. Hedge-fund strategies outperformed the S&P 500 index during these same periods. It is important to note the time periods are inexorably linked to clear and systematic policy changes. Hence, my view is the small-cap effect is due to tax sheltering, regulatory skirting, and inflation hedging. Recall tax rates increased during the 1990–1994 period, first under George H.W. Bush and then under William J. Clinton. The Clinton administration tax hikes were not as large as the president had hoped for, but if you weigh-in the threat of Hillary Clinton's massive health-care plan, the small-cap effect becomes more understandable. In 1995, the Republicans took over Congress, and the gridlock that followed was good for the market as far as taxes and regulations were concerned. The small-cap effect would, for a time, expire. Then, in 1999, Federal Reserve Chairman Alan Greenspan began to worry about the ersatz Year 2000 (Y2K) effect. He proceeded to flood the financial system with cash, only to abruptly pull the liquidity out of the system in 2000. Credit in this environment became tougher, and with the advent of the accounting scandals, the regulatory burden increased once again. The small-cap effect was back on.

The data presented here, in the framework of hedge funds, again suggest neither the pure-active nor the pure-passive strategy is optimal for asset allocation. A blend of the two either produces higher returns or lower volatility or both. At the very least, a tactical allocation between active and passive strategies should be desirable for most any investor. Given all the hedge-fund strategies embody an active strategy, my framework provides a simple explanation as to why they underperform during large-cap cycles. I was hoping the one hedge-fund exception to the rule would be the macro strategy. My rationale was macro funds are the only ones without any style- or size-specific mandate. If macro managers anticipated cycles, my reasoning went, they could morph themselves into the prevailing style. Hence, I figured if one type of hedge fund was likely to weather the large-cap cycle, it would be the macro fund. The data show this not to be the case. Two distinct possibilities explain this result: One is the macro funds did not fully anticipate the cycles. But, the second possibility can be even more important. Even if the macro managers anticipated the coming environments, hedge-fund compensation schemes would have forced them to be active. If they went passive, it would have been very difficult for them to collect their steep fees for long time periods, such as the 1994–1999 period. During that large-cap cycle, the optimal active strategy was to go long–short on the major indices (that is, going long–short on exchange-traded funds). Our Midwest hedge fund from Chapter 8, "The Cyclical Asset Allocation Strategy's Versatility," came to understand this. The long–short hedge-fund strategy captures the value-added the CAA produces.

13

MARKET TIMING OR VALUE TIMING?

One of the central themes of this book is the size effect and the relative performance between active and passive investing are directly related. As stated, these are two sides of the same coin. The interaction between the indices' weighting schemes and the size effect tells active investors and managers when to build index-like portfolios and when to pursue an active strategy.

The newer, equal-weighted S&P 500 index is tailor-made for empirically testing the desirability of a pure-passive strategy, a pure-active strategy, and a strategic asset allocation (SAA) and tactical asset allocation (TAA) to passive and active strategies. Visually analyzing the ratio of the cap-weighted to the equal-weighted S&P 500 reveals four distinct cycles of relative performance, as shown in Figure 13.1. In Table 13.1, two concrete periods are noticeable: The equal-weighted index outperformed the capweighted index during periods of a rising S&P 500 market (November 1990 to March 1994) and during periods of a falling stock market (April 2000 to March 2004). When the equal-weighted index outperformed, so did the small-cap markets.

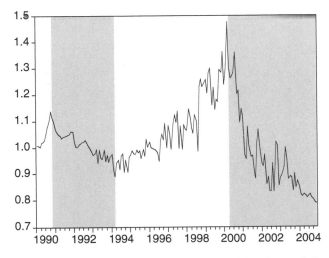

Figure 13.1   Ratio of the cap-weighted to the equal-weighted cumulative returns.

Table 13.1

Summary statistics for the cap-weighted and equal-weighted S&P 500 equity portfolios.

Selected Samples				
Market Cycle	Small	Small	Large	Large
Market Direction	Rising	Falling	Falling	Rising
Return	**November 1990 to March 1994**	**April 2000 to March 2004**	**January to December 1990**	**April 1994 to March 2000**
Equal Weighted	1.76%	0.72%	−0.86%	1.44%
Cap Weighted	1.24%	−0.35%	−0.13%	1.95%

Source: Research Insight

Value Timing Is Not a Market-Timing Story

If the insight is only weighting schemes and small-cap cycles are related, what we have is a simple market-timing story. It follows, if we can predict the small-cap cycles, we know when the odds of an active manager outperforming a passive manager will rise, as the number of stocks outperforming the active manager's benchmark will increase. But, there's more to this. In previous chapters, I set forth the argument that supply-and-demand elasticities are, in part, affected by government regulations. I also argued there are different responses to different economic shocks. Finally, I asserted the elasticities are directly related to the alpha (that is, excess return) and beta (that is, risk) stock parameters. Putting all these variables together, I can conclude *different alphas and betas exist for different economic environments.*[1] In other words, the portfolio strategy I have outlined in this book is much more than a market-timing story in which short-term-minded players attempt to buy low and sell high with anticipated market fluctuations. It is a top-down strategy designed to take advantage of the changes in alpha and beta that take place as the world changes. In practice, the well-informed cyclical asset allocation (CAA) strategy attempts to time the different asset sectors' valuations.[2] That's why I refer to the CAA strategy as a value-timing strategy. When I say investors and managers can forecast size cycles (in other words, the times when either small-caps or large-caps are the more favorable investment classes), I don't mean to imply investors and managers should be interested in predicting the size effect's day-to-day relative performance. What I have in mind is a bit different. As I have shown (in Figure 2.6 and Table 3.2), small-caps' relative performance reveals persistent cycles lasting several years at a time. These are the cycles the CAA strategy is interested in identifying. If one can spot these cycles, one can ride them and produce superior returns.

The CAA strategy also has some added advantages. Because it requires less portfolio turnover than strategies that try to anticipate daily or weekly fluctuations in relative performance, it features reduced transaction costs. Also, the CAA strategy does not mandate that practitioners act with breakneck speed. I do not believe the CAA strategy—or, in particular, the value-timing strategy—is able to identify higher-frequency cycles, but I do hold it is able to capture the lower-frequency cycles' policy changes generate. So, when the strategy practitioner correctly identifies a cycle, that identification's precise timing is not that important. Being a quarter late costs the strategy in terms of performance, but it does not doom the strategy if the cycle lasts several years.

All this, of course, is predicated on the CAA practitioners' ability to identify cycles. Chapter 5, "Linking Up," developed precise relationships between the different asset classes, and Chapter 7, "Taking It to the Tilt," outlined a clear theory as to the way to identify the asset classes' relative performance. Both chapters also discussed the way one can apply an economic forecast to these relationships to pinpoint the relative performance's different cycles. The way investors and managers develop forecasts is a matter of preference. One can easily use the economic forecasts publications, such as the *Wall Street Journal*, or one can opt to develop one's own forecast—which is my particular preference.

Table 13.2
Summary statistics for the cap-weighted and equal-weighted S&P 500 equity portfolios.

Selected Samples				
Market Cycle	Small	Small	Large	Large
Market Direction	Rising	Falling	Falling	Rising
Return	November 1990 to March 1994	April 2000 to March 2004	January to December 1990	April 1994 to March 2000
Equal Weighted	1.76%	0.72%	−0.86%	1.44%
Cap Weighted	1.24%	−0.35%	−0.13%	1.95%
Alpha	0.42%	1.06%	−0.71%	−0.43%
Alpha Standard Error	0.17%	0.31%	0.38%	0.19%
Beta	1.07	1.01	1.19	0.96
Beta Standard Error	0.05	0.01	0.08	0.04

Source: Research Insight

Should any doubt remain as to whether CAA is based on value-timing or market-timing, I have tested my hypothesis that it is indeed a value-timing strategy. To do so, I estimated the parameters of the widely used capital asset pricing model (CAPM), which describes the relationship between a security's risk and its expected return, for the equal-weighted S&P 500 during each distinct index cycle previously mentioned. Looking at the results reported in Table 13.2, a number of empirical regularities can be observed. The estimated beta terms for the equal-weighted index are not statistically different from one—indicating volatility in line with the market and also indicating the index would have been expected to move with the market. In contrast, during the two time periods when small-caps outperformed, the estimated alpha terms are positive and significantly different from zero (zero being the flat mark for alpha, indicating no extra return for the additional risk). More important, when comparing the two small-cap cycles, as the average return of the overall market improves from a declining nominal return to a rising average return, the alpha coefficient declines in magnitude.

The cap-weighted S&P 500 also outperformed during two periods: A rising S&P 500 characterizes one episode (April 1994 to March 2000), while a falling S&P 500 characterizes the other (January to December 1990). Again, some empirical regularity is evident in the data. The beta coefficients are not significantly different from one. During the large-cap cycles, however, the alpha terms are negative, with the magnitude increasing as market conditions improved. For the large-cap cycles, the estimated alphas are the mirror images of the alpha terms for the small-cap cycles.

Relative performance during the cycles clearly rules out traditional beta-related market timing as a possible explanation. By definition, we know the market beta is one. If the beta of the equal-weighted index is less than one, and all else is the same, we should see the cap-weighted S&P 500 outperform during rising-market periods (November 1990 to March 1994 and April 1994 to March 2000) and underperform during falling market periods (January 1990 to December 1990 and April 2000 to March 2004). On the other hand, if the beta is greater than one, the opposite relative performance should be observed. Yet, looking at the four periods, I find no systematic beta-related pattern. Instead, I find the equal-weighted index outperforms during periods of a rising stock market (for example, November 1990 to March 1994), as well as during periods of a falling stock market (for example, April 2000 to March 2004). Again, I find a similar pattern for underperformance, while the data uncover the lack of a systematic beta pattern—a beta pattern being a market-timing characteristic.

Beta/market timing does not explain the relative performance of the cap- and equal-weighted S&P 500 indices. Nor does a more complex analysis that takes into account a constant alpha term across cycles. Thus, the assumption of constant alphas and betas rules out market timing as a possible explanation for the indices' and size cycles' relative performance. On the other hand, an assumption of changing alphas and betas during different cycles lends support to the value-timing hypothesis.

Table 13.2 shows the estimated beta terms, while different during each subsample, are not statistically different from one. In other words, the equal-weighted index is no riskier or safer than the benchmark cap-weighted index. But, the most interesting part of this analysis relates to the estimated alpha terms: They do seem to change with the size cycles. The alpha term is positive during the small-cap cycles and negative during the large-cap cycles. During large-cap markets, the alpha term's magnitude is larger when the stock market is rising; during small-cap markets, the alpha term's magnitude declines as market conditions improve. Taken together, these results suggest the existence of an interaction between the alpha term and the market's direction.

My interpretation of these results is simple: Different environments have different vectors, and the return vectors are reflected in different alpha terms. I also contend these alpha shifts are predictable and related to the overall economic environment, and thus are amenable to exploitation in a portfolio strategy. That is the value-timing strategy. The positive alpha for the small-cap cycles supports my hypothesis that active management can add value during such cycles. The negative alpha for the large-cap cycles suggests active management does not add value during large-cap cycles and investors would be better off indexing at such times.

Table 13.3
Summary statistics of selected cap-weighted S&P 500/BARRA equity portfolios.

Selected Samples				
Market Cycle	**Small**	**Small**	**Large**	**Large**
Market Direction	**Rising November 1990 to March 1994**	**Falling April 2000 to March 2004**	**Falling January to December 1990**	**Rising April 1994 to March 2000**
S&P 400				
Return	1.12%	0.62%	N/A	1.74%
Alpha	0.42%	0.96%	N/A	−0.20%
Alpha Standard Error	0.29%	0.36%	N/A	0.34%
Beta	1.02	0.96	N/A	0.993
Beta Standard Error	0.094	0.074	N/A	0.0768

continues

Table 13.3 continued

Selected Samples				
Market Cycle	**Small**	**Small**	**Large**	**Large**
Market Direction	**Rising November 1990 to March 1994**	**Falling April 2000 to March 2004**	**Falling January to December 1990**	**Rising April 1994 to March 2000**
S&P 500/Growth				
Return	1.67%	−0.82%	0.53%	2.29%
Alpha	−0.22%	−0.45%	0.31%	0.31%
Alpha Standard Error	.187%	0.26%	0.23%	0.15%
Beta	1.09	1.05	1.07	1.02
Beta Standard Error	0.06	0.05	0.04	0.03
S&P 500/Value				
Return	−0.48%	0.14%	0.83%	1.57%
Alpha	0.22%	0.47%	−0.36%	−0.34%
Alpha Standard Error	0.19%	0.28%	0.24%	0.17%
Beta	0.90	0.95	0.92	0.98
Beta Standard Error	0.05	0.06	0.05	0.04

Source: Research Insight

How Robust Are Value-Timing Cycles?

Using the relative performance of the cap-weighted and equal-weighted S&P 500 indices again raises the possibility of sample-selection bias. So, to test the results' robustness, I decided to extend the analysis to three other cap-weighted series for which return data were available for most of the time periods in question. Summary statistics for the S&P 400, S&P 500/BARRA value, and S&P 500/BARRA growth indices are reported in Table 13.3. The results reveal a familiar pattern for alpha and beta. The estimated beta terms are not significantly different from one. The alpha terms, though positive during small-cap cycles, turn negative during large-cap cycles. Once again, the data suggest an interaction between the magnitude of the alpha term, market direction, and size cycles.

Notice, in particular, the behavior of the value index's alpha: It is similar to that of the small-cap stocks during the different cycles. In contrast, the alpha terms for growth stocks mirror the alphas of the large-cap cycles. There is an undemanding explanation for this. Recall that BARRA allocates roughly half the market cap to each style. Recall also that there are approximately twice as many value stocks as there are growth stocks. This means the average value stocks' market cap is about half the growth stocks' market cap. Thus, the alpha coefficient is capturing the interaction between the style and size effect.

I believe changes in the economic environment affect the market returns structure (that is, the alpha and beta terms). Thus, a different premium exists for each economic environment or world state. If one ignores the existence of the different world states, any regression analysis (or statistical formula for establishing relationships between the variables) tends to average the various periods. The net effect is twofold. First, the most common observation dominates the average. Second, to the extent different world states exist, the average coefficient either overestimates or underestimates the parameters characterizing the various asset classes. This represents a major problem because it suggests traditional valuation models are misspecified. Some financial economists choose to empirically deal with this issue, and they reestimate valuation models for shorter samples until the misspecification disappears. But, all this amounts to is a trial-and-error selection of the relevant subsamples. The process also presumes the relevant period for estimating parameters is the immediate past. Insofar as the process is one of trial and error, how does a researcher know when the state of the world will change? Again, the answer is empirical: when the model fails to work.

I take a different approach. Theory and common experience postulate that general economic factors impact stock prices in the aggregate. Changes in interest rates, inflation rates, oil prices, exchange rates, tax rates, regulations, and trade restrictions produce different effects across industry lines—hence asset classes. During the past three decades, these variables have covered extraordinarily wide value range. Few would doubt these economic shocks have had an overall impact on market aggregates. So, it would seem only natural such a wide value range would elicit equivalent dramatic responses from equities. In other words, in addition to an overall stock market effect, the potential should exist, at the least, for great differences in stock returns among the various asset classes.

The conception and measurement of equity responses to macroeconomic events is rooted in economic theory and is straightforward. From all I am able to uncover, it's apparent the market's reassessment of equity values is far from haphazard. Distinct patterns emerge. As I've shown, one can identify historical periods when one investment strategy dominated the rest. I've also demonstrated particular economic parameters, or environmental conditions, correspond to these dominant cycles. In the hope of estimating such cycles, it is reasonable to suggest one can ascertain the economic environment at the present moment as well as any presumed changes to it. This knowledge then dictates asset-allocation decisions. Because I believe different reaction-coefficients for each sector, size, and style exist, my CAA strategy attempts to capture what I consider to be predictable responses to economic shocks that give rise to changing alpha and beta parameters over cycles. Market timing? Hardly.

14

EVERY STRATEGY
HAS ITS DAY

A pension consultant's long-only recommendation is best described as a strategic asset allocation (SAA). The recommendation is a mix of assets based on historical estimates that will, in the long run, meet the desired plan objectives. If everything goes as expected, all a plan administrator has to do is buy the various recommended asset classes or investment buckets. In particular, an administrator only needs to select from the different exchange-traded funds (ETFs) in the recommended proportions or amounts.

One such example is of a domestic equities index in which the large-, mid-, and small-caps are weighted 70 percent, 20 percent, and 10 percent, respectively. Such a strategy's returns are reported in Table 14.1. It is interesting to point out the domestic stocks index produces a 9.71 percent average annual return, which is higher than the 8 percent long-run average stock return. It is important to note, however, the benchmark fell short of the average return in three out of eight sample years. Thus, if one is willing to stomach the domestic-index strategy's volatility, an 8 percent target return is not an outrageous demand— nor is it an unreachable goal. In addition, if investors choose superior managers who beat their benchmarks without adding additional risk, the returns of their portfolios' returns will undoubtedly increase.

Table 14.1
The feasibility of beta strategies.

	1997	1998	1999	2000
Domestic Equity Index	32.36%	23.70%	18.92%	−1.69%
	2001	**2002**	**2003**	**2004**
Domestic Equity Index	−7.78%	−19.84%	31.08%	13.18%
	Average Return	**Standard Deviation**	**Sharpe Ratio**	
Domestic Equity Index	9.71%	19.10%	0.30	

* The Domestic Equity Index consists of a weighted average of the large-, mid-, and small-cap stocks. The indices weights are 70 percent, 20 percent, and 10 percent, respectively.

Can a plan do better than an ETF-filled SAA? Quite possibly. The question now is how to pick a superior manager. The capital asset pricing model (CAPM) provides a criterion for evaluating different managers' performances. To review, one key implication of the CAPM is the market portfolio must be an efficient-market portfolio. Hence, an individual or plan manager who buys the market has an efficient portfolio. Such an arrangement, however, does not guarantee the returns to the plan are going to be high enough to generate sufficient funds to meet future obligations. This creates the opportunity for pension consultants to come in, examine contributions and expected future outlays, and (assuming the past is a good guide to the future) use historical returns and volatilities for the different asset classes to come up with the optimal asset mix most likely to satisfy future outlays with a minimal level of investor contribution. The challenge now is to create a benchmark for each manager that compares his or her performance on a risk-adjusted basis. A consultant performing this task would have to include passive and active managers in the selection process. The consultant would then search for those managers who would add alpha (that is, excess returns to a portfolio) without increasing beta (that is, the portfolio's risk). A reduction in risk (beta) without a reduction in excess return (alpha) is also a desirable outcome.

The case for active management is predicated on the individual manager's ability to beat her benchmarks. In the context of an SAA, the active/passive management-selection process boils down to whether consultants can find money managers who consistently outperform their benchmarks over the long run—in other words, managers with positive alphas.[1] Without a positive alpha—a proven excess return delivery track record—why would anyone go to the expense of hiring an active manager to perform with the market? If managers do not produce positive alphas, the optimal strategy is to buy market exposure as cheaply as possible, such as through ETFs.

The debate over whether to index or go active, when conducted in the context of an SAA, raises the bar for active managers. In this context, the active manager is required to consistently outperform the market over the long run. But, what if a manager can only consistently outperform the market during certain cycles while underperforming the rest of the time? If this is the case, it is quite possible the manager's long-run performance will not differ from an index strategy's performance. Yet, as we've discussed, selecting an active manager during an outperformance cycle enhances an asset-allocation strategy's long-run returns. The fact that the two strategies (active and passive) produce a similar long-run average does not rule out the possibility there are subperiods when one strategy is superior to the other, in which case switching from one strategy to another during cycles can give rise to superior results.[2]

Given most pension plans' focus on SAA, it is not surprising to see a lack of evidence in active management's favor. This is the reason for the backlash against active management and the push toward indexation we see in the market today. In my opinion, the focus on SAA has biased the active/passive debate against active management.

Arguing any particular strategy is superior to another at all times is a tall order. To me, a more sensible position is every strategy has its day. Sometimes, the economic environment is such that one particular strategy is superior to another. Over time, however, conditions will change and that strategy will fall out of favor. This means, over the long run, a well-designed investment strategy will alter investors' exposure to the two different strategies. The objective is to improve on SAA by tweaking it to take advantage of changing conditions over economic cycles. When we do this, we end up with a cyclical asset allocation (CAA) strategy.

So, the issue at hand is whether the CAA strategy that chooses active managers can do better than the SAA strategy invested in market indices (that is, in ETFs). An affirmative answer suggests excess returns can come from two different sources: In the parlance of the CAPM, a CAA that tilts a portfolio over a cycle is essentially making active beta bets over that cycle, while selecting active managers is an attempt to add alpha to a portfolio. Thus, CAA is best described as a strategy that makes explicit alpha and beta bets over cycles. Tactical asset allocation (TAA) strategies and, in the world of hedge funds, global macro strategies are special CAA incidences.

The asset-allocation process, as I have described it, includes explicit market exposure and does not insulate portfolios from a fluctuating market's vagaries. SAA is a great strategy for a rising market. Not only do you get the alpha of the great managers, you also get the beta of the climbing market. A rising tide lifts all boats, as the saying goes, and the positive alpha ensures an investor rides the crest of the rising tide. Such market exposure, however, proves to be the Achilles' heel of the strategy during down markets. The CAA strategy can reduce a portfolio's market, or beta, exposure in a down market all the way to zero if a portfolio is invested at the risk-free rate. Yet, although an investor can have a superior active manager, in a down market, all that manager can offer is the possibility he loses less than his peers (that is, less than the benchmark). It's only when the asset-allocation process allows for the shorting of some asset classes there is a way to reduce the market beyond zero beta and thus take advantage of a down market. In fact, that is one of the selling points of the global macro hedge-fund strategy.

During the 1990s bull market, investors had two distinct ways to capture returns: selecting superior managers and market exposure. Once the market bubble burst late in the decade, however, uncertainty abounded. Investors in that environment became increasingly concerned about capital preservation and focused more on achieving absolute returns. More specifically, the changed market conditions forced investors to think in terms of the different allocation strategies' alpha and beta components. The ideal long-run strategy became a relative performance focused on capturing both alpha and beta during up markets, and an absolute performance that captured pure alpha during down markets. Every strategy has its day. Sometimes, a relative-return strategy is desirable while, at other times, an absolute-return plan is ideal.

The ability to separate alpha and beta components gives an investor the opportunity to make explicit choices regarding market exposure as well as, hopefully, selecting superior active managers. The demand for separating services (alpha and beta) in the post-bubble days has created an opportunity for many players. The demand for both absolute-return hedge-fund strategies (pure-alpha players) and ETFs (pure-beta players) has exploded. To a large extent, the growth of the pure-alpha and pure-beta players has come at the expense of traditional mutual funds that offer the alpha and beta choices in fixed proportions. In theory, this is not a problem. The asset-allocation process can combine a mixture of funds to arrive at the proper alpha and beta for a retirement plan. The one exception to this would be when a portfolio cannot generate the alpha-beta combination desired by a pension plan. In this case, the asset-allocation solution would be inferior to the solution provided by a strategy combining the pure-alpha and pure-beta strategies.

The investment vehicles needed to implement a pure-beta strategy are readily available. Relatively speaking, it is fairly easy to replicate the market. Whether one does so using ETFs or derivatives depends on cost and institutional constraint. On the other hand, the pure-alpha strategy is not as easily identifiable or readily available. The alpha players require superior information to reach their positive alphas—and it is here where we can see the big difference between the CAA and alpha strategy. The CAA strategy argues one can identify and take advantage of relative performance cycles. Whether one can also identify exceptional managers is desirable but not essential to the strategy. On the other hand, the pure-alpha strategy argues it is very difficult to anticipate cyclical fluctuations and one is better off selecting superior managers who are uncorrelated with the market (that is, managers who invest in areas uncorrelated with the market). Either strategy requires superior information, be it in the selection of the alpha or beta providers. Hence, one strategy's superiority over another is mostly an empirical issue and not a theoretical one.

Finding Managers with Superior Knowledge

The search for a superior manager is based on the view that an active strategy is superior to a passive one. It assumes managers have superior information and can produce excess returns relative to a benchmark (that is, alpha-producing managers) and/or correctly forecast the environment to take advantage of the cyclical fluctuations in the different asset classes' relative performances (that is, the beta bets).

These questions bring us to the *portable-alpha strategy*, which hinges on being able to identify the pure-alpha plays. Alpha is portable as it can apply to any asset class. As the market has evolved, the simplest way to find pure-alpha plays is to focus on absolute-return hedge-fund strategies. Whether these hedge funds are pure-alpha players is a practical issue. Pure alpha, however, is not really essential to the strategy—it merely simplifies it. In what follows, I assume the previously mentioned hedge funds deliver the pure alpha they claim they can in their strategy literature. Once these pure-alpha players are identified, the question is whether their alphas (net of fees) are high enough to generate desired (target-rate) returns. This is not an inconsequential issue because hedge-fund fees are somewhere between a 1 percent fee and 10 percent of gains at the low-end and a 3 percent fee and 30 percent of gains at the high-end. The fee structure has a big impact on the before-fee returns the different alpha strategies must generate. The math is staggering. For a hedge fund of funds to deliver a 1 percent alpha, it has to generate a 4.4 percent before-fee return, while a 5 percent alpha strategy requires a 10.1 percent before-fee return.

One important issue is whether net-of-fees alpha generates the required investment plan rate of return. If it does not, the only way to remain in the pure-alpha strategy is to leverage the investments so they generate the required return. Smaller alphas would require larger leverage, which can carry regulatory or other types of risk.

Leverage can certainly be onerous. If alpha ranges from 1 to 4 percent, and an alpha plan's required returns are in the 8 to 10 percent range, the leverage requirement ranges from two to 10 times the plan's allocated funds. In other cases, though, leverage may not be a problem. Take, for example, the Federal Reserve's (the Fed) guarantee in the aftermath of the 2000–2001 recession that the market's short end would be low for a considerable time period. In making this pledge, the Fed created a one-sided bet and reduced the carry trade risk, whereby investors felt free to borrow short to buy long-maturity bonds, and in the process made the spread. That is the difference between the interest earned on the borrowed long-maturity bonds less the interest paid on the borrowed, short-maturity funds. The carry traders did not worry about the short rate going up. The Fed had given its guarantee. The only carry trade risk was rates at the long end would abruptly rise. To the extent, however, the economy was in a slow recovery mode and the Fed was worried about deflation, investors were not too concerned about long yields spiking. Leverage became a viable option to achieve the desired return objective—say 9 percent. If we assume a spread of only about 3 percent, to generate a 9 percent return, investors would have had to triple their original investment, which meant borrowing 200 percent of their original investment.

The issue at hand is to develop a target return for the alpha strategy (or any absolute strategy) to deliver. The term hurdle rate is also used to describe the *target return*, or the minimum target return, as this is the barrier investors need to clear in order for an investment to make sense. If an investment strategy is truly an absolute strategy, one should consider a constant hurdle rate. On the other hand, I have noticed absolute funds returns can exhibit temporary deviations from a trend, or can track the market or some aggregate returns. One simple way for investors to compensate for this is to demand an absolute strategy deliver a return in excess of the risk-free rate (such as the rate of short-term T-bills) close to or above the long-run rate of return. In practice, the average of the one-month London Interbank Offered Rate (LIBOR) plus 400 basis points is commonly used for the hurdle rate. *LIBOR* is a reference rate used by banks for lending. Surpassing the hurdle is clearly a sign of a superior investment strategy—one that delivers a higher return with lower volatility.

The next step in the process is to determine whether a pure-alpha strategy can deliver the expected target rate of return. Looking at Table 14.2, one sees, over the 1997–2004 period, the average annual rate of return for the hurdle rate would have been 7.88 percent, a figure close to the long-run historical average of 8 percent for stocks. A sample for the average of the alpha strategies would have more than satisfied the hurdle rate of returns. It would have delivered a 9.98 percent average annual return and would have fallen below the target rate only once during the eight-year sample. In contrast, looking at the data in Table 14.1, it is apparent the beta strategy would have fallen short of the hurdle rate in three of eight years. Although it appears the alpha strategy delivers a higher return than the beta strategy (9.98 percent versus 9.71 percent), the comparison is not a fair one. If one believes in the alpha strategy, one should be willing to assume one can also choose long-only managers who can outperform their benchmarks. These active managers would certainly deliver a return higher than that of an index strategy. Thus, if active managers add 27 basis points after fees, index strategies will match the alpha strategies' performance.

Table 14.2
The feasibility of alpha strategies.

Alpha Strategies	1997	1998	1999	2000	2001	2002	2003	2004	Average Return	Standard Deviation	Sharpe Ratio
Convertible Arbitrage	14.81%	3.11%	16.08%	17.77%	13.78%	8.60%	10.80%	1.10%	10.61%	6.09%	1.08
CTA Global	12.27%	14.30%	1.82%	7.32%	3.52%	14.57%	11.64%	5.17%	8.73%	5.01%	0.94
Distressed Securities	16.70%	−2.26%	19.75%	4.81%	14.65%	5.86%	27.34%	17.89%	12.73%	9.58%	0.91
Emerging Markets	22.57%	−26.66%	44.62%	−3.82%	12.52%	5.76%	31.27%	14.30%	10.56%	21.82%	0.30
Equity Market Neutral	15.43%	10.58%	13.15%	15.35%	8.18%	4.71%	6.29%	4.71%	9.72%	4.49%	1.27
Event Driven	20.98%	1.00%	22.72%	9.04%	9.32%	−1.08%	20.48%	12.43%	11.54%	9.07%	0.83
Fixed-Income Arbitrage	12.43%	−8.04%	12.63%	5.70%	7.81%	7.56%	8.35%	6.26%	6.41%	6.45%	0.37
Long/Short Equity	21.35%	14.59%	31.40%	12.01%	−1.20%	−6.38%	19.31%	8.62%	11.87%	12.22%	0.64

Alpha Strategies	1997	1998	1999	2000	2001	2002	2003	2004	Average Return	Standard Deviation	Sharpe Ratio
Merger Arbitrage	17.44%	7.77%	17.97%	18.10%	2.87%	-0.90%	8.34%	4.83%	9.33%	7.44%	0.72
Relative Value	16.51%	5.27%	17.15%	13.35%	8.63%	2.77%	12.15%	5.71%	10.08%	5.40%	1.13
Short Selling	3.07%	27.07%	-22.55%	22.80%	10.20%	27.27%	-23.87%	-4.66%	3.01%	20.76%	-0.05
Average Return	15.78%	4.25%	15.88%	11.13%	8.21%	6.25%	12.01%	6.94%	9.98%	4.36%	1.37
Funds of Funds	17.39%	4.20%	28.50%	7.84%	3.52%	1.26%	11.45%	7.08%	9.85%	8.98%	0.65
Hurdle Rate*	9.67%	9.55%	9.30%	10.44%	7.72%	5.76%	5.20%	5.54%	7.88%		

* The hurdle rate is defined as the average of one month LIBOR plus 400 basis points.

Source: EDHEC (Ecole De Haute Etudes Commerciales) Index returns

Interesting results are also delivered by hedge funds of funds, which enable investors to access a basket of hedge funds otherwise inaccessible as a result of the individual funds' various capital and net-worth requirements. Hedge funds of funds enable individual investors the ability, for a fee of course, to pool their resources to satisfy the individual hedge funds' minimum investment requirements. They also enable investors to spread around their funds and thereby diversify their investments. Although hedge funds of funds charge an additional fee of approximately 10 percent of gains plus a 1 percent management cost, they are alluring in that they apply the diversification and risk-reduction techniques outlined in earlier chapters to the individual hedge-fund strategy selection. As reported in Table 14.2, these funds deliver an average annual return that is competitive with both pure-alpha and pure-beta strategies. The average returns suggest a funds-of-funds strategy is viable. Upon closer inspection, however, it becomes apparent the strategy is more volatile than the pure-alpha strategy and has a much lower Sharpe ratio. Worst of all, the funds-of-funds strategy misses the hurdle rate in four of the eight sample years. In contrast, the pure-alpha strategy only misses in one year while the pure-beta strategy misses in three years out of eight.

By definition, a pure-alpha strategy has zero beta and is uncorrelated to a benchmark. Also, to the extent that the alpha strategy exhibits some random variation, we also know its valuation is uncorrelated to a benchmark and hopefully other alpha strategies. If this is the case, one can take advantage of the law of large numbers and pool together several alpha strategies. One can also say the variation in the expected returns of the multiple alpha strategies declines as the number of strategies increases.

To pure-alpha or not to pure-alpha? Sometimes, pension plans have regulatory constraints limiting the amount of leverage they can undertake, and thus are poor candidates for the pure-alpha play. In other cases, an alpha strategy can go through a lockup period where it holds a leveraged position for a time period, which can be an imprudent position for investors and pension plans. Another potential downside is the pure-alpha strategy is exactly that—its returns are uncorrelated with a benchmark. Yet we also know from the CAPM that *a combination of the alpha and beta strategies* will produce lower volatility for an overall portfolio.[3] So, despite the downsides, there is still good reason for investors and pension plans to add pure-alpha, and thus market exposure. If one can find managers who deliver a pure-alpha product, through the use of ETFs or derivative markets one can portion out the desired amount of market exposure. By combining the pure-alpha and pure-beta strategies, one can construct a plan both less expensive than the pure-alpha strategy and able to deliver the absolute returns desired in the long run. The exact alpha and beta strategy combination depends on an investor's hurdle rate of return and risk tolerance (that is, the volatility an investor desires or expects).

The portable-alpha and CAA strategies share the common view that an active strategy is superior to a passive one. In both cases, it assumes managers have better information. The asset-allocation and global macro strategies assume one can take advantage of the cyclical fluctuations in the different asset classes' relative performances (that is, the beta bets). On the other hand, the portable-alpha strategy argues managers have superior information and can produce excess returns relative to a benchmark. In addition, alpha strategy advocates do not believe managers can consistently anticipate the different asset classes' relative performances. In other words, they don't believe managers can make consistent beta bets.

In contrast, passive strategy advocates do not believe a manager can add alpha on a consistent basis, nor do they believe one can anticipate the asset classes' relative performances (that is, the beta bets). I take a different view. I believe every strategy has its day. Sometimes, when stock picking (that is, the alpha bet) is easier, sometimes when choosing sectors or asset classes (that is, the beta bet) best adds returns to a strategy, and sometimes when one should do nothing (that is, index) and stay on the long-run SAA path.

The portable-alpha strategy is usually sold as a very different strategy from that of a straight asset-allocation or global macro hedge-fund strategy. Yet, although philosophies and approaches to portfolio construction are quite different, there is an equivalence between the strategies under certain general conditions. I've argued, even in the context of portable alpha, pure-alpha is not always optimal and some broader market exposure is desirable. How then is a portable-alpha strategy very different from a straight asset-allocation strategy? If the optimal portable-alpha strategy is one where market exposure results in an overall portfolio beta between zero and one (a low-risk zone), one can argue the two approaches are essentially equivalent. If the beta exposure is between zero and one, the market exposure does not require any leveraged positions. Therefore, it is easy to see both strategies are focusing on choosing an allocation close to that of the long-only efficient frontier. One can certainly find an asset allocation with the same expected return and risk characteristics of the portable-alpha strategy.

Leverage is one major difference between the portable-alpha and traditional long-only asset-allocation strategies. Shorting possibilities and the ability to leverage the market more than 100 percent expand the investor's opportunity set, or efficient frontier. In effect, expanded choices enable smart investors to either increase their return or reduce their risk. One can argue, over the past two decades, most progress in investment science has been made in risk control. Developing the alpha strategies is a testament to this. Risk controls probably have a differential impact in the portable-alpha strategy's favor relative to the asset-allocation (beta) strategy.

If the various alpha strategies are truly uncorrelated, the law of large numbers suggests the increasing number of strategies (that is, bets) reduces the variability of the expected returns the strategies generate. The greater the number of managers (that is, bets), the tighter the distribution of returns around the mean expected returns. Yet whether any of the strategies—alpha, TAA, macro hedge fund, active, or passive—are viable depends on market conditions. Under some conditions, all the strategies are equivalent. Under other conditions, the alpha strategy holds more promise. In spite of this, however, from the average investor's perspective, the alpha strategy can be out of reach. Hedge funds require minimum investments. In addition, they have liquidity requirements and necessitate investors keep track of their market exposure (that is, long–short positions) to add market (beta) exposure. This is something individuals may not be willing to do or may not be able to do. The various transaction costs may in effect prevent most investors from pursuing alpha strategies.

As wealth levels increase, however, investors may be able to amortize these transaction costs over their higher net worths and hire managers who can perform all the needed services. Some portable-alpha strategies may only be available to the wealthiest investors and larger pension plans. This does not rule out the role of pure-alpha strategies in a regular asset-allocation portfolio. As I have already mentioned, the pure-alpha strategy can be uncorrelated with the various asset classes and, in the context of risk reduction alone, can merit some exposure in a global asset-allocation portfolio. New developments in the markets are providing increasing access to the hedge-fund industry, which in turn means access to the pure-alpha players. Also, because I believe there is a time for everything, a global CAA process can find the need to alter its beta and alpha exposures. As shown in Table 14.3, in the long run, the returns delivered by the alpha, beta, and hedge-funds-of-funds strategies converge, with all exceeding the hurdle rate of returns. Hence, each and every one of the strategies is viable; there is more than one way to skin a cat.

Table 14.3
The feasibility of alpha and beta strategies.

	1997	1998	1999	2000	2001	2002	2003	2004	Average Return	Standard Deviation	Sharpe Ratio
Average Return	15.78%	4.25%	15.88%	11.13%	8.21%	6.25%	12.01%	6.94%	9.98%	4.36%	1.37
Funds of Funds	17.39%	4.20%	28.50%	7.84%	3.52%	1.26%	11.45%	7.08%	9.85%	8.98%	0.65
Hurdle Rate*	9.67%	9.55%	9.30%	10.44%	7.72%	5.76%	5.20%	5.54%	7.88%		
Domestic Equity Index**	32.36%	23.70%	18.92%	-1.69%	-7.78%	-19.84%	31.08%	13.18%	9.71%	19.10%	0.30
Global Macro	23.91%	8.42%	15.73%	8.15%	5.49%	4.96%	17.25%	4.60%	10.87%	7.08%	0.97

* The hurdle rate is defined as the average of one month LIBOR plus 400 basis points.

** The Domestic Equity Index consists of a weighted average of the large-, mid-, and small-cap stocks.

The indices' weights are 70 percent, 20 percent, and 10 percent, respectively.

Table 14.3, however, also reveals it is the global macro strategy that delivers the highest rate of return over the period. This is consistent with my view that the global macro strategy is the hedge-fund version of our CAA strategy. Over cycles, as market conditions change, the CAA strategy can increase its exposure to index funds (ETFs), sectors, asset classes, and/or pure-alpha strategies.

15

PUTTING IT ALL TOGETHER: VALUE TIMING

Modern portfolio theory developments over the last 30 years provide a framework for addressing the way an investment's risk should affect its expected returns. One powerful implication of the capital asset pricing model (CAPM) is that the market portfolio is on the efficient frontier. Thus, an individual who buys the market has an efficient portfolio producing an average risk-and-return profile. The market portfolio also measures the weighted average of all market participants' individual allocations—this is another powerful implication because it means, collectively, all the world asset-allocation plans cannot deliver a return higher than that of the world portfolio in any one year or over the plans' lifecycles. Therefore, in the aggregate, any investment or actuarial calculation of these plans must choose expected returns equal to, or less than, the long-run objective. Any deviation from the portfolio, such as a portfolio holding a greater proportion of stocks than the market, implies, on net, there must be someone holding portfolios that add to a lower proportion of stocks in such a way that the two cancel one another out. The world is a good benchmark all investors, as a group, cannot evade. The investment process must begin by conceding this point: Absent any information, one wants to hold the world portfolio. Such an allocation ensures the investor will in fact receive average returns. In a static world, the implication is a zero-sum game in which one person's gains are someone else's losses.

This is not to say investing is a zero-sum game—quite the contrary. I believe investing is a positive-sum activity. Through investment, one expands society's opportunity set. In turn, those investments result in net wealth increases. It is the investors' collective actions determining the net increments to wealth, and it is our investment decisions determining what share of the increments we receive. Again, in a dynamic sense, whether we do better than the average depends on the way we position our portfolios to take advantage of that net wealth creation. It is through collective investment investors expand the world pie and, by correctly positioning our portfolios, we simultaneously affect world investments, rates of returns, and our shares of the pie. If we as investors make the right decisions, everyone benefits. We receive a higher rate of return in the process of expanding the rest of the world's opportunities.

Just as it is true individual investors can differ from average investors in terms of their risk tolerances and preferences, it's also true individual asset-allocation plans can differ from those of the aggregate economy. Collectively, however, investors cannot avoid economy-wide constraints. A weighted average of the individual asset-allocation plans must ultimately add up to the market allocation. The market allocation is a good starting point in any strategic asset allocation (SAA) program. One can argue it is the relevant allocation for the seemingly infinite number of foundations and trust funds. The market allocation can also be optimal for retirement plans, such as 401(k)s, that boast many participants. Hence, a market SAA must be considered the appropriate starting point for any investor who hopes to do better than average.

So, let's review our global market benchmark. The equity/fixed-income split is the most important decision made in determining a portfolio allocation. Conventional wisdom and the two asset classes' market capitalization suggest a 60/40 split between equities and fixed income. In Figure 15.1, the asset-allocation tree's last column shows our final equity/fixed-income allocation, as per the global market-weight approach I propose. The global portfolio's equity allocation is approximately 60 percent. According to the Morgan Stanley Capital Index (MSCI), which I use as a rough guideline for a global equity allocation, the U.S. is approximately 50 percent of the world equity markets. Hence, 30 percent of our benchmark portfolio is allocated to domestic stocks and 30 percent to international stocks. The U.S. allocation is further subdivided by size and style. Large-, mid-, and small-caps account for almost 70 percent, 20 percent, and 10 percent of the U.S. equity markets, respectively (if we use the Russell Investment Group as our guide). Hence, the 30 percent of the global portfolio allocated to domestic stocks is split as follows: 21 percent large-cap, 6 percent mid-cap, and 3 percent small-cap.

From BARRA, we know approximately 50 percent of U.S. stocks are value and 50 percent are growth. The large-cap allocation is thus equally split into value and growth stocks, with 10.5 percent of portfolio assets going to large-cap value stocks and 10.5 percent to large-cap growth stocks. Mid-cap value stocks and mid-cap growth stocks each receive a 3 percent allocation, and only 1.5 percent is allocated to small-cap value and small-cap growth stocks.

For international stocks, we focus on only three regions, or groups: Europe, Asia, and the emerging markets. Depending on the index used, the three regions account for 50 percent, 30 percent, and 20 percent of the rest of the world's (that is, non-U.S.) market capitalization, respectively. Because only 30 percent of our benchmark portfolio's assets are going to international equities, it follows the portfolio allocates 15 percent to Europe, 9 percent to Asia, and 6 percent to the emerging markets.

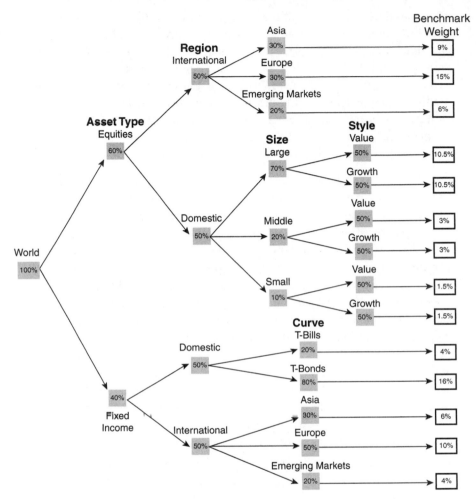

Figure 15.1 Strategic asset allocation.

The fixed-income allocation of our global portfolio is 40 percent of total assets. Different indices can give a slightly different allocation to the different countries, but (on average) most major global indices would put the U.S. fixed-income share around 50 percent. This means 20 percent of the overall portfolio is allocated to U.S. fixed-income instruments. Within the U.S., a 20/80 split between short- and long-term bonds seems reasonable. This gives us a final allocation of 4 percent short-maturity U.S. fixed-income instruments and 16 percent long-maturity U.S. fixed-income instruments.

Again, within most indices, the rest-of-the-world breakdown is 50 percent Europe, 30 percent Asia, and 20 percent emerging markets. So, as was the case with international equities, our regional fixed-income exposure is 15 percent Europe, 9 percent Asia, and 6 percent emerging markets.

With our basic global market benchmark set, some issues arise as to the way to best implement the SAA strategy. I now address several of these head-on.

The portable-alpha strategy is usually sold as very different from an asset-allocation strategy. Portable-alpha strategies enable investors to take a modular approach toward investing, combining a variety of alpha sources with the market, or beta, exposure they desire in a highly risk-controlled environment. I have argued, when the market exposure (beta) of the pure-alpha strategy is between zero and one, a traditional asset-allocation approach can match it in terms of expected returns and risk. In effect, the two strategies can be each other's equivalent at such times. The argument in the pure-alpha strategy's favor rests on hedge-fund managers' ability to make leveraged investments as opposed to traditional asset allocations that do not normally allow for leveraged investments. Yet, when leverage is ruled out on theoretical grounds, whether one chooses an alpha strategy over an asset-allocation strategy is a matter of indifference because the two are equivalent. Transaction costs, however, tilt the balance in one strategy's favor over the other. For small investors, the transaction costs of implementing a portable-alpha strategy with some market exposure may not be feasible. Most hedge funds have liquidity constraints, net worth conditions, and leverage requirements, all which combine to exclude many investors from pursuing a full fledged alpha strategy. The transaction-cost barrier alone keeps many investors in a pure asset-allocation strategy. This does not mean, however, alpha strategies cannot play a role in asset-allocation plans.

By definition, a pure-alpha strategy has zero beta and is uncorrelated to a benchmark. We also know from the CAPM that an alpha and beta strategy combination produces an overall lower volatility in a portfolio. So, investors and pension planners have many reasons to choose to add market exposure to their portfolios. More, to the extent the alpha strategy has some random variation, we also know its valuation is most likely uncorrelated to other alpha strategies. Under these conditions, one can take advantage of the law of large numbers and pool together several alpha strategies. If we do this, we can say the variation in the multiple alpha strategies' expected returns declines as the number of strategies increases. All this means adding a pure-alpha-strategy allocation to a portfolio may not only be desirable, but also necessary.

With these guidelines in mind, we can now modify the SAA to include some alpha strategies. Accounting for the fact alpha strategies really do not deliver pure alphas, it follows historical relationships overestimate the alpha strategies' contribution by adding some beta effect, especially during periods when the market is rising. For this reason, we scale down the optimal alpha allocation derived using historical relationships and use our benchmark allocation for the nontraditional asset classes. My experience suggests a 20 percent allocation to alpha strategies is desirable in a portfolio. So, all we need to do is determine which vehicle to use to fill our alpha bucket. Because many hedge funds are sold as absolute strategies, hedge funds and some closed-end funds are most likely pure-alpha strategies. Figure 15.2 describes the benchmark inclusive of the nontraditional/pure-alpha strategies.

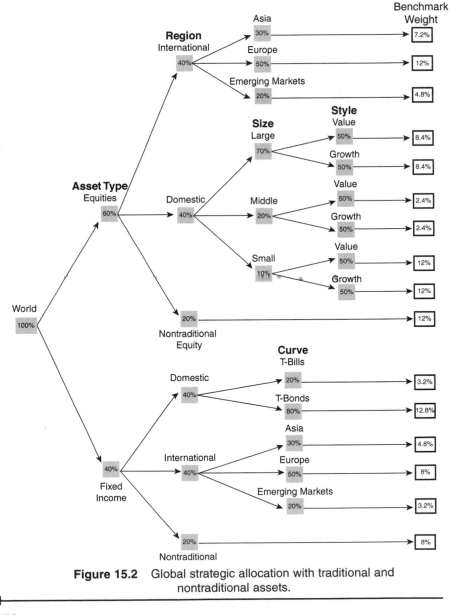

Figure 15.2 Global strategic allocation with traditional and nontraditional assets.

Next, we'll return to the active versus passive debate. Constructing major stock indices holds the key to deciding whether to go active or passive. In general, stock indices are capitalization weighted. This means larger stocks tend to get more weight in an index. For example, during the mid-1990s, the ten largest holdings of the S&P 500 at one time accounted for roughly 50 percent of the index's capitalization. Thus, when the top-ten holdings outperformed the index, the 490 stocks in the bottom 50 percent would have underperformed, on average. The odds an active manager would have outperformed during that time would have been low. The implication is an index strategy during large-cap cycles is the superior strategy.

On the other hand, during a small-cap cycle, the 490 stocks would have out-performed, on average. Once again, even a monkey throwing darts at the S&P stock board would have had a good chance at beating the market during such a period. Hence, an active strategy may be the desirable strategy during small-cap cycles. Notice this is not an inefficient-market story, such as the argument smaller issues have a smaller number of analysts following them and thus are not as efficiently priced as larger issues. This view would support my asset-allocation story, but there's no need to depend on it. The point is the odds of outperforming the market over size cycles are not constant. Alpha, as tradi-tionally measured, increases during small-cap cycles and declines during large-cap cycles. More important, the alpha coefficient does not really capture a manager's true skill in picking stocks. Even managers with no special insight have an excellent chance at outperforming an index during a small-cap cycle. In summary, size and weighting schemes alter the odds of an active manager outperforming an index. I believe, when the odds are in your favor, you should take the chance.

Size Cycles

Size cycles also have implications for the different style, size, and location strategies. For example, to the extent small-cap indices are closer to being equally weighted than other indices, it follows the number of stocks outper-forming in a small-cap index is close to the 50 percent mark at all times. This means there is little or no fluctuation in the number of stocks outperforming or underperforming during small-cap cycles. Cyclical size fluctuations are thus less important for small-cap managers, and whether these managers outper-form is more closely related to their stock-picking abilities than to size cycles. On the other hand, large-cap managers—even if they are exceptional stock-pickers—have great difficulty outperforming during large-cap cycles.

Irregardless of a manager's superiority, one may be better off indexing during large-cap cycles to avoid damaging relative performance. To sum up, even if one identifies superior alpha-generating managers, an SAA or continuously selecting small-cap active managers may be the optimal strategy. In contrast, a continuous allocation to large-cap managers may not be desirable, even if the managers are superior alpha-generators.

This analysis is consistent with the popular belief one is better off indexing large-cap allocations and going to active managers for small-caps. I agree this is the best-case scenario for a basic SAA, but I also believe one can do better. By strategically tilting between active and passive managers over cycles—this goes for large- and small-cap, value, growth, and hedge-fund managers—the probability of generating above-average returns is very high.

Style Differences

Is one style (that is, value or growth) better than the other? If so, why? *Style differences* certainly interact with the size effect to produce their own relative performance cycles. Take any index, such as the S&P 600, 500, or 400. The number of value stocks in each is much larger than the number of growth stocks. Because we know the style split used in these indices is such that each style's market-cap is about 50 percent, the larger number of value names means value stocks have, on average, smaller capitalizations than growth stocks. I have already shown the capitalization weightings of most indices tilt the balance in active management's favor during the small-cap cycles. So, it follows small-cap cycles tilt the odds not only in all active managers' favor, but value managers in particular.

The style differences also offer a likelihood of success unrelated to the size effect. Numerous studies show value stocks, on average, tend to beat their respective broad-based indices. However, even if the result of value stocks outperforming holds true, it may not be advisable to pursue an active value strategy. Here's why: An active strategy invariably leads to a concentrated portfolio in relation to the value stocks universe. Equally important is the fact that by the value-selection criteria's very nature, when misses occur, they can be disastrous to a portfolio. A simple example illustrates this point. Assume a stock is undervalued at $15, but its price declines to $12. Is it even more undervalued at this point? Should you increase your exposure to the stock? No and no. In short, the value approach can sometimes induce an investor to double-up on a loser, and such self-destructing stocks can have dire implications for portfolio performance. On the other hand, growth investors have a natural way of preserving all their gains. When growth slows down, they get out.

My argument makes the case for indexing the bulk of a value portfolio during value cycles because this is when the likelihood of blow-ups is the highest. This line of reasoning suggests an active strategy is more apt to be successful when applied to a portfolio's growth portion. Ironically, if growth cycles are associated with rising stock prices, it follows the chance of stock blow-ups is greatly reduced during growth cycles. Hence, the odds of an active value strategy being successful are highest during small-cap and growth cycles.

With the increasing market globalization, should investors persist in making the U.S./non-U.S. designation? The California example used in Chapter 10, "Location, Location, Location?," answers this best. When California experienced an energy crisis not so long ago, corporations in the state had to choose between paying a higher price for energy and doing without the energy. During blackout periods, those without their own power-generating facilities had to shut down. Yet, whether the California companies paid for the energy or not, the profitability of their in-state facilities declined relative to the rest of the U.S. The multiplant California corporations, however, could minimize higher energy costs' impact by shifting production to out-of-state or out-of-country facilities where energy was readily available at the right price. California's single-plant facilities meanwhile took it on the chin. If you compare that time period's California-headquartered nontech stocks' performances to their respective indices, the following is revealed: California large-caps were within 20 basis points of the S&P 500's performance during the energy crisis, California mid-caps lagged the S&P 400 by 312 basis points, and California small-caps fell behind the S&P 600 by 683 basis points. The data clearly show while all stocks underperformed their respective indices, underperformance increased the further you went down the size scale.

This simple example returns us to a very important point: Mobility and location matter a great deal. Immobile production factors bear a burden when bad things happen in their locality, and they reap the benefits when good things occur. In some cases, consumers are immobile and, in other cases, production is stationary. Either way, both consumers and investors have a vested interest in protecting themselves against adverse shocks. Those who choose not to move away from an unfavorable local situation can protect themselves through their investments. Immobility can be the result of natural barriers, such as transportation costs (for example, you cannot move your real estate) and artificial barriers, such as immigration restrictions, taxation, and even the portability of pension plans across state and national borders. As long as geographic and fiscal and monetary policies persist across countries, there will be a location effect.

Size and location also interact. Not taking this relationship into account can put a portfolio in jeopardy, while being mindful of it can play to an investor's advantage. Looking at the example of Japan over the last decade, we can see the size–location effect in action. Most global managers knew Japan was an under-performer waiting to happen, but most did not greatly reduce their allocations to the country. Instead, most chose to buy the largest companies in Japan. In doing so, they minimized their exposure because these companies were multi-national and had a large chunk of their production facilities outside the coun-try. Yet, although the global allocation to Japan appeared neutral, it was effectively an underweight. The Japanese exposure was much less than the allo-cations to the large Japanese companies. To conclude, a sound international strategy can best be described as a location strategy applied to small-cap com-panies, where size is just a proxy for the location factor.

If one compares asset classes on a pair-wise, risk-adjusted basis over the long term, neither asset class in a pair dominates the other. Yet, a great deal of value can be added by departing from long-run market weights from time to time. Sometimes, these departures can persist for quite a while when cycles persist and have been correctly identified. Why should a plan constrain itself as if it had one of its hands tied behind its back? A sound plan shouldn't. Instead, it should have all the invest-ment alternatives at its disposal at all times. Such a plan would also need a strate-gy for identifying the relative attractiveness of the different investment strategies over cycles. Committing to a single strategy only guarantees mediocrity in the long run. More often than not, this is because the ex post optimal result is a corner solu-tion. As reported in Chapter 2, "The Case for Cyclical Asset Allocation," the Sharpe ratio reveals the optimal size, style, location, and/or equity/fixed-income allocation is a corner solution (that is, between a 90 percent and 100 percent allocation to one of the choices) approximately 80 percent of the time:

- The balanced, or equity/fixed-income, allocation produced a corner solu-tion in 19 of the 30 sample years. The optimal allocation was 100 percent stocks for 11 of the years and 100 percent bonds for eight other years.
- The style choice produced a corner 28 times. During 14 years, a 90 percent or better allocation to growth stocks was optimal. For 15 other years, a 90 percent or better allocation to value stocks was best.
- The size choice produced 24 corner solutions equally split between large- and small-cap allocations.
- The domestic/international choice also produced 24 corner solutions. During nine of the years a 90 to 100 percent allocation to international stocks would have been the right call. For 15 of the years, a 100 percent allocation to domestic stocks would have been the most advantageous.

These results implicitly suggest an all-or-nothing strategy over cycles maximizes any plan's risk-adjusted returns. But, risk's realities loom large here. When you miss on a corner solution, you miss big. Hence, for the risk-averse investor, it can be desirable to minimize long-run volatility relative to the long-run average return. The benchmark SAA allocation does just that: It allocates funds in proportion to asset-class market weights. Yet, although deviating from the long-run solution entails some risk, it also promises added reward.

Without question, the more random the deviation, the greater the risk. But, notice our all-or-nothing strategy would have been successful 80 percent of the time—a very high success rate over the long haul. Notice, in particular, there appears to be a persistent patterning of the corner solutions. This is very useful information easily exploited in a cyclical asset allocation (CAA) strategy. The process has only three general guidelines: 1) Ensure that the strategy returns to the long-run allocation. 2) Develop a way to identify cycles. 3) Identify the signals that will tilt a portfolio in the proper direction.

Ensure That the Strategy Returns to the Long-Run Allocation

The simplest way to do this is to tilt around the long-run values. Doing so provides a time-consistent active strategy, while holding the world weights is a reliable way to produce a long-run, mean-reverting, and sensible outcome.

Develop a Way to Identify Cycles

Changes to the economic environment (whether caused by taxation, regulation, or monetary policy) impact the market and asset prices. In turn, one can find distinct patterns to the market's asset prices reassessment. Visually, these are your cycles.

Identify the Signals That Will Tilt a Portfolio in the Proper Direction

Once the linkages between the economic environment and the various asset classes' relative performances are identified, that outline, combined with a reliable economic forecast, suggests the portfolio tilts need to take advantage of the foreseen economic environment.

One must also understand navigating the various investment opportunities around the world requires a logical framework that clearly lays out all the investment choices. With logic and choice on their side, investors need not only a return assumption as they select between asset classes, but also a conviction in the their success's likelihood. That's why the CAA process is probability based. Armed with probability information, the CAA strategy develops decision rules for determining how and when to choose an investment's style, location, and/or size, and whether to do so in a passive or active mode. This whole process is the value-timing approach to asset allocation.

The first decision investors who are about to embrace this approach must make is whether they have any opinion about the asset classes. Let's assume sample investors have no strong feelings about any one asset class. In this case, their allocation probabilities are set at 50 percent on a pair-wise basis. In other words, the 50 percent probability suggests there is an equal chance any one asset class will outperform the other in the future. Hence, because these investors have no strong opinions about the economy's or any one asset class's future, they should buy the market. This is their default allocation and there is no reason to change it. Now, because our sample investors have embraced the CAA style, they should only deviate from their market SAAs when they have strong convictions to do so. As I have argued, probabilities represent that degree of conviction. If one is 100 percent certain large-caps are going to outperform small-caps, the size allocation should be as follows: 100 percent to large-caps and 0 percent to small-caps. Allocations of 0 percent and 100 percent convey certainty in a conviction, while a 50 percent allocation conveys an absence of conviction. It follows the deviations from a basic allocation should be in direct proportion to how much the probabilities deviate from the 50 percent mark. Using a factor of two produces some familiar results. If an asset-class outcome's probability is 100 percent, the difference between the 100 percent and the 50 percent neutral position multiplied by two gives us the new allocation for that asset class: 100 percent. This is exactly the way one correctly deviates from a long-run SAA. This simple allocation procedure produces tilts designed to take advantage of a changing economic environment.

If the CAA theory can only offer the insight that weighting schemes and small-cap cycles are related, all we have in our hands is a simple market-timing story. If this is the case, all the CAA strategist needs to do is predict small-cap cycles to determine the odds of an active manager outperforming a passive manager. But, there is more to this story. I presented the argument in Chapters 11, "Eye on Elasticity," and 12, "Keeping the Wheels on the Hedge-Fund ATV," government regulations affect the industries' supply and demand. I also argued there are different responses to different economic shocks. Finally, I set forth the idea supply-and-demand elasticities are directly related to the alpha (that is, excess return) and beta (that is, risk) stock parameters. Putting this together, one can come to the conclusion different alphas and betas exist for different economic environments. *So, the portfolio strategy outlined in this book is much more than a market-timing story. It is a strategy that takes advantage of the changes in alpha and beta that take place as the world states change.* Rather than time the market, the CAA strategy times the different sectors' valuations. In practice, this value-timing strategy identifies periods and conditions when one investing style is dominant (see Figure 15.3). More, particular economic parameters, or environmental conditions, correspond with these dominant cycles. To estimate these cycles, it becomes reasonable to ascertain the current economic environment as well as any presumed changes to it. The current environment and the estimated changes then dictate asset-allocation decisions. Because I believe different reaction coefficients exist for the different asset sectors, sizes, and styles, the CAA decision attempts to capture what I consider to be predictable responses to economic shocks. It is these shocks that give rise to changing alpha and beta parameters over cycles.

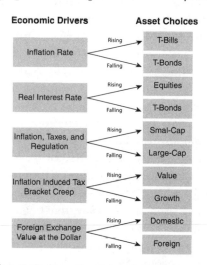

Economic Drivers   **Asset Choices**

Inflation Rate — Rising → T-Bills / Falling → T-Bonds

Real Interest Rate — Rising → Equities / Falling → T-Bonds

Inflation, Taxes, and Regulation — Rising → Smal-Cap / Falling → Large-Cap

Inflation Induced Tax Bracket Creep — Rising → Value / Falling → Growth

Foreign Exchange Value at the Dollar — Rising → Domestic / Falling → Foreign

Figure 15.3   Asset choices: the link between economic drivers and relative economic performance.

Once again, this is not a black-box process. In practice, it is much more than a simulator digesting a large number of statistical variables and spitting out an investment plan. The CAA framework logically formulates asset-class returns' probability. The probabilities are then applied to an investor's long-term goals, producing a recommended asset allocation that, once run through a quantitative framework, overweights the opportunistic sectors and underweights the overvalued sectors. Doing so removes any unintended bets from a portfolio. Where many asset-allocation approaches argue the same combination of expected returns and the variance–covariance matrix produces the same allocation each and every time, the CAA process goes the extra step of deriving the probability asset classes can provide returns in excess of the long-run, mean-reverting allocation. These probabilities are derived from, or are related to, the overall economic environment and the investor's outlook. If the allocation these probabilities suggest does not match an investor's outlook, either the allocation or the outlook must change so the two are aligned. More than likely, an allocation is changed to fit an outlook. This approach's importance is that CAA allocations are intuitive—investors can see and understand the needed adjustments. Black boxes provide average returns. The CAA strategy captures the above-average returns predictable cycles generate.

Investors embracing the CAA approach enjoy both choice and a likelihood of success. To see this, consider the inputs, or probabilities, generated by an investment counsel following a value-timing strategy (see Table 15.1). The probability of equities outperforming fixed income in this example is 74 percent. The probability of cash outperforming bonds is 55 percent. Figure 15.4 illustrates the way these probabilities tilt the benchmark allocation and produce a final allocation used in the CAA value-timing strategy. The 74 percent probability of stocks outperforming bonds leads to an increased exposure for equities at the expense of fixed income. Ultimately, the equity allocation is increased to 71.15 percent from a neutral 60 percent. Meanwhile, the fixed-income allocation is reduced to 28.85 percent from a benchmark 40 percent. Absent any additional information, the scaling back of the fixed-income portion would be done proportionately. For instance, the cash allocation would be reduced to 2.3 percent from 3.2 percent. Because the probability estimates suggest cash will outperform bonds (the probability of this is 55 percent), however, we need to reallocate fixed income away from bonds and into cash. Hence, the cash exposure is increased in this example to 2.42 percent from 2.3 percent. This final allocation to cash is part of a two-step process: First, determine the new allocation to fixed income. Second, within fixed income, determine the new allocation to cash.

The probabilities' net effect reported in Table 15.1 can be viewed in Figure 15.4's next-to-last column. The differences between columns one and two are the overall asset-allocation tilts that the model produces. These tilts can be generally described: The strategy increases the exposure to U.S. equities at the fixed-income instruments' expense. Notice also the exposures to each international component of the portfolio, as well as to nontraditional equities, are all increased. Within the U.S., the exposures of large-caps and in particular growth stocks are higher. All fixed-income allocations are reduced, with the largest proportionate reduction coming for U.S. and European bonds.

Table 15.1
The conviction level.

Bonds > Cash	**45%**
Equities > Bonds	**74%**
Value > Growth	**40%**
Large-Cap > Mid-Cap	**65%**
Mid-Cap > Small-Cap	**54%**
Large-Cap > Small-Cap	**62%**
Nontraditional > Bonds	**64%**
Nontraditional > Equities	**58%**
Equity	
U.S. > International	**53%**
U.S. > Europe	**59%**
U.S. > Asia Ex-Japan	**48%**
U.S. > Japan	**59%**
U.S. > Emerging Markets	**46%**
Fixed Income	
U.S. > International	**53%**
U.S. > Europe	**59%**
U.S. > Asia Ex-Japan	**48%**
U.S. > Japan	**59%**
U.S. > Emerging Markets	**46%**

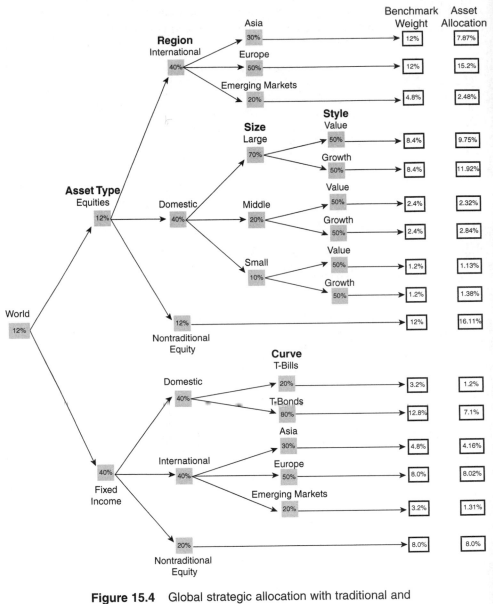

Figure 15.4   Global strategic allocation with traditional and nontraditional assets.

Working backward, we can easily derive the implicit outlook generating this asset allocation. The strategy is bullish on stocks—in particular, foreign stocks. It also assumes dollar appreciation. On the domestic front, large-cap growth stocks are favored.

Given the current outlook for U.S. growth and the appreciating dollar's prospects, it is easy to see the bullish bias in this asset allocation. The growth outlook also produces the expectation of a rising or higher real interest rate, so it is not surprising the allocation reduces the exposure to fixed-income instruments.

Looking at the final allocation and deriving the implicit forecast is intended to ensure no unintended bets are made. The derived implicit forecast must agree with the probability estimates and the overall macroeconomic outlook. Only then can one have a consistent asset allocation free of unintended bets.

Historical experience more than confirms general economic factors impact stock prices in the aggregate. Changes in interest rates, inflation rates, oil prices, exchange rates, tax rates, regulations, and trade restrictions produce different effects across industry lines and hence asset classes. During the past three decades, these variables have covered an extraordinarily wide value range. It thus seems natural such a wide value range elicits equivalently dramatic and diverse responses from equities. In other words, in addition to an overall stock market effect, there exists at least the potential for great differences in stock returns among the various asset classes. Yet the market's equity values reassessment is far from haphazard. Indeed, the conception and measurement of equity responses to macroeconomic events is straightforward. Distinct patterns have emerged over time, patterns that can guide the asset-allocation process.

Over the years, as I have come to identify and understand the asset classes' cyclical swings, I have also developed a few rules to help guide the asset-allocation process. For example, if one increases an exposure to a particular region or country, my analysis suggests one shift to the small-cap stocks in that region or country. Similarly, when a region is being deemphasized or underweighted, I recommend tilting toward the large-caps.

Another insight is when small-cap markets are anticipated in the U.S., one should tilt toward active managers—in particular, active large-cap managers. Selecting small-cap active managers is not as sensitive during small-cap cycles, no matter the hedge-fund or alpha strategies selection. Another simple rule is investors must be careful with regard to value management during volatile markets. The reasoning is a declining stock price does not necessarily lead a value manager to bail out of that stock, but a growth manager will likely do so. Each example brings us back to the idea the CAA value-timing strategy is built on a logical framework incorporating the predictable tilts of asset classes with the decision-rule of whether to go active or passive. Armed with this strategy, you will do better.

ENDNOTES

Chapter 1

1. A very nice and complete half-century financial economic development survey can be found in Fama and French (2004) and Perold (2004).

2. Sharpe (1992).

3. The CAPMs can be traced to Lintner (1965), Mossin (1966), Sharpe (1964), and Treynor (1962).

4. One CAPM application is to assess and measure fund managers' performance. See Jensen (1968), Sharpe (1964), and Treynor (1965). This application largely coincides with the establishment of the Employee Retirement Income and Security Act (ERISA). The legal structures that fell upon trustees as a result of the new law, combined with financial economic developments, resulted in a wider use of benchmark managers. The benchmarks began as a legal firewall for trustees operating under personal legal liability as a result of ERISA. Over time, the benchmark became more restrictive, requiring smaller tracking errors and style drifts.

Chapter 2

1. There is extensive literature on the size and style effects, such as Banz (1981); Barber and Lyon (1997); Chan and Lakonishok (2004); Chan, Jegadeesh, and Lakonishok (1995); Fama and French (1995 and 1998); La Porta, Lakonishok, Shleifer, and Vishny (1997); Liew and Vassalau (2000); Piotroski (2000); and Reinganum (1981).

2. I chose the 1975–2004 sample period for a number of reasons. The various data indices used in this period are mutually

exclusive. That is, if a stock belonged in the large-cap index (that is, the S&P 500), it would not have been in the small-cap index (that is, the S&P 400). Similarly, if a stock was a domestic stock (that is, included in the S&P 1500), it would not have been in the international stock universe. If a stock was considered a value stock, I did not want it to also be included in the value universe. The BARRA value and growth classifications ensured this was the case. A final reason for choosing this specific sample period is the bulk of the asset data is only available from 1975 on. This is the longest sample period for which I could get the data in the classifications that match the current exchange-traded funds' (ETFs) availability to satisfy the mutual-exclusion constraint I find essential.

3. Harry Markowitz's seminal paper (1952) marks modern financial literature's beginning. Subsequent publications by Jensen (1968), Lintner (1965 and 1969), Sharpe (1964), and Treynor (1962) led to modern financial risk metrics' development.

4. S&P/BARRA Indexes, Research and Indices description, BARRA.com (2005).

5. Sharpe (1992).

6. Many of the citations in endnote 1 for this chapter document this point.

7. See Jeremy Siegel (1998). The professor's views are not universally accepted, however, as noted in Bernstein (1996).

8. Chan and Lakonishok (2004).

9. A somewhat related problem occurs in empirical literature focusing on risk and volatility measurement. Because, in this literature, volatility is estimated using historical data, it poses many of the same problems. What is the right length for a historical period? If too long, it won't be relevant; if too short, it will be too noisy. The right balance tilts the estimation toward the hotter time period. The solution to this problem can be found in the time-series analysis Robert Engle (2004) pioneered and discussed in his Nobel lecture. The value at risk is one such solution. This is somewhat ironic as the opposite problem

occurs in the financial literature focusing on different asset classes' long-run rates-of-return measurements and economic policies' impact on long-run valuations. Thus, for the latter purpose, the Engle approach focuses on a much higher data frequency than necessary. Fortunately, Engle's colleague and Nobel Prize winner, Clive Granger, identified the problem's solution. His pioneer work (2004) focuses on lower event frequencies. Granger's approach is tailor made for cyclical asset allocation (CAA) purposes. Rather than trying to capture short-term fluctuations, this book's approach focuses on long-lasting changes in relative performance. The price paid for this approach is one must endure the short-term volatilities high-frequency events cause. Correctly identifying the turning points in the high-frequency events is of paramount importance to the success of the strategy set forth in this book. On the other hand, during low-frequency event periods, the relative performance differential lasts a longer time. Therefore, correctly timing the turning point is less important. If one gets in a little late or a little early, the value-timing strategy underperforms for a while, but (in due time) the differential performance makes up the difference—and then some.

Chapter 3

1. Fisher and Lorie (1964) are credited with the first careful historical stock returns study. Their follow-up study (1968) inspired a couple of former students, Ibbotson and Sinquefield (1976), to continue and expand on the original work. The latter team has become the source of the historical rates of returns for the different asset classes.

2. There is extensive literature on the stock/bond choice. See, for example, Bernstein (1996 and 1997), Fama and French (1993), and Sharpe (1973).

3. See endnote 1 in Chapter 1, "In Search of the Upside."

4. *Barrons* (1998).

5. See endnote 1 in Chapter 1, "In Search of the Upside."

6. Sharpe (1992).

7. My framework is described in Canto and Webb (1987 and 2001).

Chapter 5

1. The capitalized earnings model and the La Jolla Economics (LJE) modifications to it are only two of the many valuation models used to determine the equity risk premium and whether the market is overvalued or undervalued or the P/E ratio too high or too low.

   Other examples are Asness (2000), Campbell and Shiller (1998), Canto (2000), Fairfield (1994), Good (1991), Nicholson (1960), and White (2000).

2. A detailed version of the model is presented in Canto and Webb (2001).

Chapter 9

1. There is extensive literature on the market efficiency issue. For a range of opinions and views, see Barton (2004); Fama (1970); Grinold (1989); Gruber (1996); and Lanstein, Reid, and Rosenburg (1985).

2. For studies documenting persistent effects and other anomalies, see Blake, Das, Elton, and Gruber (1996); Goetzman and Ibbotson (1994); Grinblatt and Titman (1992); and Narasimhan (1990).

3. In general, these strategies aim to take advantage of perceived predictable cycles in relative performance. Market timing and tactical asset allocation (TAA) are only two tools used. A discussion of these strategies' pros and cons can be found in Bauer and Dahlquist (2001), Droms (1989), Jeffrey (1984), Sharpe (1975), and Shilling (1992). Lee and Phillips (1989) discuss the

differences between market timing and TAA. The following discuss the existence of patterns in mutual fund performance: Blake, Das, Elton, and Gruber (1996); Goetzman and Ibbotson (1994); Grinblatt and Sheridan (1992); and Hendrick, Patel, and Zeckhouser (1993). Other patterns are discussed in Asness (1997); Eleswarapu and Reinganum (2004); Grinblatt, Titman, and Wermers (1989); Hong, Lim, and Stein (2000); Liew and Vassalou (2000); Narasiman (1990); and Perez-Quiros and Timmerman (2000). All these studies are variations the cyclical strategy may exploit.

4. Sinquefield (1995).

Chapter 10

1. For an extension of the CAPM to an international framework, see Adler and Dumas (1983), Bekaert and Harvey (1995), Solnik (1974), and Stultz (1991).

2. There is extensive literature on economic integration's impact on the correlation among markets and industry groups. See, for example, Beckers, Connor, and Curds (1996); Beckers, Grinold, Rudd, and Stefek (1989); Canto and Webb (1987 and 2001); and Freeman (1998).

3. Canto and Webb (2001) provide a full model description.

4. An analysis of fiscal policies' impact on state economies with mobile and immobile factors can be found in Canto and Webb (1987).

5. Ibid.

6. See Canto (1982) and Bollman et al (1982) for an analysis that is applicable to the oil industry.

7. There is extensive literature focusing on the same topic: Dabora and Froot (1999); Diermier and Solnik (2001); Geert and Heston (1994 and 1995); Hoffman, Kopp, Lin, and Thurston (2004); Lessard (1974 and 1976); and Solnik (1974) represent a nice cross-section.

8. Canto and Webb (1987 and 2001).

9. La Jolla Economics (1999).

Chapter 11

1. Financial literature is full of industry studies both at the national and international levels. See, for example, Aked, Brightman, and Cavaglia (2000); Baca, Garbe, and Weiss (2000); Fama and French (1992 and 1997); Geert and Heston (1994); Griffin and Karolyi (1998); and Lessard (1974 and 1976).

2. Bollman, Canto, and Melich (1982); Canto (1982 and 1984); Canto and Kadlec (1985 and 1986); Canto and Melich (1982); and Canto, Dietrich, Jain, and Mudaliar (1986).

3. Samuelson (1973).

4. Canto (1986, 1987, and 1988).

5. Bollman, Canto, and Melich (1982).

Chapter 12

1. There is extensive literature on the survivor bias's effect on the reported hedge fund performance. On this and related issues, see Brown, Goetzman, and Ibbotson (1999); Brown, Goetzman, Ibbotson, and Ross (1992); Fung and Hsieh (1997); and Liang (2000).

Chapter 13

1. Campbell and Vuolteenaho (2004) present a similar argument. They use a weighted average of two distinct betas that changes depending on market conditions.

2. Canto (2000).

Chapter 14

1. Black (1993), Grinold (1994), and Siegel (2004) address some of these issues.

2. Empirical literature is full of evidence of persistent patterns and anomalies in returns. See Asness (1997); Carhart (1997); Eleswarapu and Reinganum (2004); Goetzman and Ibbotson (1994); Grinblat and Titman (1992); Hendrick, Patel, and Zeckhouser (1993); Hong, Lim, and Stein (2000); and Perez-Quiros and Timmerman (2000). From my perspective, however, this literature fails to discuss any linkage between policy changes and relative return patterns. Absent this linkage, one needs to develop some mechanical rules to take advantage of the anomalies. The question I pose is: Can one do better than that? I think one can.

3. On this issue, see Bova and Leibowitz (2005). In their approach, the alpha core becomes a portfolio's core asset and the traditional benchmarks (betas) become the swing assets. For traditional portfolio construction, the latter represent the predominant factor risks.

BIBLIOGRAPHY

Adler, Michael, and Bernard Dumas. "International Portfolio Choice and Corporation Finance: A Synthesis." *Journal of Finance* 38 (June 1983): 925–84.

Aked, Michael, Christopher Brightman, and Stefano Cavaglia. "The Increasing Importance of Industry Factors." *Financial Analysts Journal* 56, No. 5 (September/October 2000): 41–54.

Asness, Clifford S. "The Interaction of Value and Momentum Strategies." *Financial Analysts Journal* 53, No. 2 (March/April 1997): 29–36.

———. "Stocks Versus Bonds: Explaining the Equity Risk Premium." *Financial Analysts Journal* 56, No. 2 (March/April 2000): 96–113.

Baca, Sean P., Brian L. Garbe, and Richard A. Weiss. "The Rise of Sector Effects in Major Equity Markets." *Financial Analysts Journal* 56, No. 5 (September/October 2000): 34–41.

Banz, Rolf W. "The Relationship Between Return and Market Value of Common Stocks." *Journal of Financial Economics* 9 (1981): 3–18.

Barber, Brad M., and John D. Lyon. "Firm Size, Book-to-Market Ratio, and Security Returns: A Holdout Sample of Financial Firms." *Journal of Finance* 52 (1997): 875–83.

BARRA (2005). Research and Indices are at www.barra.com.

Barrons. "Smoking Gun," Up and Down Wall Street, Barron's Online (Monday, September 14,1998).

Barton, Waring M. "The Future of Active Management." *CFA Institute Conference Proceedings—Points of Inflection: New Directions for Portfolio Management* (February 2004).

Bauer, Richard J., Jr., and Julie Dahlquist. "Market Timing and Roulette Wheels." *Financial Analysts Journal* 57, No. 1 (January/February 2001): 28–40.

Beaver, William, and Dale Morse. "What Determines Price-Earnings Ratios?" *Financial Analysts Journal* 34, No. 4 (July/August 1978): 65–76.

Beckers, Stan, Gregory Connor, and Ross Curds. "National Versus Global Influences on Equity Returns." *Financial Analysts Journal* 52, No. 2 (March/April 1996): 31–39.

————, Richard Grinold, Andrew Rudd, and Dan Stefek. "The Relative Importance of Common Factors Across the European Equity Markets." *Journal of Banking and Finance* 16, No. 1 (February 1992): 75–95.

Beebower, Gilbert, Gary P. Brinson, and L. Randolph Hood. "Determinates of Portfolio Performance." *Financial Analysts Journal* (January–February 1995): 133–138.

Bekaert, Geert, and Campbell R. Harvey. "Time-Varying World Market Integration." *Journal of Finance* 50, No. 2 (June 1995): 403–444.

Bernstein, Peter L. "Are Stocks the Best Place to Be in the Long Run? A Contrary Opinion." *Journal of Investing* 5, No. 2 (Summer 1996): 6–9.

————. "Stock/Bond Risk Perceptions and Expected Returns." *Newsletter* (February 1, 1997).

Black, Fischer. "Beta and Return." *Journal of Portfolio Management* 20 (1993): 8–18.

Blake, Christopher R., Sanjiv Das, Edwin J. Elton, and Martin J. Gruber. "The Persistence of Risk-Adjusted Mutual Fund Performance." *Journal of Business* 69, No. 2 (April 1996): 133–57.

Bollman, Gerald, Victor Canto, and Kevin Melich. "Oil Decontrol: The Power of Incentives Could Reduce OPEC's Power to Boost Oil Prices." *Oil and Gas Journal* 80, No. 2 (January 11, 1982): 92–101.

Bova, Anthony, and Martin Leibowitz. "The Efficient Frontier Using 'Alpha Cores.'" *Morgan Stanley Equity Research North America* (January 7, 2005).

Brown, Stephen J., William N. Goetzmann, and Roger G. Ibbotson. "Offshore Hedge Funds: Survival and Performance 1989–95." *Journal of Business* 72, No. 1 (January 1999): 91–117.

————, ————, ————, and Stephen A. Ross. "Survivorship Bias in Performance Studies." *Review of Financial Studies* 5, No. 4 (Winter 1992): 553–80.

Campbell, John Y., and Robert J. Shiller. "Valuation Ratios and the Long-Run Stock Market Outlook." *Journal of Portfolio Management* 24, No. 2 (1998): 11–26.

———— and Tuomo Vuolteenaho. "Bad Beta, Good Beta." *The American Economic Review* (December 2004): 1249–1275.

Canto, Victor. "Deconstructing Market Returns." *The Journal of Wealth Management* 3, No. 3 (Winter 2000): 19–23.

————. "Fine-Tuning the CATS' Meow." *Financial Analysts Journal* 43, No. 6 (November/December 1997): 56–66.

————. "Substitution Effects: Perilous to Ignore." *Financial Analysts Journal* 44, No. 5 (September–October 1988): 12–164.

————. "The CAT'S Meow: A Portfolio Strategy for the Modified Flat Tax." *Financial Analysts Journal* 42, No. 1 (January/February 1986): 35–48.

————. "The Fat CATS Strategy for Portfolio Selection." *Financial Analysts Journal* (January/February 1987): 43–51.

————. "Volatility and Valuation." *The Journal of Wealth Management* 4, No. 1 (Summer 2001): 83–6.

————. "The Effects of Voluntary Restraint Agreements: A Case Study of the Steel Industry." *Applied Economics* 16, No. 2 (April 1984): 175–86.

————. "Fuel Use Patterns in the United States: The Outlook for the 1980s." *Oil and Gas Journal* 80, No. 34 (August 23, 1982): 125–43.

————, Richard V. Eastin, Charles W. Kadlec, and Arthur Laffer. "A High Road for the American Automobile Industry." *The World Economy* 8, No. 3 (September 1985): 267–86.

————, Adish Jain, Dietrich J. Kimball, and Vishwa Mudaliar. "Protectionism and the Stock Market: The Determinates and Consequences of Trade Restrictions on the U.S. Economy." *Financial Analysts Journal* 42, No. 5 (September/October 1986): 32–42.

———— and Charles W. Kadlec. "The Shape of Energy Markets to Come." *Public Utilities Fortnightly* 117, No. 1 (January 9, 1986): 21–8.

———— and Kevin Melich. "Natural Gas Decontrol: The Road to Lower Energy Prices." *Public Utilities Fortnightly* 100, No. 9 (October 28, 1982): 31–9.

———— and Robert I. Webb. "Financial Markets and the Euro." *EMU, Financial Markets and the World Economy* (2001): 143–56.

———— and ————. "The Effect of State Fiscal Policy on State Relative Economic Performance." *Southern Economic Journal* 54, No. 1 (July 1987): 186–202.

Carhart, Mark M. "On Persistence in Mutual Fund Performance." *Journal of Finance* 52 (1997): 57–82.

Chan, Louis K.C., Narasimhan Jegadeesh, and Josef Lakonishok. "Evaluating the Performance of Value Versus Glamour Stocks: The Impact of Selection Bias." *Journal of Financial Economics* 38, No. 3 (July 1995): 269–96.

———, ———, and ———. "New Paradigm or Same Old Hype in Equity Investing?" *Financial Analysts Journal* 56, No. 4 (July/August 2000): 23–6.

——— and Josef Lakonishok. "Value and Growth Investing: Review and Update." *Financial Analysts Journal* 60, No. 1 (January/February 2004): 71-86.

Cordes, Joseph J., Robert D. Ebel, and Jane G. Gravelle. *The Encyclopedia of Taxation and Tax Policy.* Washington, D.C.: Urban Institute Press, 1999. 215–16.

Dabora, Emil, and Kenneth A. Froot. "How Are Stock Prices Affected by the Location of Trade?" *Journal of Financial Economics* 52, No. 2 (August 1999): 182–216.

Davis, James L. "Mutual Fund Performance and Manager Style." *Financial Analysts Journal* 57, No. 1 (January/February 2001): 19–27.

De Santis, Giorgio, and Bruno Gerard. "International Asset Pricing and Portfolio Diversification with Time-Varying Risk." *Journal of Finance* 52, No. 5 (December 1997): 1881–1912.

Diermeier, Jeff, and Bruno Solnik. "Global Pricing Equity." *Financial Analysts Journal* 57, No.4 (July/August 2001): 37–47.

Droms, William G. "Market Timing as an Investment Policy." *Financial Analysts Journal* 45, No. 1 (January/February 1989): 73–7.

Eleswarapu, Venkat R., and Marc R. Reinganum. "The Predictability of Aggregate Stock Market Returns: Evidence Based on Glamour Stocks." *Journal of Business* 77, No. 2 (2004): 275–94.

Engle, Robert. "Risk and Volatility: Econometric Models and Financial Practice." *The American Economic Review* 94, No. 3 (June 2004): 405–20.

Ezra, D. Don, Chris R. Hensel, and John H. Ilkiw. "The Importance of Asset Allocation Decision." *Financial Analysts Journal* 47, No. 4 (July/August 1991): 65–72.

Fairfield, Patricia M. "P/E, P/B, and Present Value of Future Dividends." *Financial Analysts Journal* 50, No. 4 (July/August 1994): 12–31.

Fama, Eugene F. "Efficient Capital Markets: A Review of Theory and Empirical Work." *Journal of Finance* 25, No. 2 (1970): 383–471.

———— and Kenneth R. French. "The Capital Asset Pricing Model: Theory and Evidence." *The Journal of Economic Perspectives* 18, No. 3 (Summer 2004): 25–46.

———— and ————. "Common Risk Factors in the Returns on Stocks and Bonds." *Journal of Financial Economics* 33 (1993): 3–56.

———— and ————. "Size and Book-to-Market Factories in Earnings and Returns." *Journal of Finance* 50 (1995): 131–55.

———— and ————. "Industry Costs of Equity." *Journal of Finance* 43, No. 2 (1997): 153–93.

———— and ————. "The Cross-Section of Expected Stock Returns." *Journal of Finance* 47, No. 2 (1992): 427–65.

———— and ————. "Value Versus Growth: The International Evidence." *Journal of Finance* 53 (1998): 1975–99.

Fisher, L., and J. H. Lorie. "Rates of Return on Investments in Common Stocks." *Journal of Business* 37 (January 1964): 1–21.

———— and ————. "Rates of Return on Investments in Common Stocks: The Year-by-Year Record, 1926–1965." *Journal of Business* 41 (July 1968): 291–316.

Freiman, Eckhard. "Economic Integration and Country Allocation in Europe." *Financial Analyst Journal* 54, No. 5 (September/October 1998): 32–41.

Fung, William, and David Hsieh. "Survivorship Bias and Investment Style in the Returns of CTAs." *Journal of Portfolio Management* 24, No. 1 (Fall 1997): 30–41.

Goetzmann, William N., and Roger G. Ibbotson. "Do Winners Repeat? Patterns in Mutual Fund Performance." *Journal of Portfolio Management* 20, No. 2 (Winter 1994): 9–18.

Good, Walter R. "When Are Price/Earnings Ratios Too High-or Too Low?" *Financial Analysts Journal* 47, No. 4 (July/August 1991): 9–12, 25.

Granger, Clive W.J. "Time Series Analysis, Cointegration, and Applications." *The American Economic Review* 94, No. 3 (June 2004): 421–25.

Greene, Kelly, and Jeff D. Opdyke. "Is Your Retirement Money Safe?" *Wall Street Journal* (May 12, 2005): D1.

Griffin, John M., and G. Andrew Karolyi. "Another Look at the Role of the Industrial Structure of Markets for International Diversification Strategies." *Journal of Financial Economics* 50, No. 3 (December 1998): 351–373.

Grinblatt, Mark, and Sheridan Titman. "The Persistence of Mutual Fund Performance." *Journal of Finance* 42, No. 5 (December 1992): 1977–84.

———, ———, and Russ Wermers. "Momentum Investment Strategies, Portfolio Performance, and Herding: A Study of Mutual Fund Behavior." *American Economic Review* 85, No. 5 (1989): 1088–1105.

Grinold, Richard C. "Alpha Is Volatility Times IC Times Score, or Real Alphas Don't Get Eaten." *Journal of Portfolio Management* 20, No. 4 (Summer 1994): 9–16.

———."The Fundamental Law of Active Management." *Journal of Portfolio Management* 15, No. 3 (Spring 1989): 30–7.

———, Andrew Rudd, and Dan Stefek. "Global Factors: Fact or Fiction?" *Journal of Portfolio Management* 16, No. 3 (Fall 1989): 79–88.

Gruber, Martin J. "Another Puzzle: The Growth in Actively Managed Mutual Funds." *Journal of Finance* 51, No. 3 (1996): 783–810.

Hendricks, Darryll, Jayendu Patel, and Richard Zeckhauser. "Hothands in Mutual Funds: Short Run Persistence of Performance, 1974–88." *Journal of Finance* 48, No. 1 (March 1993): 93–130.

Heston, Steven L., and K. Geert Rouwenhorst. "Industry and Country Effects in International Stock Return." *Journal of Portfolio Management* 21, No. 3 (Spring 1995): 53–8.

——— and ———. "Does Industrial Structure Explain the Benefits of International Diversification?" *Journal of Financial Economics* 36, No. 1 (June 1994): 3–27.

Hoffman, Phillip, Lisa Kopp, Wenling Lin, and Mark Thurston. "Changing Risks in Global Equity Portfolios." *Financial Analysts Journal* 60, No. 1 (January/February 2004): 87–99.

Hong, Harrison, Terence Lim, and Jeremy C. Stein. "Bad News Travels Slowly: Size, Analyst Coverage, and the Profitability of Momentum Strategies." *Journal of Finance* 55, No. 1 (2000): 265–95.

Ibbotson, Robert G., and Rex Sinquefield. "Stocks, Bonds, and Inflation: Year-by-Year Historical Returns (1926–1974)." *Journal of Business* 49 (January 1976): 11–47.

——— and Paul D. Kaplan. "Does Asset Allocation Policy Explain 40, 90, or 100 Percent of Performance?" *Financial Analysts Journal* 56, No. 1 (January/February 2000): 26–33.

Jeffrey, Robert H. "The Folly of Stock Market Timing." *Harvard Business Review* (July/August 1984): 102–10.

Jensen, Michael C. "The Performance of Mutual Funds in the Period 1945–1964." *Journal of Finance* 23 (May 1968): 389–416.

La Jolla Economics. "The Rise of the Yen Is Bullish for the World Economy." Economic Study (September 28, 1999).

La Porta, Rafael, Josef Lakonishok, Andrei Shleifer, and Robert Vishny. "Good News for Value Stocks: Further Evidence on Market Efficiency." *Journal of Finance* 52, No. 2 (June 1997): 859–74.

Lanstein, Ronald, Kenneth Reid, and Barr Rosenburg. "Persuasive Evidence of Market Inefficiency." *Journal of Portfolio Management* 11 (1985): 9–17.

Lee, Joan, and Don Phillips. "Tactical Asset Allocation: Differentiating Tactical Asset Allocation from Market Timing." *Financial Analysts Journal* 45, No. 2 (March/April 1989): 14–16.

Leibowitz, Martin. "The β-Plus Measure in Asset Allocation." *Journal of Portfolio Management* (Spring 2004): 26–35.

Lessard, Donald. "World, Country, and Industry Relationships in Equity Returns: Implications for Risk Reduction Through International Diversification." *Financial Analyst Journal* 32, No.1 (January/February 1976): 32–8.

———. "World, National, and Industry Factors in Equity Returns." *Journal of Finance* 29, No. 3 (May 1974): 379–91.

Liang, Bing. "Hedge Funds: The Living and the Dead." *Journal of Financial and Quantitative Analysis* 35, No. 3 (September 2000): 309–26.

Liew, Jimmy, and Maria Vassalou. "Can Book-to-Market, Size and Momentum Be Risk Factors that Predict Economic Growth." *Journal of Financial Economics* 57 (2000): 221–45.

Lintner, John. "Security Prices, Risk and Maximal Gains from Diversification." *Journal of Finance* 20 (December 1965): 587–615.

————. "The Aggregation of Investors Diverse Judgments and Preferences in Purely Competitive Security Markets." *Journal of Financial and Quantitative Analysis* 4 (December 1969): 347–400.

Markowitz, Harry. "Portfolio Selection." *Journal of Finance* 7 (1952): 77–91.

Mossin, Jan. "Equilibrium in a Capital Asset Market." *Econometrica* 34 (1966): 768–83.

Narasimhan, Jegadeesh. "Evidence of Predictable Behavior of Security Returns." *Journal of Finance* 45 (1990): 881–98.

Nicholson, S. Francis. "Price/Earnings Ratios." *Financial Analysts Journal* 16 (1960): 43–5.

Perez-Quiros, Gabriel, and Allan Timmermann. "Firm Size and Cyclical Variations in Stock Returns." *Journal of Finance* 55 (2000): 1229–62.

Perold, Andre F. "The Capital Asset Pricing Model." *The Journal of Economic Perspectives* 18, No. 3 (Summer 2004): 3–24.

Piotroski, Joseph. "Value Investing: The Use of Historical Financial Statement Information to Separate Winners from Losers." *Journal of Accounting Research* 38, Supplement (2000): 1–41.

Reinganum, Marc R. "A New Empirical Perspective on the CAPM." *Journal of Financial and Quantitative Analysis* 16 (1981): 439–62.

Review & Outlook. "United We Default." *Wall Street Journal* (May 12, 2005): A16.

Samuelson, Paul. *Economics*. McGraw-Hill (1973).

Sharpe, William F. "Asset Allocation: Management Style Performance Measurement." *Journal of Portfolio Management* 18, No. 2 (Winter 1992): 7–19.

————. "Bonds Versus Stocks: Some Lessons from Capital Market Theory." *Financial Analysts Journal* 29, No. 6 (November/December 1973): 74–80.

————. "Likely Gains from Market Timing." *Financial Analysts Journal* 31, No. 2 (March/April 1975): 60–9.

————. "Capital Asset Prices: A Theory of Market Equilibrium Under Conditions of Risk." *Journal of Finance* 19 (1964): 425–42.

————. "The Sharpe Ratio." *Journal of Portfolio Management* (Fall 1994): 49–58.

Shilling, A. Gary. "Market Timing: Better than a Buy-and-Hold Strategy." *Financial Analysts Journal* 48, No. 2 (March/April 1992): 46–50.

Siegel, Jeremy J. *Stocks for the Long Run, Second Edition.* McGraw-Hill, 1998.

Siegel, Laurence. "Distinguishing True Alpha from Beta." *CFA Institute Conference Proceedings—Points of Inflection: New Directions for Portfolio Management* (February 2004).

Sinquefield, Rex A. "Active Versus Passive Management." *Schwab Institutional Conference in San Francisco* (October 12, 1995).

Solnik, Bruno H. "An Equilibrium Model of the International Capital Market." *Journal of Economic Theory* 8 (August 1974): 500–24.

———. "Why Not Diversify Internationally Rather Than Domestically?" *Financial Analysts Journal* 30, No. 4 (July/August 1974): 48–54.

Stulz, René M. "A Model of International Asset Pricing." *Journal of Financial Economics* 9 (September 1981): 383–406.

Treynor, Jack. L. "How to Rate the Performance of Mutual Funds." *Harvard Business Review* 43 (January/February 1965): 15–22.

———. "Toward a Theory of Market Value of Risky Assets." *Unpublished Manuscript* (1962). Final version in Robert A. Korajczyk, ed. *Asset Pricing and Portfolio Performance.* London: Risk Books, 1999: 15–22.

White, C. Barry. "What P/E Will the U.S. Stock Market Support?" *Financial Analysts Journal* 5, No. 6 (November/December 2000): 30–9.

GLOSSARY

absolute return strategy   The objective of the absolute return strategy is to provide investment returns higher than the Consumer Price Index (CPI) in addition to some prespecified returns amount (for example, 6 percent). These strategies are expected to produce positive absolute returns in excess of the inflation rate with low volatility. The managers' investment objective is to seek positive returns in both up and down markets. This contrasts with the relative return, which measures a fund manager's performance as compared to a market benchmark.

active management   A money-management approach based on informed, independent investment judgment. This is opposed to passive management.

alpha   A coefficient that measures risk-adjusted performance, factoring in risk due to the specific security, rather than the overall market.

BARRA growth stocks   Stocks included on the BARRA Growth index; stocks with higher price-to-book ratio.

BARRA value stocks   Stocks included on the BARRA Value index; stocks with lower price-to-book ratio.

benchmark   A standard used for comparison. For example, the S&P 500 is a benchmark for large capitalization stock and the Russell 2000 is a benchmark for small capitalization stocks

beta   A quantitative measure of the volatility of a given stock, mutual fund, or portfolio, relative to the overall market. A beta above one is more volatile than the overall market; a beta of less than one is less volatile.

black box   A device or theoretical construct with known or specified performance characteristics but unknown or unspecified constituents and means of operation. Or, something mysterious, especially in regard to function.

bracket creep   Slowly moving into higher tax brackets as one's income rises to keep up with inflation.

capital asset pricing model (CAPM)   An economic model for valuing stocks by relating risk and expected returns. Based on the idea investors require additional expected return if asked to accept additional risk.

capital gains (cap gains)   The amount by which an asset's selling price exceeds its initial purchase price.

capital intensity   A measure of the general use of capital, compared to other factors, in a production process.

capitalization-weighted (cap-weighted)   Assigns greater value to companies' stocks with the highest market value, calculated by multiplying the number of existing shares by the current market price.

capitalized earnings model   Estimates a company's value by calculating the adjusted accounting earnings' present value in perpetuity. The value is simply computed by dividing earnings by a capitalization factor expressed as a percentage.

carry trade   A speculation strategy that borrows an asset at one interest rate, sells the asset, and invests those funds into a different asset that generates a higher interest-rate yield. Profit is acquired by the difference between the borrowed asset's cost and the purchased asset's yield.

corner solution   A choice an agent makes that is at a constraint and not at the tangency of two classical curves on a graph (one graph characterizing what the agent could obtain and the other characterizing the imaginable choices that would attain the agent's objective's highest reachable value).

corporate debt   The short-term and long-term debt a company issues. Short-term debt is issued as commercial paper, while long-term debt is usually issued as bonds or notes.

cyclical asset allocation (CAA)   A strategy allowed to deviate from the long-run allocation to take advantage of predictable fluctuations in the market.

cyclical stocks   The stock of a company sensitive to business cycles and whose performance is strongly tied to the overall economy. Such companies tend to make products or provide services in lower demand during economic downtimes and higher during upswings.

demand shift   Movement of the entire demand curve (as opposed to movement along the demand curve) based on income, tastes and preferences, substitute and complement prices, and expectations for the future.

discount rate   Interest rate used in discounting future cash flows; also called the capitalization rate.

dividends   A taxable payment a company's board of directors declares and gives to shareholders out of the company's retained earnings.

double taxation   Taxation of the same earnings more than once.

earnings management   A company's management strategy used to deliberately manipulate the company's earnings so figures match a predetermined target.

economies of scale   Describes the fact that as output increases, the average cost of each unit produced falls. One reason is that overheads and other fixed costs can be spread over more units of output.

efficient frontier   A set of portfolios that is optimal both because it offers the maximum expected return for a given risk level and because minimal risk is given an expected return level.

efficient market theory   The theory that all market participants receive and act on all the relevant information as soon as it becomes available.

efficient portfolio   A portfolio providing the greatest expected return for a given risk level or the lowest risk for a given return.

employee stock ownership plan (ESOP)   A plan by which a company contributes to a trust fund that buys stock on the employees' behalf.

equal weighting   Gives equal emphasis so every company's price movement has the same effect on the index.

equity risk premium   The extra return the overall stock market or a particular stock must provide over the rate of Treasury bills (T-bills) to compensate for market risk.

exchange traded funds (ETFs)   Baskets of securities traded, like individual stocks, on an exchange. They can be bought and sold throughout the day, they tend to have lower expenses, and they can be bought and sold on the margin.

fair market value   The price an interested (but not desperate) buyer is willing to pay and an interested (but not desperate) seller is willing to accept on the open market—assuming a reasonable time period for an agreement to happen.

financial engineering   Creating new and improved financial products by innovatively designing or repackaging existing financial instruments.

growth stock   Stocks with high price-to-book or price-to-earnings ratio. A company's stock that is growing earnings and/or revenue faster than its industry or the overall market.

hedge fund   A fund, usually used by wealthy individuals and institutions, that is allowed to use aggressive strategies unavailable to mutual funds. Includes selling short, leverage, program trading, swaps, arbitrage, and derivatives. They are also exempt from many of the rules and regulations governing other mutual funds.

high-yield bonds   A debt instrument issued for a period of more than one year with high rates of return because there is a higher default risk.

hurdle rate-of-return   The required rate of return in a discounted cash flow analysis, above which an investment makes sense and below which it does not.

index   In economics and finance, an index (for example, a price or stock-market index) is a benchmark of activity, performance, or evolution in general. Consumer price indexes (an inflation measurement), or a country's gross domestic product (GDP) index (an economic growth measurement) can be used to adjust salaries, Treasury bond (T-bond) interest rates, and tax thresholds. Index funds manage their portfolio so their evolution always mirrors a stock-market index's evolution. A passive investment strategy in which the portfolio is designed to mirror a stock-market index's performance.

inflation hedging   An investment designed to protect against inflation risk. Such an investment's value typically increases with inflation.

information ratio   The expected return-to-risk ratio as measured by standard deviation. This statistical technique is usually used to measure a manager's performance against a benchmark.

interest rate parity   Relationship that must hold between the spot rate currencies' interest rate if there are to be no arbitrage opportunities.

interest rate spread   The difference in yield between two distinct securities, such as corporate bonds and government securities.

investor's horizon   The time length a sum of money is expected to be invested.

law of one price   The economic rule that states that, in an efficient market and absent transaction or transportation costs, a security and/or a commodity must have a single price, no matter how that security is created.

leverage buyouts (LBOs)   A transaction used to privatize a public corporation financed through debt, such as bank loans and Treasury bonds (T-bonds). Due to the large amount of debt relative to equity, the bonds are usually rated below investment grade.

lifecycle fund   A type of a fund structured between stocks and fixed income. Its overall asset allocation automatically adjusts to become more conservative as your expected retirement age approaches.

long–short strategy   A portfolio construction technique that traditionally has long positions in stocks, as well as short positions, resulting in portfolios that have reduced systematic risk.

mark-to-market   Daily recording the price or value of a security, portfolio, or account to calculate profits and losses or to confirm margin requirements are being met.

market breadth   The fraction of the overall market participating in the market's up or down move.

market portfolio   A concept used in Modern Portfolio Theory referring to a hypothetical portfolio containing every security available to investors in a given market in amounts proportional to their market values.

mean reversion   The process is mean reverting. Ultimately, asset class returns converge along their long-run historical averages.

Modern Portfolio Theory   A theory on how risk-averse investors can construct portfolios to optimize market risk for expected returns, emphasizing risk is an inherent part of higher reward. Also called portfolio theory or portfolio management theory. According to the theory, it's possible to construct an "efficient frontier" of optimal portfolios offering the maximum possible expected return for a given risk level. This theory was pioneered by Harry Markowitz in his paper "Portfolio Selection," published by the Journal of Finance in 1952.

Monte Carlo simulation   An analytical technique in which a large number of simulations are run using random qualities for uncertain variables and looking at the distribution of results to infer which values are most likely. Used to calculate value above risk.

net present value (NPV)   The future stream of benefits and costs converted into today's equivalent values.

nominal interest rate   Interest rate not adjusted for inflation.

passive management   A money management strategy that seeks to match the return and risk characteristics of a market segment or index by mirroring its composition.

passively managed low-cost index funds   Owning all or almost all of the stocks in a certain index rather than actively buying and selling stocks based on different recommendations. The result is if the market does well, these funds do well; if the market doesn't do well, neither do these funds. The main benefit is the low overhead costs because there is little buying and selling.

Phillips curve   Based on the theory there was a trade-off between inflation and unemployment. The lower the unemployment rate, the higher the inflation rate.

portable alpha strategy   Process of investing in alpha-generating strategies of any type without affecting the underlying market positioning or the portfolio's asset allocation.

price rule   Requires that the monetary authority attempt to maintain a chosen price index at a particular level by varying the stock of money. In other words, the sole function is to prevent the price index from deviating substantially from a predetermined level.

price/earning (P/E) ratio   The most common measure of how expensive a stock is. It is equal to a stock's market capitalization divided by its after-tax earnings over a 12-month period. The higher the P/E, the more the market is willing to pay per annual-earnings dollar.

probability density function   A statistical function that shows how the density of possible observations in a population is distributed.

purchasing power parity (PPP)   The theory that, in the long run, identical products and services in different countries should cost the same in different countries.

rate of return   The amount returned per unit of time expressed as a cost percentage.

real exchange rate   An exchange rate that takes into account the inflation differential among countries.

regulatory burden   Any aspect of legislation, regulation, or policy that could be made more efficient without dismissing the intended level of protections.

regulatory skirting   An attempt to get around rules or regulations.

relative performance   A measure of performance that indicates how well it is doing relative to some gauge (such as market, industry, other stocks or funds).

residual risk   Risk remaining after risk-management techniques have been applied. Risk cannot be diversified away.

retention rate   Retained after-tax income expressed as a percentage of before-tax income.

risk free rate (return)   A theoretical interest rate that is returned on an investment completely free of risk. The three-month Treasury bill (T-bill) is sometimes used because it is virtually risk free.

secular upswings   A long-term (as opposed to temporary or cyclical) rally or rebound following a decrease in price.

Sharpe ratio   A risk-adjusted measure developed by William Sharpe, calculated using standard deviation and excess return to determine reward per unit of risk. The higher the Sharpe Ratio, the better the fund's historical risk-adjusted performance.

spread   Reflects the difference between the price the sellers are asking and the price the buyers are offering for the product.

standard deviation   A statistical measure of a mutual fund's or portfolio's historical volatility. More generally, a measure of the extent to which numbers are spread around their average.

supply shift   Moving the entire supply curve (not movement along) based on changes in costs of production, random shocks, expectations of future prices, and technology.

survivor bias   The tendency for failed companies to be excluded from performance studies due to the fact that they no longer exist. It causes the studies to skew higher because only companies successful enough to survive until the period's end are included.

systematic risk   Risk common to an entire class of assets or liabilities. Investments' value may decline over a given time period simply because of economic changes or other events that impact large portions of the market.

tactical asset allocation (TAA)   The shifting of capital between asset classes in relationship to a policy benchmark, based on perceived valuation discrepancies in a reasonably efficient market.

tax sheltering   Any legal means of postponing or reducing the tax amount due.

Treasury bill (T-bill)   A negotiable debt obligation issued by the U.S. government and backed by its full faith and credit, having a maturity of one year or less.

Treasury bond (T-bond) A negotiable coupon-bearing debt obligation issued by the U.S. government and backed by its full faith and credit, having a maturity of more than seven years.

value stocks Stocks with low price-to-book or price-to-earnings ratios. A stock considered a good stock at a great price, based on its fundamentals, as opposed to a great stock at a good price.

INDEX

Page numbers followed by *n* indicate endnotes.